The Paradox of Suicide and Creativity

The Paradox of Suicide and Creativity

Authentications of Human Existence

M. F. Alvarez

Foreword by
George Atwood

LEXINGTON BOOKS
Lanham • Boulder • New York • London

Published by Lexington Books
An imprint of The Rowman & Littlefield Publishing Group, Inc.
4501 Forbes Boulevard, Suite 200, Lanham, Maryland 20706
www.rowman.com

6 Tinworth Street, London SE11 5AL, United Kingdom

British Library Cataloguing in Publication Information Available

Library of Congress Control Number: 2020946608

ISBN 978-1-4985-2382-0 (cloth)
ISBN 978-1-4985-2383-7 (electronic)

Contents

Acknowledgments

The writing of a book is never a solitary endeavor, and I owe a debt of gratitude to those who have journeyed alongside me throughout this wild ride. These include friends and family who bring color and levity to my life, mentors and colleagues who are steadfast in their support and appreciation of my work, and students who genuinely believe that my writings will impact the world in some way. I am also thankful to my agent, Jennifer Chen Tran, whose enthusiasm about my work often exceed mine, and my editor, Kasey Beduhn, for her patience and generosity with time.

An earlier version of the Robin Williams chapter has been published in the Mad in America webzine, and I have presented my research at various Creativity and Madness conferences and workshops at Goddard College. The opportunity to engage in productive conversation at such venues with members of the academic community and the general public has only encouraged me to be daring and stretch the boundaries of my thought.

The people who have nurtured me in mind, body, and spirit and reminded me to care for myself throughout the writing process are many, but this acknowledgment would not be complete without my partner, Benjamin Cleaves. Thank you for enduring my bouts of madness, my outbursts, my long silences, and for greeting me warmly upon my return from the inner recesses of my thoughts.

Foreword

Mike Alvarez has written a wonderful book, and it explores a mystery: Why should it be that the lives of those who give the world extraordinary creative works so often come to an end in an act of self-destruction? One might think that creative activity is the highest expression of the life impulse and yet, the people responsible for astonishing achievements in the arts and sciences very frequently spiral into the darkness of despair and choose to end their lives.

Mike's interest in this paradox traces back to his undergraduate years at Rutgers University. He had passed through an extraordinary personal crisis of his own in his late teen years, one that included a nearly successful suicide attempt and psychiatric hospitalization. As part of his recovery he searched for an understanding of what had befallen his young life, and his search expanded into an interest in the phenomenology of suicide in general. He came to me in the last year of his college studies and made a proposal for a senior honors thesis. He proposed conducting a series of case studies of artists who after great success had opted to kill themselves, with a goal of identifying the relationship between their creativity and their suicides.

I was unsure of the feasibility of Mike's idea at first, so I asked him which artists he was thinking of studying. Among the many he listed was Yukio Mishima, whose quasi-autobiographical *Sun and Steel* I happened to have just recently been studying. Mishima's committing *seppuku* in a highly ritualized way, vividly imagined before being carried out, was a way of substantiating himself and overcoming a devastating sense of personal unreality. Our ensuing discussions of Mishima's life and death were so interesting that I approved Mike's proposal and he went on to write a magnificent thesis focusing on three great artists: Yukio Mishima, Sylvia Plath, and Diane Arbus.

Mike's honors thesis was so good that it was unexpectedly given the Charles Flaherty Award at Rutgers for outstanding undergraduate research in psychology. Professor Flaherty, now deceased for many years, was a behaviorist and positivist, and he is undoubtedly still spinning in his grave about this award having been given to research using psychobiographical interpretive methods.

Mike never gave up on his writing and on this beautiful, important theme. For the next 13 years he and I kept in touch as his work on creativity and suicide expanded and deepened to include a wide range of creative persons working in many domains. *The Paradox of Suicide and Creativity* takes the reader on a journey, at times harrowing, at times heartbreaking, through the discoveries made in this expanded search. Theories of suicide are so often detached from the phenomenology of suicidal despair, but this book dares to venture close. Mike's writing is elegant, his psychological insight into his subjects profound, and his project as a whole is itself a creative work of the first magnitude.

This book will be of wide interest to students and scholars in the social sciences and humanities and more generally to the educated public. And it will be of incalculable value to anyone engaged with people whose circumstances have brought them to the threshold of life and death.

George Atwood, PhD
Professor of Psychology (Emeritus)
Rutgers University

Introduction

According to the myths of ancient Greece, it was fire that gave birth to civilization, that sculpted human achievement from the natural world that had always been. The fire was a gift from Prometheus, a titan from Mount Olympus who witnessed the plight of humanity. With this gift the creative arts flourished, as did scientific innovation, and Zeus, the king of all Olympian gods, was enraged. The gift was a threat to his dominion over humankind, who might someday rival and tower over the gods. Fire belonged to divinity, not mere mortals. As punishment for his crime, Zeus bound Prometheus to Mount Caucasus and condemned him to an eternity of suffering, his liver in a perpetual state of repair so that vultures may feed on it to no end. Fortunately for Prometheus, Chiron, a compassionate centaur, took pity on him and gave up *his* immortality so that the titan may walk the Earth once more, shattering the chains that kept him in captivity.

Humans carry inside them the seeds of growth, the limitless potential to transform themselves into whatever or whomever they wish to be. We are limited only by our finitude, the horizon toward which we are steadily moving, which defines our being and becoming. However, the creative act itself allows us to confront the subjective experience of death and reach beyond our own finitude (May, 1975). Just as Prometheus rebelled against Zeus by stealing fire from Mount Olympus and bestowing it upon humans, just as Chiron's courageous sacrifice allowed Prometheus to transcend the suffering to which he'd been sentenced, creativity is rebellion against forces that limit our existence. In this day and age, however, the expression of creativity challenges not the Olympian gods but the gods of our society—apathy, materialism, conformity, greed—which provide the masses illusory comfort because they have form. What is formless is frightening to human beings; it is an abyss that stares back. For this reason, the generative act of creation requires a great deal of courage, what Rollo May (1975) calls *creative courage.*

But the creative *encounter*—surrendering oneself to a purpose with an intensity of commitment—is not without peril. Creative individuals sense the alienation of our time, and because creativity challenges the relationship between self, world, and other, the act of creation may cause anxiety, the anxiety of nothingness. One wonders if this is partly responsible for why so many creative persons end their lives.

The list of creative men and women who challenged the status quo and ultimately succumbed to suicide is endless, and an impersonal catalog of names, creative domains, means of demise, and circumstances leading to death will not do this tragedy justice. Many book-length treatises have been written about the creativity and madness connection (e.g., Jamison, 2003; Kottler, 2006; Ludwig, 1995; Nettle, 2001; Sass, 1994), each from a particular theoretical, methodological, and epistemological stance. However, to my knowledge, only one book exists on the creativity and suicide connection, and that is David Lester's *Suicide in Creative Women* (1993), written more than a quarter of a century ago. As the title suggests, the book compares six creative women who committed suicide, with six creative women who did *not* and six creative men who *did.* Useful as that book may be, it remains deeply entrenched in the epidemiological language of risk and protective factors, missing the once ripe opportunity to deeply explore the lifeworlds of the persons featured therein.

The book you hold is a modest but serious attempt to understand highly creative persons who ended their lives *in their own subjective terms.* Though the creativity-suicide connection is related to the creativity-madness connection, the former is a special case of the latter and deserves its own treatment. But first, some words on the driving force behind this book.

INSPIRATION FOR THE BOOK

Thirteen years ago, when I was an undergraduate, I found myself in the waiting room of a mental hospital. I had made plans and attempts to terminate my own life, and when I disclosed this to my psychiatrist, the ambulance was summoned. I was fortunate enough not to remain trapped inside the revolving doors of the mental health system, and upon release, I was overcome with a compulsion to study suicide, to understand how and why the fierce instinct to self-preservation can be and often is surmounted. This avenue led me to study exceptionally creative individuals who committed suicide, in whom I saw the tragedies of my own life reflected, and whose tragedies are inscribed in their own creative productions. But I didn't want to commit the injustice of viewing their lives through the reductive lens of contemporary psychiatry or much of academic psychology. Their lives, their deaths, and their enduring contributions to humankind beckoned to be understood in *their* own terms.

In the ensuing years, I journeyed far and wide, literally and imaginatively, in my quest to study highly creative people and understand the coexistence of creativity and self-destruction. Literally in that I traveled across state lines to museums, archives, and other places of biographical importance; imaginatively in that I immersed myself in these individuals' lifeworlds, letting their stories and the symbolic content of their creations wash over me like a waterfall as I struggled to make sense of their underlying patterns and meanings. To study suicide up close demands vulnerability, an open mind and heart. It's no wonder that it is often studied at a remove, the distance between the observer and the observed achieved through diagnostic jargon and ruthless quantification. The subject drowns in numbers and labels, killed a second, third, or fourth time, while the researcher walks away unscathed.

The study of suicide and creativity is the study of a central paradox. Creativity is the ultimate celebration of existence, of one's own and that of humanity. When words are put on paper, when paint is applied to canvas, when feelings are turned into music, and when ideas, no matter how abstract or inchoate, are given concrete form, the conscience of the individual is given expression, as is the conscience of the entire human race. Suicide, on the other hand, is the cessation of that very existence. Whereas creativity generates limitless possibilities, suicide precludes the possibility of possibilities. Creativity is the lifeblood that animates persons and civilizations; suicide is the spilling of that blood. And yet, these two seemingly dichotomous forces of creation and destruction, perpetuation and termination, coalesce in exceptionally creative individuals who resist, wrestle with, and ultimately succumb to the call of self-destruction. That in itself is paradoxical.

When I set out on this path, I wanted to find that golden thread (a grand theory, if you will) that elegantly, and parsimoniously, linked creativity with suicide. Modest as it may be, one recurring thread that emerged is this:

> *Creativity fulfills various ontological needs that have been thwarted by nuclear crises in a person's life. If creativity loses its potency, or forces beyond the person's volition impinge upon creativity's restitutive powers, other creative pathways may emerge. If these too are rendered impotent or choked off, suicide may surface—as a final stand against forces of negation, and as the ultimate resolution of the original crises.*

The idea that tragic life experiences that lead to creative acts may also lead to suicide is not surprising in and of itself, though it is worth reiterating in the context of rampant medicalization. But the important point here is that creativity and suicide are joint pathways to the realization of being or preemption of its negation, with suicide taking over when creativity fails—in the lives of the 11 individuals featured here, and in other lives as well. I revisit this thread throughout the book, but it must be noted that the central paradox houses several other paradoxes.

One paradox sees creativity as a branching path, with one pathway headed toward healing and plenitude of being, and another pathway leading to trauma, retraumatization, and/or death by suicide. In some cases, the paths do not run parallel but intersect at critical junctures in a person's life. Another paradox relates to suicide as authentication and suicide as surrender: the ultimate declaration of agency, or absolute compliance to a negating force. One last paradox concerns the medicalization of lived experience itself. In this day and age, suicide prevention is synonymous with its medicalization. But when death is medicalized, so too are the myriad expressions of life's vitality. In other words, contemporary efforts to thwart death and perpetuate life, often lead to the disavowal of life. I address these paradoxes in the case studies and in digression chapters (referred to as "interludes"), but golden thread or no, what this endeavor ultimately teaches is that there is priceless value in understanding an individual life, in its own terms, in its rich complexity and humanity.

A BRIEF OVERVIEW OF THE LITERATURE

There are many theories on suicide and just as many theories on human creativity. I will not reiterate those theories here, though I invoke them throughout the book as they become relevant in individual case studies. Instead, let us briefly turn our attention to how the creativity-suicide connection has previously been studied.

There have been numerous attempts to quantify the prevalence of suicidality among creative populations, though these rates vary widely across studies, depending on how creativity is operationally defined (Lester, 1998a; Preti, de Biasi, & Miotto, 2001), the designation of attempted versus completed suicide as the outcome variable (Ludwig, 1995), and weighted comparisons against national averages (Stack, 1997). Though these studies as a whole seem to agree that creative individuals are at heightened risk of suicide, they neither explain why this may be so nor illuminate the deep meanings of creativity and self-destructiveness to those who exhibit both.

Enter studies on risk factors among creative persons. One study finds that creative people who are less rigid about traditional moral values are more likely to espouse a nonjudgmental attitude toward suicide, seeing it as a natural phenomenon rather than a violation of divine or natural laws (Domino,

1988). In other words, they are more likely to act on suicidal impulses because they are less inhibited by societal conventions and taboos. Another study implicates divergent thinking and problem generation fluency, that is, the ability to identify a large number of problems, which makes one prone to finding faults in one's personal life (Mraz & Runco, 1994). A third study implicates the conflation of achievement with self-worth, especially among those who believe that love and affection are contingent upon critical or material success (Willings & Arseneault, 1986).

The role of sociodemographic and environmental factors has also been studied. For example, it appears that creative women and African Americans are more likely to attempt suicide than creative men and Caucasians, but this trend is reversed with respect to completed suicides (Ludwig, 1995). The lifespan of creative homosexuals who die by suicide is noticeably shorter than their heterosexual counterparts (Ludwig, 1995). Drug use by the mother, attempted suicide by the father, rejection by a father figure in adolescence, and divorce by multiple spouses also confer greater risk (Shneidman, 1971), as do early loss, oversensitivity to criticism (Lester, 1990), and rapid changes in one's lifestyle (Tabachnik, 1975).

There is value to each of these observations, but we must be careful not to absolutize, to commit the ecological fallacy of generalizing from large samples to particular cases. This snapshot of the literature comes from nomothetic (i.e., top-down) approaches, which are primarily concerned with generalizability and external validity. Though idiographic (i.e., bottom-up) case studies of creative suicides are numerous, there have been no attempts to study enduring patterns and variations *across* individual cases. What's missing is a multiple-case psychobiographical study, one that is deeply rooted in the spirit of phenomenological inquiry, to which I now turn. Readers who are interested in the theoretical and methodological underpinnings of this book may forge ahead, whereas those eager to immerse themselves in the individual narratives that, collectively, form the heart of this book may jump to chapter 1. But first, a few words of caution are in order.

As I mentioned, writing about and studying suicide up close demands vulnerability on the writer's part. It follows that the stories that emerge, in order to be more fully appreciated, demand the reader to be vulnerable as well. Each story details human suffering—from childhood loss, to fractured relationships, to witnessing unimaginable cruelty and violence—with candor and without reservation. There is no holding back, because to sugarcoat suffering is to deny its felt reality. With this in mind, I urge readers to care for themselves, to take necessary breaks when reading becomes overwhelming, and to return to the communality of the larger human and social surround.

ON PHENOMENOLOGICAL CONTEXTUALISM

Throughout, my endeavor has been guided by the spirit of *phenomenological contextualism* (Stolorow & Atwood, 2019). Phenomenology is the study of the first-person perspective and places human subjectivity at the center of inquiry, whereas contextualism, as its name suggests, highlights the role of context in understanding phenomena. Combined, this depth psychology seeks to illuminate the human meaning of subjective experiences and their embeddedness in the world, from the point of view of the experiencing subject. One may ask, for example, what suicide means *to* the person wrestling with thoughts and feelings of suicide, and from that person's perspective, what life circumstances produced such anguish.

As an intellectual enterprise, phenomenological contextualism is a *human science*, one that eschews the myth of the isolated mind perpetuated by Cartesian thought. Cartesian dualism envisions the mind as radically separate from the body, from other minds, and from a stable external reality, which the mind apprehends or distorts. The mind is reified, pictured as an enclosed container, its contents readily cataloged. It is an atomistic epistemology that hews closely to the natural science criteria of reducing the influence of confounding variables, eliminating personal bias from the analysis, and arriving at knowledge that is certain and pure, without any shred of humanity. In contrast, phenomenological contextualism does away with these mind-body, self-other, and self-world splits, for relatedness, community, and intersubjectivity are at its heart.

As its earlier moniker, *psychoanalytic phenomenology*, suggests, phenomenological contextualism draws upon, yet is distinct from, psychoanalysis and phenomenological systems of philosophy (Stolorow, Atwood, & Brandchaft, 1994). It does not discard the contributions of classical psychoanalysis or its offshoots (e.g., psychodynamic and object-relations theory), but deabsolutizes their overstated findings, so that they are more sensitive to context rather than beholden to the natural science criterion of external validity. Like its philosophical counterparts, phenomenological contextualism is concerned with the experiencing subject, but the key difference here is that its interest lies in the subjective worlds of *particular* persons, not knowledge of subjectivity in universal terms.

A key concept of phenomenological contextualism is the *experiential world*, the sum total of an individual's experience, which is subject to continuing (re) organization (Stolorow, Atwood, & Orange, 2002). The relational contexts that we inhabit shape the way we assimilate experiences and organize our experiential worlds. Some life experiences, such as a nurturing upbringing, expand our *world horizons*, whereas others, such as intensely traumatic ones, may cause our world horizons to contract, limiting what we are able to know and feel.

There is a deep human need to maintain the way our experiences are organized, and this is accomplished via a process called *concretization* (Atwood & Stolorow, 1993). Concretization assumes a variety of forms, including, but not limited to, dream imagery, behavioral enactments (including self-destructive behaviors), and creative endeavors, all of which serve as "royal roads" to the principles that unconsciously thematize and organize a person's psychological life. In other words, through symbols and actions, concretization makes "concrete" the felt reality of our lived experience.

Concretization can be *prereflectively* relied upon (without our realizing it) to "shore up an imperiled subjective world" (Atwood & Stolorow, 1993, p. 92), to restore or maintain structures of experience that are disintegrating, thus serving a restitutive function. We see this, for example, in the artist who writes her way through loss so catastrophic that it calls into question her sense of inviolability. But symbolic concretizations are seen not only where structures are breaking down; they are also apparent in situations where world horizons are expanding and new structures are coming into being. Moreover, the sensorimotor symbols of concretization may encapsulate both threats to the self and efforts at self-restoration. For instance, via the act of painting, an artist may exorcise, however fleetingly, the toxic influence of past trauma on the present—by inscribing the trauma itself in the visual language of the artwork, holding it captive in the canvas.

From the standpoint of phenomenological contextualism, psychological disorders may involve the consolidation of pathological structures that restrict experiencing, thereby preventing emotional conflict from rising (Stolorow, Atwood, & Brandchaft, 1994). We see this, for example, in the avoidance of situations that elicit anxiety, sometimes so blown out of proportion that the person never leaves the safety of their home. Insufficient structuration may also be involved, so that persons prone to self-fragmentation must rely on others to sustain the cohesion of experience, because they are incapable of doing so on their own. Inner cohesion, or the sense that one is unitary and whole, is but one of many dimensions of self-experience that are called into question, or even annihilated, in the face of unbearable trauma. Other dimensions include, but aren't limited to: temporal continuity, the sense that one's past, present, and future are linked; psychosomatic unity, the sense that one's mind and body are entwined, not irrevocably split; self-other differentiation, an understanding of where "I" end and "you" begin; affectivity, which refers to our capacity to feel; human volition, or agency; and authenticity, the experience that one is real rather than artificial (Orange, Atwood, & Stolorow, 2001).

Implicit in the concepts of *experiential worlds* and *world horizons* is that of *double-inhabiting*—that the world we inhabit inhabits us (Stolorow, Atwood, & Orange, 2002). It follows that from the point of view of the experiencing subject, self-loss is tantamount to world-loss, and vice versa. As mentioned, phenomenological contextualism is context-sensitive; just as there is no such thing as a *view from nowhere* (Nagel, 1986), there is also no such thing as *meaning-in-itself*, because "statements of truth or falsehood are meaningful only within systems" (Stolorow, Atwood, & Orange, 2002, p. 116). Context is crucial to interpretation.

To work contextually is to recognize that all phenomena are embedded within a larger historical matrix; that past and future are implicated in all present moments (we have come from somewhere, and we are going somewhere); and that the meaning of an utterance can only be discerned from its use in a particular dialogic context. To work contextually is to also work *structurally*. It involves understanding (psychological) phenomena in relation to other phenomena, and how these in turn constitute a structural whole.

Phenomenological contextualism is guided by the spirit of hermeneutics, which suggests "taking any strange-sounding utterance as true, then seeking to understand how a reasonable person could think in this way . . . so we can begin a dialogue with what seems to us strange" (Stolorow, Atwood, & Orange, 2002, pp. 27–28). It is an endeavor that values the truth of the other's experience. To proceed hermeneutically is to see how individual parts give rise to a whole, which in turn serves as the context against which each part becomes interpretable and intelligible. When studying human lives, this translates to collecting relevant pieces of biographical (and historical) information to arrive at a fuller picture of a life, against which individual life events attain meaning and coloration, with each new revelation calling for reinterpretation.

Phenomenological contextualism is also guided by the epistemological attitudes of *fallibilism* and *perspectival realism*, respectively. The observer's interpretations "may at any time be mistaken" (p. 27), and his or her subjective reality is no more true than that of the observed. The narrative account that emerges is self-contained, capable of being understood on its own terms, but it is by no means final. The subjective reality of another is never fully knowable; we can only approximate it from within our particularized perspective.

This epistemological stance is invaluable because in order to understand the central paradox of our concern in a *humanly* intelligible way, the path forward lies not in reduction to symptoms and abstractions but immersion in lifeworlds. Let us now turn to the method animating this endeavor: the psychobiographical method.

ON PSYCHOBIOGRAPHY

Psychobiography refers to both the method of collecting and interpreting "data" about individuals, and the narrative account that is formulated as a result. In spirit, psychobiography is a partial "cure" for the "sickness" of reductionism and triviality that has plagued academic psychology; as Schultz (2005a) argues, the individual is at least as important a unit of analysis as faceless undergraduates participating in lab experiments for class credit. In highlighting what makes people unique, irrespective of their group affiliation, we in turn come to better understand the human condition and *ourselves*. Most psychological theories that drive research do not emerge from nothingness, but are actually inspired by the study of individual lives. Therefore, one of psychobiography's most important contributions is the formulation of theory itself: "Psychobiographies produce strong hunches, or insights, leading in time to formal propositions that can be tested against larger groups of people" (Schultz, 2005a, p. 4).

Psychobiography draws together disparate webs of knowledge, integrating different disciplines as well as the split selves of psychology. Like phenomenological inquiry, it is a structuralist endeavor that requires interpretation and meaning-making, and that which is not directly observable, such as dreams, unconscious ideas, and motives, are presumed to be just as real and amenable to analysis. Unlike biography, which seeks to chronicle an entire life, the goal of psychobiography is more modest: to illuminate one or a small handful of related episodes, actions, or events in a person's life. Psychobiographical inquiry is iterative: "The process unfolds according to its own timetable, until one achieves what feels like the best fit, the most elegant coherence between the life, the work, and the link between the two" (Schultz, 2005a, p. 9). More "data" lead to more robust interpretations, which in turn lead to more refined ways of configuring the "data."

Throughout, I endeavored to follow the hallmarks of good psychobiography, including cogency, sound logic and structure, comprehensiveness (multiple facets of an action or event are illuminated), convergence of evidence (a single interpretation is supported by multiple "data" sources), and elegance (e.g., Runyan, 2005; Schultz, 2005a). Good psychobiography exhibits careful selection of theory and does not let the subject drown in jargon and metaphysical conceit. It is not beholden to a single theoretical framework; the details of the subject's life should dictate the theories selected, not the other way around. As mentioned, psychobiography is interpretive; it is *not* diagnostic. The worst kind of psychobiography, "pathography," is one that diagnoses, because it does not interpret at all but merely substitutes names for behaviors. Rather than leave things in, pathography leaves things *out*, and it reduces artistic and creative productions to disease symptoms. The book you are reading is as far from that as you can imagine.

What you hold is a multiple-case psychobiography, which is more than a collection of single-subject psychobiographies. When writing psychobiography with multiple subjects, one has a choice between *serial* and *parallel* iteration (Isaacson, 2005). The former treats each subject separately, while the latter generates a single narrative about all subjects; this book falls in the former camp. A single narrative about all 11 creative suicides featured here would have been ill-equipped to deal with the nuances of each person's life, not to mention the micro-, meso-, and macro-contexts that each inhabited. But as with any multiple-case psychobiography, comparisons are made between subjects (in brief interludes and in the culminating chapter), making this approach "morphogenic." While it benefits from the strengths of the nomothetic approach by means of a comparison group, a meaningful understanding of individual lives is not lost, because each subject is approached ideographically. Thus, each case study is self-contained, and they can be read in any order.

THE CHAPTERS AHEAD

This book examines the creativity and suicide of 11 individuals across 10 chapters. In order, they are (1) Iris Chang, journalist, historian, and author of *The Rape of Nanking*, which chronicled Japan's gruesome atrocities in China's former capital during World War II; (2) Kevin Carter, Pulitzer Prize–winning photographer who documented the "hostel wars" of apartheid South Africa; (3) Phyllis Hyman, jazz, blues, and R&B singer; (4) Kurt Cobain, lead singer and songwriter of Nirvana; (5) Sylvia Plath, confessional poet and author of *The Bell Jar*; (6) the digital artist Jeremy Blake, and his lover, (7) video game designer and filmmaker Theresa Duncan; (8) Alan Turing, scientist, mathematician, and father of the modern computer; (9) Yukio Mishima, Japanese postwar author and playwright; (10) Reinaldo Arenas, Cuban author and vocal critic of Castro's regime; and (11) Robin Williams, beloved actor and stand-up comedian.

These individuals were selected for a variety of reasons. First, they represent a wide range of creative domains and subdomains, with some working in multiple or hybrid domains. As Schultz (2005b) notes, there is an abundance of psychobiographies on writers, mainly because verbal materials, such as poetry, fiction, and plays, are more accessible and transparent than other types of material. More attention needs to be funneled toward nonwriters, and this book is a modest attempt at that. Second, as Sass (1992) remarked, prevailing conceptions of creativity in psychology derive from Romanticist ideas, and this statement holds purchase even today. The inclusion of documentary (Chang, Carter) and scientific (Turing) domains decenters artistic and expressive creativity, even if only slightly. Third, the subjects are diverse in terms of gender, sexual orientation, class, race-ethnicity, and ability. One of the elephants in the room in the psychobiographical enterprise is the extensive focus on white subjects. Consider the inclusion of Iris Chang (Chinese American), Phyllis Hyman (African American), Yukio Mishima (Japanese), and Reinaldo Arenas (Cuban) a modest intervention. Lastly, the selected individuals come from different sociocultural and historical milieus. Thus, we are not only able to see how the micro- and macro-contexts interact for each subject but we are also able to see which aspects of the creativity-suicide connection endure across time and across space.

For each individual, I studied the life and the work *together* rather than separately, and I read every published biography I could get my hands on, to gain as full a picture as possible. For those who do not have a single biography written about them (Kevin Carter, Jeremy Blake, Theresa Duncan), I conducted a systematic LexisNexis search for news and popular press articles printed *after* their deaths. Given their retrospective nature, these are biographically more complete than articles published during the individual's lifetime. One exception is Reinaldo Arenas, who does not have a biography but had published a memoir shortly before his death; in his case, a LexisNexis search was not necessary. Whenever the opportunity presented itself, I traveled to museums and archives where personal artifacts of the decedent are stored. These include the Herbert Hoover Archives in Stanford University, where Iris Chang left over 300 boxes of such documents, and the Seattle Art Museum retrospective *Kurt*.

As for the work, each creative mode of production—written, oral/aural, visual, bodily/performative, digital, hybrid—"presents its own special complexities for the psychobiographer" (Schultz, 2005a, p. 18). The full range of creative productions I examined, and the ways I approached them, are beyond the scope of this brief introduction. Suffice it to say, I adapted my methods to the medium and endeavored to be comprehensive in the quantity and variety of works analyzed. For example, I listened to every song written and sung by Phyllis Hyman and Kurt Cobain; read the complete collection of Sylvia Plath's poems; played one of Theresa Duncan's video games on an old personal computer, watched a handful of her animated films on YouTube, and read all entries in her blog *The Wit of the Staircase*; viewed over 30 films Robin Williams had starred in; and read the major writings of Reinaldo Arenas and Yukio Mishima. While only the most exemplary and illustrative works are mentioned in the book and cited in the bibliography, bear in mind that the number of total works I examined over the last 13 years is far more extensive.

Chapter 1

"You Will Rescue Objects from Oblivion"

The Case of Iris Chang

A few hours before dawn on Tuesday, November 9, 2004, Iris Chang, best-selling author of *The Rape of Nanking* (1997), quietly slipped out of her house. She left behind three notes addressed to her parents, brother, and husband Brett of nine years, with whom she had a son.

The first note, titled "Statement of Iris Chang," read:

> I promise to get up and get out of the house every morning. I will stop by to visit my parents then go for a long walk. I will follow the doctor's orders for medications. I promise not to hurt myself. I promise not to visit Web sites that talk about suicide. (quoted in Benson, 2005)

A few months ago in August 2004, during a research trip to Louisville, Kentucky, Iris had been involuntarily admitted to the psychiatric unit of Norton Hospital. Because she was behaving erratically and exhibiting flagrant symptoms of paranoia (the CIA was out to get her, she'd claimed), the doctors diagnosed her with bipolar disorder, with psychotic features. They placed her on a regimen of tranquilizers and the antipsychotic Risperdal, but she didn't like how the drugs made her feel: zombified, unalive, and not herself. Iris then attempted group therapy, but the vacant and soulless expressions of the other patients scared her away from continuing treatment.

In the second note, Iris wrote: "I had considered running away, but I will never escape from myself and my thoughts. I am doing this because I am too weak to withstand the years of pain and agony ahead" (Benson, 2005).

Weeks ago, Iris checked into a hotel room in the middle of the afternoon, carrying a bottle of wine and a paper bag full of pills. She had intended to die then, but exhausted, she fell asleep instead. Her family managed to find her and continued to monitor her every behavior for potential signs of suicide. But this time, they would not find her soon enough.

"Each breath is becoming difficult for me to take—the anxiety can be compared to drowning in an open sea," she wrote in her third and last note. "I know that my actions will transfer some of this pain to others, indeed those who love me most. Please forgive me. Forgive me because I cannot forgive myself" (Kamen, 2007, p. 57).

Iris drove down Highway 17 and in Los Gatos, California, pulled over on a desolate section of the road. Yesterday, she'd stopped by Reed's Sport Shop in San Jose. Although firearms dealers are required by state law to run background checks on customers, an exception is made for the purchase of antique guns. Knowing that she'd fail the check because of her stint in a mental hospital, Iris told the clerk that she was a historian researching antique guns. She bought the biggest one she could find—a frontier-type gun with ivory handles—and gave a local gunsmith 10 dollars to teach her how to load and fire it.

Iris pulled out the gun and loaded it with gun powder and a lead ball. She put the gun in her mouth and squeezed the trigger. Her body was found some time after daybreak. She was 36.

THE WORLD ON THE OTHER SIDE

The death of Iris Chang was unthinkable to those who viewed her as a "warrior" woman, someone unafraid to expose wartime atrocities that had been buried for decades under lies. People called her "a beacon for Chinese Americans" (Mueller, 2004), "a stoic and heroic warrior, who illuminated the world with her writings and vigilance" (Chu, 2004). The most frequently enlisted rhetoric to explain her death was that she suffered from mental illness—specifically, bipolar disorder. While this diagnosis is not inaccurate (after all, she did cycle between mania and depression), it is also not profound. It tells us very little about her as a person: her craft, her vocation as a historian and social activist, and her commitment to the preservation of justice, no matter the cost. "Bipolar" diverts attention *away* from her life. But if we are to understand Iris Chang as a human being, it is precisely the nuances of her life to which we must turn. Not so that we can gather more evidence of her bipolar tendencies, but so that we can understand more fully the humanity of her actions.

Iris was born on March 28, 1968, to Chinese parents who came to the United States to become prominent scientists. Naturally, they wanted to raise her to be a gifted child. To teach her vocabulary, for example, they read to her every night and labeled everything in the house with index cards. But it would be erroneous to give them full credit for her success, for even as a little girl, Iris possessed a degree of autonomy uncharacteristic of most children. She had an insatiable love of learning that only widened her curiosity about the world. She cared less about grades and more about learning for learning's sake. She was also very diligent.

As a child, Iris liked to picture herself in the role of the detective. She spied on friends and family members and wrote what she observed in her "Secret Spys Notebook" (n.d.d). But instead of using the 26 letters and 10 digits of the alpha-numeric system, she created an elaborate system of pictographs that no one else could decipher. She wrote her first mystery story at age four, and many others thereafter: of evildoers receiving just punishment for their wrongdoings; of two brothers who unravel a case involving the mysterious theft of ancient artifacts ("Racing the Hail Storm," n.d.c); of a man seeking retribution for having been sentenced to life in prison under the false charge of murder ("From the Files of the FBI," n.d.b). These stories invite readers to solve the mystery alongside the narrator, sometimes teasing them with red herrings (e.g., "The Case of the Meat Grinder," n.d.e). She would then compile her writings into self-made books, from which she would give "public" readings at school and at home.

Given her precociousness, it's hardly surprising that Iris became a member of Mensa and scored in the 99th percentile of an IQ test at age 15 ("Mensa correspondence," 1983). The local and university libraries of her hometown, Urbana, Illinois, were uniquely special to her. She believed that books—the thicker the dust on the jacket, the better—contained the answers to some of the world's greatest mysteries. All she had to do was pry them open.

As with many gifted children, Iris possessed an insight and emotional maturity that were well beyond her years, which caused her to feel alienated at times. Her writings from adolescence reveal an awareness of the transitory nature of life, the inevitability of death, and the world's dire state, plagued by one unremitting war after another. In a poem titled "The Invasion" (n.d.g), for example, she writes about a World War III, in which planet Earth was so busy "battling with itself" that people were trampled like ants by extraterrestrials. In a story called "The Halloween Prince" (1988a), the narrator ponders whether a "short life threatened by a million things" is necessarily worse than "a secluded long one . . . able to see the world on the other side, but never able to reach it." And lastly, in "The Fiasco" (n.d.f), a female artist deems herself to be such a failure in life that she commits suicide by drug overdose. In a cruel twist of fate, the artist's last painting receives posthumous praise from art critics.

Although these stories suggest a growing attraction to dark subjects, one must be careful not to confuse the loneliness and sensitivity so often experienced by gifted children with manifestations of an underlying mental disorder. But one can view these childhood artifacts as *prototypes* of Iris Chang's social justice and investigative work. As an adult, she would enthusiastically describe archival research as "detective work" (Kamen, 2007, p. 67) and passionately devote her career to championing the rights of the downtrodden.

THE SHADOW SIDE OF HUMAN NATURE

Iris was not one to shy away from exposing injustice, whatever form it took. *Thread of the Silkworm* (1995), her first book, which she began writing at age 23, is a biography of Tsien Hsue-shen. Tsien was a Chinese scientist whose expertise in jet propulsion and aerodynamics helped strengthen American military defense during World War II. But in spite of his contributions to the scientific community, Tsien was accused of being a member of a Communist cell in Pasadena, California, where he and his family resided, during the McCarthy era's "Red Scare." His careers in government, industry, and academia were crushed, and the flimsiest evidence became grounds for his deportation. In a strange twist of irony, by deporting Tsien the United States made his talents available to the Communist regime in China, where he revolutionized space development and oversaw the creation of the Silkworm missile.

The Chinese in America (2003), the third and last book published under Iris's name, recalls the struggle of Chinese immigrants and their American-born descendants to find acceptance in the face of institutional racism and discrimination. Over the course of 150 years, the Chinese triumphed over a series of exclusionary acts and secured the right to naturalize, vote, own land, participate in labor unions, and testify against whites in court. But as Iris astutely observed, injustice on the basis of race still lingers. At the time of the book's writing, Chinese American employees received 20% less in wages than whites with similar credentials. Mattel's millennium collection of future female presidents included white, Black, and Hispanic, but not Asian, Barbie dolls. And relative to other ethnic minorities, a disproportionately greater percentage of Chinese high school seniors were (and continue to be) denied admission to the most prestigious universities, despite stellar academic records and involvement in extracurricular activities.

But the visage of injustice had never been uglier than in Iris's second and arguably most important book, *The Rape of Nanking* (1997), which documented the seemingly endless atrocities committed by Japanese soldiers in China's former capital during World War II. In a matter of six weeks—and in most brutal fashion—the massacre leveled Nanking's population from over half a million to less than two hundred thousand. On her own, Iris traveled to China, Hong Kong, and Taiwan to interview elderly survivors, whom she called "the last human links to the past" (Chang, 1998, p. 183). She critically examined documents in four different languages and tracked down letters and diaries penned by those who had witnessed the massacre.

The horrific story of Nanking was one familiar to Iris from a young age, passed down to her by her grandparents, who had lived there and managed to escape before the city fell. She learned, for example, that the Japanese military "sliced babies not just in half but in thirds and fourths" (p. 8), and that the Yangtze River, a dumping ground for thousands of fresh corpses, "ran red with blood for days" (ibid.). These stories were never forgotten but relegated to the deeper recesses of her memory, only to be reawakened with force nearly two decades later by poster-sized photographs of the Rape at a conference for the preservation of World War II history. Iris was not prepared for the gruesome black-and-white images she saw: stomachs torn open, heads separated from torsos, the contorted faces of women forced into rape and submission.

For too long, the massacre had been reduced to a mere footnote in history. Iris insisted on writing *The Rape of Nanking* to purge the world of its collective amnesia, even if it was the last thing she ever wrote. But instead, the project "ended as a personal exploration into the shadow side of human nature" (p. 220). Never before had human existence seemed so fragile and the faces of evil so innumerable.

Through her research and interviews with survivors, Iris learned the extent to which the 300,000 slaughtered civilians suffered at the hands of their captors. Pregnant women who tried desperately to fight off their assailants were disemboweled, the squirming fetuses inside their bellies ripped out. Infants met bayonet point and were tossed alive into pots of boiling water. Men were buried to the waist, then hacked to pieces with swords, run over with horses and tanks, or fed to packs of ravenous German shepherds. Labor workers were mummified alive with ropes, then stoned to death with heaps upon heaps of bricks, leaving the corpses disfigured beyond recognition. Victims were propped up on wooden poles and used for bayonet practice, the thrusts continuing long after they stopped breathing. Sometimes, they were hanged by their tongues, stabbed with hundreds of needles, or had long strips of flesh carved from their bodies. Nails were extracted from fingers and joints ripped from their sockets. Prisoners of war (POWs) were fed and injected lethal substances, including snake venom, and had water or kerosene pumped into their orifices until their stomachs and bladders ruptured.

The atrocities did not end there.

Iris discovered that Japanese soldiers murdered the Chinese for no other reason than pleasure. They performed vivisections (cutting people open while alive); decapitated thousands during infamous killing contests; gang-raped

Buddhist nuns and elderly women to death; forced men to commit necrophilia and rape their own mothers, sisters, and daughters; and impaled women's vaginas with broken beer bottles, golf clubs, bamboo shoots, and lit firecrackers. Iris estimated that up to 80,000 women from all social classes were raped, including girls under the age of 10, who were cut down in half when they could no longer satisfy the sexual requirements of their assailants. The Japanese raped virginal young girls under the preposterous belief that it would render them impervious to bullets. Men were not exempt from torture of the sexual kind. They were brutally sodomized by laughing Japanese soldiers and stripped naked on the streets, their genitals exposed to packs of hungry canines.

The atrocities mentioned represent only a small fraction of the horrors that took place within China's former capital, which in turn comprise a mere sliver of Japan's war crimes in the Pacific theater. "There seemed to be no limit to the Japanese capacity for human degradation and sexual perversion in Nanking" (Chang, 1997, p. 94), wrote Iris, calling such disrespect for the dead and dying a "reversion in human and social evolution" (p. 10). But what she found most detestable was Japan's refusal as a nation to acknowledge that the massacre ever took place, a massacre so unbelievably horrific, it could not have possibly been true.

The murder of innocent civilians is a clear violation of the Geneva and Hague Conventions. But after the atomic bombs fell on Hiroshima and Nagasaki, the Japanese government orchestrated the myth that its people were the primary victims of World War II, and therefore, bore no responsibility for the wholesale massacre of innocent civilians elsewhere. There was no Japanese equivalent to the Nuremberg Trials, which prosecuted the military and political leaders of the Third Reich for Holocaust atrocities. Instead, names of class-A war criminals were inscribed in Tokyo's Yasukuni Shrine, where their souls are installed and worshipped as *kami*, or gods of the battlefield. The Japanese were prolific in photographing the crimes they committed against humanity, with pictures of beheading contests amid an enthusiastic crowd splashed on the front pages of the widely read *Asahi Shimbun* (trans. *Morning Newspaper*). And yet, despite overwhelming evidence that reports of the Rape appeared in both Western print media *and* Japanese newspapers, the Japanese Ministry of Education continues to remove references to the Rape from history textbooks, and this whitewashing extends to other forms of cultural production. For instance, a 30-second scene depicting the massacre was deleted from Bernardo Bertolucci's 1987 film *The Last Emperor* by Shochiku Fuji, a distribution company in Japan, without the director's consent. Those who dare suggest that history books are propagating lies, or that the Imperial family should be held liable for the massacre, receive death threats from right-wing extremists and ultranationalists.

As one of the first to capture on videotape the oral testimonies of Nanking's elderly survivors, Iris saw with her own eyes the repercussions of Japan's "selective amnesia" (Chang, 1998, p. 205). Believing that the People's Republic of China had long forfeited the right to seek reparations, most survivors lived in conditions of abject poverty, "in dark, squalid apartments . . . heavy with mildew and humidity" (p. 183). Some were unable to make a decent living because of the injuries they had sustained. Wrote Iris: "even a minimal amount of financial compensation from Japan could have greatly improved the conditions of their lives" (ibid.). She described Japan's historical revisionism as a second rape and warned her readers that "to forget a holocaust is to kill twice" (p. 16).

Iris was determined to put an end to Japan's ongoing burial of massacre victims—"not under the soil, as in 1937, but into historical oblivion" (p. 220). However, the price she paid for her efforts was immense. As a result of her work on *The Rape of Nanking*, Iris felt especially hopeless about the state of humanity. She began to wonder if people are, at their core, actually good. Iris had always been (hyper)sensitive to the pain of others. In college, she broke down in tears in front of a journalism class when describing her experiences writing about a man who had died of AIDS. It is not surprising, then, that she found listening to the oral histories of massacre victims "so physically and psychologically draining" (Kamen, 2007, pp. 76–77).

"AN EVIL FORCE WILL HURT ME"

In a study of staff workers at the Holocaust Memorial Museum in Washington, D.C., McCarroll and colleagues (1995) found that handling traumatic materials produced symptoms resembling that of post-traumatic stress: anger, nightmares, social withdrawal, emotional numbing, grief. Though the staff had never experienced war trauma directly, prolonged contact with archival materials and survivor histories was enough to leave an indelible imprint on their minds.

Mental health professionals refer to *indirect* exposure to traumatic events as secondary, or vicarious, traumatization—as opposed to *primary* trauma, which implies direct exposure. It results from empathic engagement with painful material, often brought by victims to the listener or viewer. It is an accumulative process, meaning that single exposure is not enough. Several factors contribute to vicarious trauma, including the duration of exposure, the intensity and severity of the raw materials encountered, the listener's (in)ability to change the victim's predicament, and the extent to which the listener is empathetic (Baird & Kracen, 2006; Chouliara, Hutchison, & Karatzias, 2009; Dunkley & Whelan, 2006; McCann & Pearlman, 1990). Horrific stories passed down by families to future generations, and the listener's own history of primary trauma can also render one susceptible to vicarious trauma (Baranowsky et al., 1998). As someone "hypersensitive" and "vulnerable" by her own admission (Chang, 2000), and who met all the aforementioned qualifications, Iris was in an especially precarious position.

While writing *The Rape of Nanking*, Iris experienced tremor and moments of intense physical pain, for which there was no underlying physiological cause. She also felt "strapped to a roller coaster," unable to get off, and spent countless hours in tears (Kamen, 2007, pp. 76–77). But the pain lingered long after the book had been written. Images of the Rape would "float" in front of her and bleed into every marginal space of her waking life: while she was shopping, taking a bath, or walking through the park. Not wanting the events to "spill over" and "poison" the rest of her life, she would chide herself, "Put it out of your mind" (ibid.).

But Iris Chang was a woman who never stopped. At the behest of her mother to pick a lighter topic for her next book, she wrote *The Chinese in America*, but soon after its completion, she found herself thrust into another dark moment in World War II history: the Bataan Death March.

For two years, Iris collected oral testimonies from American POWs who had been held captive by the Japanese in the Philippine peninsula of Bataan. Specifically, she wanted to write about the 192nd battalion from the Midwest states of Illinois, Kentucky, Ohio, and Wisconsin. Their ordeals would have been the subject of her fourth book had she lived to complete it. The transcriber of her interviews said, "She had cried all the way through the work because it was so intensely sad" (Kamen, 2007, p. 16). POWs recounted grisly stories of being ordered by their captors, at bayonet point, to bury their comrades alive, and amputees with suppurating wounds being forced to walk the entire length of Bataan's Old National Road, a distance of no less than 60 miles. According to other authoritative sources (e.g., Norman & Norman, 2009), Japanese "cleanup crews" and "buzzard squads" split open the heads of dehydrated soldiers who broke formation to fill their canteens. Those who did survive the March were then shipped to Japan, to slave under life-threatening conditions in mines and factories.

The trauma of being a secondary witness to unimaginable violence filled Iris with immense pain, and she could not expel the horrific images of death and dying from her thoughts. Prolonged confrontation with evil made the world a more terrifying place for Iris, possibly as terrifying as it had been for the victims of Nanking and Bataan. She began to see the world through trauma-tinted lenses. She trusted others less and became preoccupied with her and her loved ones' personal safety.

Her fears began to metastasize around the time *The Rape of Nanking* was published. In November 1997, *Newsweek* delayed a scheduled excerpt from the book in response to backlash from Japanese advertisers, which Iris perceived as an attempt by corporations to undermine her work. Before long, Japan sympathizers who deemed her book libelous were harassing her by mail, on the phone, and in person during book tours. One man came up to her and said, "You will NOT continue writing this" (Benson, 2005). Another created a website called "Iris Chang and Her Lies." Iris never received death threats herself, but her ex-Japanese publisher, the liberal Kashiwa Shobo Company, received several from right-wing extremists. As a result, her book's publication in Japan was suspended indefinitely, and any plans to travel there would have been unsafe, to say the least.

Iris soon became convinced that her phones were bugged. She kept her home address a secret, even from friends, and warned her husband and family members that an "evil force" would harm her if she told the world of the alleged conspiracy. She found respite during the writing of *The Chinese in America*, but her fears resurfaced and spiraled out of control years later, in the midst of her research on the Bataan.

In a December 24, 2001, *New York Times* article, "Betrayed by the White House," Iris criticized the Bush administration for blocking efforts by Bataan veterans to seek reparations from Japanese corporations. She writes: "Our leaders must not be permitted to sell out the men who gave so much for our freedom. . . . If we are to have another 'greatest generation' we must duly honor the rights of the first one."

The long-standing debt to Bataan veterans goes as far back as 1947. Immediately after World War II, the United States found itself in the grip of the Cold War. To make a long story short, tables turned and Japan suddenly became an ally of strategic importance against the former Soviet Union. Following a series of negotiations between the United States and its former nemesis, high-ranking Japanese officials were granted immunity from the Tokyo War Crimes Trial, absolving Japan from facing full moral accountability for its crimes in the global theater. As a consequence, Japan was never obligated to dole out reparations to Bataan veterans and their surviving families.

Iris had fought on behalf of Nanking's elderly survivors, and she was determined to do the same for the men of Bataan. However, she was convinced that the magnitude and controversial nature of the story she had unraveled was beyond imagining. She confessed to her friend and biographer: "People in high places are not going to like it. Frankly, Paula, I fear for my life" (Kamen, 2007, p. xi). Thinking that the Bush administration had orchestrated a plot to discredit her work—which was tantamount to negating her—Iris became visibly upset when in 2004 President G. W. Bush was reelected for a second term.

Telltale signs of the evil plot surrounded her—from damaged mail arriving at her P.O. Box to a mysterious white van parked outside her house. She and she alone sensed that she was being followed in the streets and that strange people were looking up at the windows of her room. Later that year, while she was conducting interviews with Death March survivors in Louisville, Kentucky, Iris panicked when a colonel entered her hotel room and said, "I want you to join our organization" (p. 186). She accused him of being a confederate of the U.S. government, when in fact he was referring to an advocacy group lobbying for the remuneration of Bataan veterans. When he offered her a glass of water, she accused him of trying to poison her. Iris was involuntarily admitted to the psychiatric ward of Norton Hospital, which she saw as further evidence of the conspiracy, saying, "They recruited me and I turned them down, and now they're out to get me" (p. 187).

A PIECE OF ETERNITY

Iris's fears were not without basis in objective reality. Sometime after her death, her biographer, Paula Kamen (2007), filed a Freedom of Information Act request to the State Department and received 26 multipage documents marked "sensitive" and "immediate." The files were dated between May 1998 and December 2005, spanning almost the entire length of Iris Chang's writing career. They had been sent to the White House, to defense and intelligence agencies, and to U.S. embassies all over Asia—apparently, to mitigate the impact of *The Rape of Nanking* on U.S.-Japan diplomatic relations.

In other words, Iris's suspicions were correct, to the extent that she was indeed on the radar of two global powers. To borrow the words of Fingleton (2008): "In essence Chang was poking a stick in the eyes of two of the world's most powerful governments at once." Yet one cannot deny that her work with dark subjects colored her perceptions. Her vigilance to real and imagined threats, and her reaction to the colonel when he walked into her hotel room, are consistent with the worldview of traumatized individuals.

Several factors exacerbated Iris's condition, one of which was an unforgiving schedule. During her book tour for *The Chinese in America*, which lasted a mere five weeks, Iris attended 35 events across 20 cities, crisscrossing the continent four times. She hardly ate, hardly slept, and was mentally fatigued. Simply put, she worked herself tirelessly, a trait she possessed since childhood. But one must be careful not to reduce her drive and "enormous passion" to mania, as her biographer does, which severely undermines her commitment to the preservation of justice. Iris never once believed she was so-called bipolar. Neither did her family, and one must respect that.

Then there was the issue of her treatment with antidepressants and antipsychotics during the last year of her life. In her memoir *The Woman Who Could Not Forget*, Ying-Ying Chang (2012), Iris Chang's mother, writes that not only did high doses of Risperdal and Depakote *not* improve her daughter's condition, but they produced all sorts of frightening side effects, including bizarre suicidal ideation and akathisia, a state of extreme restlessness. For Ying-Ying, it is no coincidence that Iris's first suicide attempt on September 2004, and her attempt to buy a gun a month later, both took place within days of her starting a new medication (Celexa). According to Ying-Ying, the violent nature of Iris's death was "uncharacteristic." This is unsurprising, in light of recent scientific findings that antidepressants (compared to placebo) can paradoxically multiply the risk of suicide, and in light of FDA black box warnings that psychotropic drugs can induce the very symptoms they were meant to alleviate.

However, it's worth noting that Iris's depression and persecutory beliefs intensified even before she was treated with said drugs. In fact, they took on a life of their own during those years when she was trying desperately to conceive a child.

It is not unreasonable to think that prolonged confrontation with grotesque images of death, and with insidious forces that seek to erase millions from the pages of history, made Iris realize the finitude of her own life. Human beings, when faced with the reality of their own mortality, perpetuate themselves by leaving behind a replica of their body or spirit (Becker, 1997). For Iris, the miracle of conception and birth was the ultimate creative act, the means by which to forestall or undo her own dying. She referred to the human progeny as "a piece of eternity," and in a letter to her friend and biographer, she writes: "It's important that somebody lives on after me with a piece of me . . . men come and go, but your children are always going to be your children. They're part of you. They're your flesh and blood" (Kamen, 2007, p. 145). Bearing children may have been a way for Iris to redeem what was left of her finite existence—and to affirm life itself, for it takes courage of the highest degree to give birth after witnessing human nature's darkest terrains.

But Iris had difficulty getting pregnant. According to blood tests, she had suffered four miscarriages without even knowing it. Apparently, she and her husband Brett had mismatched immune systems. Whenever the egg was fertilized or the embryo was formed, Iris's body would see it as a foreign entity and reject it. The thought of being unable to bear a child made Iris intensely sad. Once, while waiting for her order inside a restaurant, tears flowed from her eyes at the sight of a mother and child sharing a meal together, and another child bobbing up and down its mother's lap.

Iris didn't want to adopt; she wanted a child of her blood. She explored alternative medicine and attended a support group for couples with infertility issues. Ultimately, she and Brett decided that experimental drugs and intravenous immune globulin therapy were too risky, opting instead for a surrogate mother to carry her egg and his sperm to term. Their son Christopher (named after the doctor who'd diagnosed the immunity-incompatibility problem) was born to a surrogate on August 31, 2002, the year before she began her research on the Bataan.

The months leading up to Christopher's birth were shrouded in secrecy. During that time, she rarely stepped outside her townhouse. She avoided contact with friends and relatives so as not to disclose the details of her complicated pregnancy. Some speculate that Iris was too ashamed of being unable to conceive, but the fact that she kept Christopher's existence secret even *after* his birth only proves that she genuinely feared for his safety. She had to keep him alive, in order to keep her *self* alive. She said as much in a personal letter to her biographer, in which she repeats the words of her then-editor Susan Rabiner: "The worst thing you could do to hurt a woman is to take her children away. . . . That's even worse than having her husband killed. That's the worst thing that could ever happen to you" (Kamen, 2007, p. 145).

Paradoxically, the real basis of her concern for her son was her continuing aliveness, that Christopher would be in danger for as long as she lived. And that is why Iris felt remorse beyond absolution when he was diagnosed with Asperger's syndrome, a less severe form of autism. At the time, it was believed that the combined measles, mumps, and rubella vaccine could lead to autism when administered to infants during critical periods of brain development. This was later debunked when Andrew Wakefield, the author of the research paper that spread such findings, was discovered to have falsified the results. Wakefield had backdoor deals with lawyers and made nearly half a million pounds from compensation claims by parents of autistic children. Unfortunately, the results weren't debunked soon enough. Iris blamed herself for having had Christopher vaccinated. "I've made serious mistakes with my son," she said to her biographer, who described the tone of her voice as "firm, like she was proclaiming an unassailable guilty verdict on herself from the voice of the highest possible authority" (Kamen, 2007, p. xii). By convincing herself that she'd given Christopher autism, Iris came to believe that she extinguished the only part of her self that would live on.

CONCLUDING REMARKS

At the age of 20, when Iris was still an aspiring journalist, she wrote in her journal:

> Think: I'm going to write a story, a story the world has never [heard] of before. This story will be special to me, whether it win prizes or sell well. It will be my creation, my child. Something that never existed before [and] now because of me, exists. (Chang, 1988b)

This story, of course, would be *The Rape of Nanking*, but while it did win prizes and sell well, this creation also heralded her descent into madness, and ultimately, suicide. This descent is chillingly captured by an unpublished poem, titled "End of the Mirror Tunnel" (Chang, n.d.a) which conjures the image of two mirrors placed in front of one another. What is reflected on each surface stretches infinitely inward, and for the narrator, to see oneself "spiraling forever" is maddening, like a tightrope walker on "thin ladder bars," with no end or landing in sight and a "bottomless" abyss threatening to swallow one whole.

Tracing the pathway from creativity to suicide: Iris Chang's encounter with the photographic inventory of Japan's wartime atrocities compelled her to direct her creative energies toward the preservation of historical truth. In dealing with collective trauma, she herself became traumatized, her sense of ontological safety breached. Though she continued to write prolifically, another creative pathway surfaced, and that was the creation of an offspring that would endure long after she is gone. Unfortunately, her son was diagnosed with autism, for which she blamed herself. As a final stand against forces of negation, and as punishment for her perceived crime against her child, she extinguished her own life.

As we have seen, the human meaning of Iris Chang's suicide is multiplex, irreducible to a singular cause. It was the outcome of sustained confrontation with human evil, and of being a secondary witness to unimaginable violence. It was the means by which she could preserve her agency, against forces—both real and imagined—that threatened to negate her work and her *self*. It was the product of pharmacologic interventions that intensified rather than ameliorated her suffering. And it was atonement, for having had her son vaccinated before the age of two. By putting an antique gun between her lips, Iris took on the role of both jury and defendant, and in squeezing the trigger, she became her own executioner.

Contrary to claims of Japanese extremists—that Iris committed suicide because she could no longer live with her "lies"—her death does not discredit her work, but instead, underscores its seriousness and global import. By venturing into the dangerous interstice where creativity, on one hand, and death, on the other, meet, Iris was able to rescue moments of paramount importance from oblivion, thereby restoring them to their proper place in history. In doing so, she taught both her readers and survivors of wartime atrocities that remaining silent about oppression only invites further injustice.

Incidentally, her story also breached the long-standing taboo surrounding Asian American mental health. Asian Americans are far less likely than whites and the general population to seek professional help for psychological distress. Doing so is culturally perceived as a sign of weakness and invites ridicule from friends, family members, and relatives. If and when one does seek help, it is carried out in secrecy, divorced from crucial networks of support.

But the pressures of being Asian American are manifold: racial discrimination, parental demands to succeed academically, internalization of the "model minority" stereotype. For recent migrants, especially those who escaped oppressive regimes, there is the added stress of *acculturation*, of acclimatizing to a new social and cultural surround. Despite successful transitions, many report feeling stuck between two places: as foreigners in their adopted country, and as strangers in their native homelands. In light of these challenges, distress is to be expected, but because of a reluctance to seek help, suicide is a leading cause of death among Asian Americans, generally, and Asian American women, especially.

To this day, Japan has yet to issue a formal apology to the citizens of Nanking and survivors of Bataan. The true impact of Iris Chang's legacy has yet to be felt.

Chapter 2

"Haunted By the Vivid Memories of Killings"

The Case of Kevin Carter

Kevin went from one drugstore to another until he has accumulated enough sleeping pills, painkillers, and rat poison. He then treated himself to a chocolate milkshake and a Wimpy burger, after which he ingested the drugstore items, washing them down with a bottle of Coke. Lying in bed, he asked himself, "Why had I failed so miserably?" (Marinovich & Silva, 2000, p. 40).

Kevin Carter was born on September 13, 1960, to a white middle-class family in the affluent suburbs of Johannesburg, South Africa. Growing up, he had little confidence in himself. He was an irritable child who often quarreled with his father, and, according to his mother, was prone to "moods and outbursts" that his parents found "impossible to deal with" (p. 39). After graduating from high school, he tried to pursue a degree in pharmacy but soon dropped out with unsatisfactory marks. He was then drafted into the army's infantry unit—ironic given his conscientious objection to war—but later switched to the air force, where he would spend the next four years of his life. Needless to say, he disliked life in military service so much that he went AWOL after fellow soldiers ganged up on him for defending a Black waiter. Desperate to start fresh, he assumed the name "David" and became a radio disc jockey in the coastal city of Durban. However, his plans for a new life fell through when he couldn't open a bank account with his fake name. With his life at a standstill, he became severely depressed, contemplated suicide day and night, and finally decided to take action.

He left his room and went to the beachfront to play a few games in the arcade. When he was down to his last few rands, he walked into a phone booth determined to bid someone, anyone, farewell. He couldn't die "without saying just one goodbye" (p. 41). Though he looked forward to his death "as an upcoming relief, a total escape from my solution, my problems, and the mess I felt I had made of my life" (p. 40), his actions suggest a faint connection to life that had not dissolved entirely. What he wanted was to cease to be a burden on anyone and be free of other people's expectations. But before he could pick up the phone, his vision went black.

Kevin regained consciousness in the emergency room and felt shame upon seeing his mother: "I shall never forget facing my mother again. It is living through a suicide that is the hardest part" (p. 41). To resume the life he had almost forsaken, he decided to see through the rest of his military commitment. One afternoon, outside the military headquarters where he was stationed, militant members of the African National Congress (ANC), the antiapartheid liberation party, detonated a bomb. The explosion sent Kevin flying through a window. As he was assisting wounded personnel, he realized that he himself had been struck by shrapnel. Bearing witness to the ANC attack filled him with an excitement he'd never before felt. Barely 23 years old, he decided then that he wanted to be a part of and record history.

Within a year, Kevin would become a photojournalist, a documentarian of the National Party's regime, and the violence and injustice of apartheid. The South Africa he inhabited was one where the majority Black population had no human rights, where three hundred years of white rule kept Blacks from receiving education, and where Blacks remained in labor and service jobs, living in sprawling townships in poor health and unsanitary conditions. Though whites made up only 14% of the population, 80% of the country was reserved for them (Schaffer & Smith, 2004). The National Party, the all-white ruling party, limited Black aspirations and reproduced relations of subordination by segregating Blacks according to ethnolinguistic divides, keeping them from massing and curtailing their movements to other parts of the country. The party also fomented much violence between different Black factions and tribes, and it was this violence that Kevin captured with his camera, violence that would haunt him until the end of his life.

"A DARK PLACE WITH DARK IMAGES"

The camera helped renew Kevin's connection to life by imbuing it with newfound purpose, but it also spurred him into a realm where the frightening possibility of death awaited at every turn. He and three other photojournalists, together known as the Bang Bang Club, ventured into South Africa's townships to cover the "hostel wars"—gruesome blood baths that erupted between militant factions of the ANC, the liberation party that opposed apartheid, and the Inkatha Freedom Party (IFP), Zulu nationalists who were covertly funded by white supremacists to uphold the National Party's white dominion over the nation.

Not long after he started working for the papers in the mid-1980s, Kevin witnessed the first known public execution by "necklacing." The victim was Maki Skosana, a woman accused of dating a policeman, an instrument of the white state. Deemed a traitor to the Black community, a tire doused with gasoline was placed around her neck and ignited. Her head in flames, Maki was kicked and beaten by an angry ANC mob as she writhed in agony on the ground, the last moments of her life filled with blood-curdling screams. The mob continued to beat her long after her body stopped moving, and long after haloes of smoke ceased to emanate from her head.

Kevin captured the entire incident on film. Years later, he would write:

> I was appalled at what they were doing. I was appalled at what *I* was doing. But then people started talking about those pictures; they created quite a stir. And then I felt that maybe my actions hadn't been all bad. Being a witness to something this horrible wasn't necessarily such a terrible thing to do. (Marinovich & Silva, 2000, p. 39)

By showing everyone, including white South Africans, how gruesome township deaths actually looked, Kevin hoped to snap people out of their apathy and help stop the killings. According to his sister, he "could never understand how people carry on as if all the world's suffering didn't exist" (MacLeod, 2001), an indictment that extended to his liberal parents.

The art critic Susan Sontag wrote that one's "first encounter with the photographic inventory of ultimate horror" divides one's life into two parts (quoted in Berger, 1991, p. 61). Although Sontag was writing from the viewer's perspective, her statement holds purchase for the image-maker. Kevin's life was irrevocably divided in half the moment he pressed the shutter: He was no longer a detached observer, but an active participant in the hostel wars. He was (in Lacan's terms) thrust from mundane Reality into the Real, a world "loaded with horror and threatening possibilities" (quoted in Zizek, 1991, p. 88).

As the decade came to a close and paved the way for the 1990s, Kevin witnessed the birth of his daughter Megan. Though life was full of promise when he cut this tiny miracle's umbilical cord, the carnage in the townships was intensifying in anticipation of the first nonracial, democratic election ever to take place in South Africa. Hostel dwellers met with increasingly gruesome deaths: gunfires, fatal bludgeonings, bodies impaled with wooden poles, skulls cleaved in half with rusted machetes. Kevin's photographic inventory swelled with images of the dead from both sides of the conflict as well as those caught in the crossfire, children included. In one such image, a wounded ANC fighter on the brink of death is rushed by his comrades to safety, his tattered pants and white sneakers drenched in fresh blood; in another, a dead man is lifted off the ground on all fours by armed militia.

It would be a mistake to assume that Black South Africans were the sole perpetrators of township violence. As mentioned, white supremacists covertly funded IFP operations in their efforts to undermine democracy. Their involvement reached flagrant proportions as the elections, which would finally permit Blacks to vote, drew closer. White extremists calling themselves "neo-Nazis" went on armed excursions, shooting Blacks point-blank without remorse and instigating more Black-on-Black violence by terrorizing sleeping civilians while disguised in black face paint. Needless to say, their savagery did not escape Kevin's viewfinder.

Kevin photographed the execution of three such right-wingers in one of few instances during apartheid in which Blacks retaliated against whites. In this episode, members of the Afrikaner Weerstands-Beweging, in an effort to derail the upcoming election, went on an outing and shot many Black people along the road to Mmabatho in Bophuthatswana, then an independent state that resisted reincorporation into South Africa. Their efforts were thwarted by Bophuthatswana police, who took justice into their own hands. Recounting the incident to a friend: "Lying there in the middle of the gunfight, I was wondering about which millisecond next I was going to die, about putting something on film they could use as my last picture" (MacLeod, 2001).

It's surprising that Kevin himself was not killed in the townships. However, taking photos of the brutal killings exacted a terrible toll on his psyche. In an essay titled "Photographs of Agony," John Berger (1991) wrote that it is impossible to emerge unscathed from looking at images that depict human suffering. To resume one's life is a morally inadequate response to what one had just seen, and one's inadequacy becomes just as shocking as the war crimes themselves. These words certainly ring true for Kevin, who felt his own inadequacy each time the shutters came down. His inability to save or improve the lives of Black South Africans tormented him as much as the atrocities being committed before his eyes. He felt ashamed of his privileged upbringing in the white suburbs of Johannesburg, and he felt much empathy for Black people, whom he treated as his "reference points." Paging through negatives often brought him to tears. "Look at this, look at this," he once implored a friend. "It's all dead people, and it's all Black South African dead people that I'm photographing" (Krauss, 2005).

There would be no respite from the atrocious sights, not even in sleep. His surviving friends recount one of his recurring dreams as follows:

> In the dream, he was near death, lying on the ground, crucified to a wooden beam, unable to move. A television camera with a massive lens zoomed closer and closer in on his face, until Kevin would wake up screaming. (Marinovich & Silva, 2000, p. 55)

Apparently the dream had variations: "sometimes Kevin was the photographer, not the victim, and in that version, the 'dead' man would roll over and grab him by the ankle, holding him captive with bloody hands" (p. 55). The dream imagery is loaded with meaning, to say the least. Both variants convey his and his subjects' shared feelings of helplessness, anger, and fear, and both concretize survivor guilt over his inability to rescue the people he'd photographed, which demanded that he pay the price (i.e., death). The messianic imagery in the first variant is indicative of his Catholic upbringing, and here the psychological toll of his *sacrifice* is laid bare.

Of all the members of the Bang Bang Club, Kevin was said to be the most affected. He could not "shut off completely" (p. 60) as most seasoned photographers were trained to do. Describing a shoot-out:

> I had to think visually. I am zooming in on a tight shot of the dead guy and a splash of red. Going into his khaki uniform in a pool of blood in the sand. The dead man's face is slightly gray. You are making a visual here. But inside something is screaming, "My God." But it is time to work. Deal with the rest later. If you can't do it, get out of the game. (MacLeod, 2001)

But there was no getting out of the game; he was compelled to take those pictures. At nights, Kevin made phone calls to his closest friends and wept for hours "until he had been soothed or grown exhausted enough to sleep" (Marinovich & Silva, 2000, p. 54); they overlooked his sensitivity because of his "openness to pain," "generosity with his time and affection" (pp. 54–55) and childlike honesty. One of his colleagues compared him to her two-year-old son:

> There was no cover. When he's happy, he dances up and down and kisses me all over. And when he's upset, he throws things and he kicks things. And when he's lonely, he just bursts into tears. And Kevin was like that. (Krauss, 2005)

Kevin depended on others to contain his emotions because he could not do it himself, but witnessing and photographing such atrocities put him in a quandary, for the experience of singularity is built into trauma. He did not feel comfortable talking about township incidents with people outside the Bang Bang Club since they were either disgusted by or incapable of understanding the true nature of his work. He was, as his mother described him, "very impatient with people who didn't understand what was going on with what he was doing" (Krauss, 2005). Of this, he wrote:

> I suffer depression from what I see and experience nightmares. I feel alienated from "normal" people, including my family. I find myself unable to relate to or engage in frivolous conversation. The shutters come down and I recede into a

dark place with dark images of blood and death in godforsaken dusty places. (Marinovich & Silva, 2000, p. 53)

He could find no refuge from the horrible sights he witnessed. No matter how far he was from the townships, all he had to do was close his eyes in order to see the brutal killings. Desperate to get away from all the violence in South Africa, however briefly, he accepted an assignment to cover a civil war in the Sudan. There, he would capture the singular image around which the remaining year of his life would revolve.

THE PRIZE-WINNING IMAGE

In March 1993, Kevin joined a United Nations cargo plane that was bringing food and medical supplies to an area of the Sudan known as the Famine Triangle. The genocidal conflict between the Islamic Khartoum government and the Christian Dinkas and Nuer tribes had left tens of thousands either dead or on the brink of starvation—a scene ripe for the activities of war correspondents and photojournalists.

Escorted by armed locals, Kevin would discover upon arriving that the images he was sent to capture were no less ghastly than those of the hostel wars. Scattered on the ground under the sun's fiery canopy were hundreds of famished children left by mothers who were trying to secure food from a nearby feeding center. He described the scene as a "horrible pornography" (Marinovich & Silva, 2000, p. 190), a slide show of human deprivation from which he could not avert his eyes. He photographed cadaverous children in the arms of their mothers, their faces hollow from malnutrition, and hospice children waiting patiently for food rations unaware that death was fast approaching.

Kevin was about to photograph one of the children when a vulture entered his viewfinder. Though tempted to chase the bird away, he immediately recognized that very powerful symbols had just arranged themselves in front of him. It was an opportunity he could not pass. He approached the scene very carefully, zooming in and out from various angles, waiting (to no avail) for the bird to flap its wings. Twenty minutes later, when the vulture and the child fit the frame perfectly, he pressed the shutter.

In the resulting image, the vulture appears to be waiting for the life of its target to expire. The target is a bald little girl with skeletal arms and legs, her skin almost as black as the scavenger's feathers. She is down on all fours, her face buried in her hands, unaware of the bird behind her. The space she and the vulture occupy is a scorched wasteland with few traces of green. In the horizon are huts with thatched roofs from which she had presumably crawled. Her destination (and her fate) is left to the viewer's imagination.

Upon taking the photo, Kevin was completely devastated. The sight of starving children filled him with an intense longing to see his daughter, whom he missed terribly. He took her picture out of his wallet, sat under a tree, and sobbed. He was thankful she was not the girl in the photograph. A lapsed Catholic, he promised God that he would turn his life around should He ensure his safety back home. "I see all this, and all I can think of is Megan . . . I can't wait to hug her when I get home," he would later tell a friend (Marinovich & Silva, 2000, p. 118).

On March 26, 1993, "The vulture and the little girl," as the photo came to be known, appeared on the front page of *The New York Times*, generating worldwide interest. (It was revealed much later that the little girl was in fact a little boy.) NGOs and UNICEF would utilize the image in their campaign against world hunger. It would also win Kevin the Pulitzer Prize for Feature Photography, the highest accolade a photojournalist can aspire to. When he collected the prize a year later at Columbia University's Low Memorial Library, he wrote excitedly to his mother: "I swear I got the most applause of anybody. I can't wait to show you the trophy. It is the most precious thing and the highest acknowledgement of my work I could receive" (Marinovich & Silva, 2000, p. 187). For Kevin, the award represented an opportunity to compensate for his past failures and win the approval of his parents, whom he'd disappointed time and time again. It was also confirmation that the work he was doing was meaningful to others.

However, proof of his newfound success turned into proof of his failure as a human being when viewers began to inquire about the fate of the young girl. Thousands condemned him for not carrying the child to safety, with some calling *him* a vulture. He couldn't tell them that vultures don't prey on living things, or that the child was unlikely to die. After all, the feeding center, where the child's mother had presumably gone, was barely a hundred meters away. Nor could Kevin tell viewers that physical contact with natives was prohibited due to the high risk of disease transmission. Instead, he told them that "as a photojournalist my first instinct was to make the photograph" (Krauss, 2005). He would later revise his story to reflect that he *did* chase the bird away, and that the child got back on her feet to resume her trek: "I know she made it, I saw her" (Marinovich & Silva, 2000, p. 120).

Looking at the photograph, it is not difficult to see why he received such criticisms. According to Vivian Sobchack (2004), documentary filmmakers—and by extension, photojournalists—are forgiven by viewers if it's apparent that personal risk was taken to capture a horrific image (such as photos of the hostel wars). They are also forgiven if the image was captured accidentally or from a position of helplessness, or if an interventional or humane gaze was employed. But the vulture picture did not follow rote ways of provoking feeling and sentiment. It was a candid shot of a terribly harsh reality, steely in its gaze and technically masterful in its composition. Although Kevin did succumb to feelings of helplessness after pressing the shutter, such feelings are not apparent in the image. From the perspective of viewers, an event that should have elicited a more humane response was instead treated with technical and machinelike competence by the photographer.

According to Julia Lloyd, Megan's mother, the criticisms "really affected him. He wept over comments. He was shattered" (Krauss, 2005). In his defense, she asked rhetorically: "Who's gonna stop and pick up a child? Is Kevin supposed to go there on a mission of mercy? He's there as a photographer, and he's got to keep his emotions in check and do his job." But no defense could allay his doubts about his own humanity, a test that he believed he failed by walking away. Though the vulture picture was his most prized image 10 years into his profession, he would not even hang it on his wall.

DESCENT AND DEATH

After his return from the Sudan, and prior to claiming the Pulitzer Prize, Kevin was arrested for drunk driving, kicked out of the apartment he'd been sharing with his then-girlfriend, and fired by Reuters for sabotaging one too many assignments. Just days before the first democratic election in South Africa, Reuters sent him to cover Nelson Mandela speaking at a Johannesburg hotel. Bored and high on drugs, he left in the middle of Mandela's speech, but not before telling another photographer: "If the old man catches a bullet, phone me" (Marinovich & Silva, 2000, p. 147). Everyone present was speechless, to say the least. Although the Pulitzer initially gave him the confidence (and credential) he needed to thrive as a freelancer, one by one the doors that it opened slammed shut in his face: "No one is going to want to use me because I'm unreliable" (p. 199).

The death of Ken Oosterbroek, his best friend and a fellow member of the Bang Bang Club, was especially devastating. Kevin was being interviewed by a local journalist about the prize he'd just won when Oosterbroek took a bullet to the head in the township of Thokoza. Upon hearing of the shooting, he rushed to the hospital where Ken's body had been taken. Up to that point, the deaths Kevin had witnessed, though horrifying, belonged to others—specifically, impoverished Black others. They weren't of his own. With Oosterbroek's death, the sense of inviolability that had been breached only in dreams was now breached in physical reality. "All at once he felt fear . . . The boys were no longer untouchable," wrote Greg Marinovich and Joao Silva, the two surviving members of the club (p. 3). The boys, including Kevin, were no longer protected by the privilege of being middle class and white.

Kevin harbored guilt for having survived Oosterbroek's death. He believed that the bullet that killed his friend should have struck him instead: "I should have stopped that fucking bullet. It should have been me, not Ken" (Krauss, 2005). This statement is especially poignant because Kevin saw Ken as his "good twin . . . a good person, with a stable home life" (Marinovich & Silva, 2000, p. 188), a better version of him in every aspect of life. Ken had a stable marriage and a loving daughter that waited for him back home. Ken was chief photographer of *The Star* and thrice recognized as South Africa Press Photographer of the Year. And Ken very much looked like Kevin, only more self-assured. That same afternoon, Kevin went to the exact spot where Ken had been killed, hoping to catch a stray bullet himself. If his better half could not continue living, what right did he.

The end of apartheid on May 10, 1994, made Kevin feel impotent. Nelson Mandela's rise to presidency signaled the extension of human rights to the majority Black population and acknowledgment of the indignities they suffered in official discourse. It would also usher the Truth and Reconciliation Commission, a project of individual and collective remembering in which victims offered personal accounts of civil rights violations (Schaffer & Smith, 2004). Seeing the curtain close on apartheid, with Mandela sworn in as president behind bulletproof glass, left Kevin feeling purposeless. It had been his avowed mission to expose the National Party's evil regime, after all. With apartheid finally over, he felt as aimless in life as he had been 10 years prior, when he first attempted suicide. He felt despondent and would refuse to come out of his apartment for days at a stretch. Panic would set in at dusk and at dawn, the two times of the day during which the Bang Bang Club once photographed township violence. He likened his predicament to falling into a black hole, though perhaps it would be more accurate to say that he felt as empty as a black hole, one that threatened to implode.

He accepted other assignments, but their outcome only frustrated him. For instance, his photographs of Mandela's visit to Cape Town alongside then French president François Mitterand shipped too late for deadlines and were of too poor quality to show to clients. The final straw was an assignment from *Time* magazine to cover Mandela's trip to Mozambique, his first state visit to another country as South Africa's president.

Kevin was afraid he'd botch the assignment. Despite setting three alarm clocks, he woke up late and almost missed his flight. It is conceivable that he himself *wanted* to miss the flight so that his photographic ability, on which his precarious sense of self hinged, would not be put on trial. The biggest tragedy, however, was that after six days in Mozambique he actually felt proud of the pictures he'd taken, only to realize upon returning to South Africa that he left more than 15 rolls of film on the plane. When the airline failed to find the missing items, he looked inside every trash bin within the airport's vicinity. His search turned up empty.

On July 27, 1994, only two days after his return from Mozambique, Kevin called to tell his parents that he was going to be late for their monthly family dinner. How late, he did not say. But instead of driving straight to their place, he parked his pickup truck next to a blue gum tree overlooking the Braamfontein Spruit River, where he used to play as a child. He uncoiled a green garden hose and attached it to the pickup's exhaust pipe, leaving a narrow slit at the top of the windows for the hose. Once inside, he began smoking a white pipe and hastily wrote the following note:

> I'm really, really sorry. I have got to the point where the pain of life overrides the joy to the point that joy does not exist . . . I am depressed . . . without phone . . . money for rent . . . money for child support . . . money for debts . . . money!!! I am haunted by the vivid memories of killings and corpses and anger and pain . . . of starving or wounded children, of trigger-happy madmen, often police, of killer executioners . . . and I am haunted by the loss of my dear friend Ken . . . I have gone to join Ken if I am that lucky . . . I have always had it all at my feet—but being me just fucks it up anyway. (MacLeod, 2001)

By the time his vehicle was found by the police, Kevin Carter, who only three months earlier claimed the Pulitzer Prize, was already dead. He was 33 years old, barely 10 years into his career as a war photographer.

One need not look beyond Kevin's suicide note to arrive at his reasons for ending his life. In fact, the note itself encapsulates his subjective life history: a privileged upbringing ("I have always had it all at my feet"); an inherent sense of worthlessness ("being me just fucks it up"), which became tied to money and material possessions, or what Kohut (1971) calls "narcissistic supplies"; the horror of bearing witness to humankind's worst tendencies; and the trauma of losing a dear friend who represented his own untapped potential for a better life. Photography rescued Kevin Carter from a hollow existence by giving him purpose, but it also propelled him face-to-face with death, including his own. When critics twisted his prize-winning photograph into a signifier of his failure to be human, his sense of moral inadequacy in the face of carnage deepened. It's no coincidence that his suicide occurred shortly after the anticlimactic end of apartheid and his return from Mozambique. Both events communicated that there was nothing left for him in the world.

Interlude I

Is Creativity Intrinsically Healing?

In Greek myths, there once was a man with a beautiful voice and lyre named Orpheus. So mesmerizing was his voice that it could tame the most savage of beasts, and so skillfully did he pluck the strings of his lyre that even the searing flames of Apollo, and the fierce Dionysus, succumbed to his music. As legend has it, the siren's song, which had lured countless seafarers to the ocean's depths, was no match for the songs of Orpheus, for his voice could restore the senses to those who had lost it.

The magic of Orpheus's music was matched only by the beauty of Eurydice, whom he asked to be his wife. Sadly, their blissful marriage came to an abrupt end when the nymph fell ill and died from a snake's venomous bite. But all glimmer of hope was not lost. Devastated, Orpheus sought entrance to the Underworld and sang to Hades and Persephone a plaintive plea to have his beloved resurrected. Moved by his music, Hades agreed to grant him his wish, under one condition: Orpheus was not to look at Eurydice until they *both* have returned to the mortal realm. He was to look forward, and only forward, as she trailed behind him.

The terrains of the Underworld were cavernous and the path to the world above treacherous. But with his voice and the sound of Eurydice's footsteps, Orpheus overcame the trials ahead and reached the gateway to the land of the living. He crossed the divide in one quick stride. The sun was warm on the other side, and feeling triumphant, he cast one glance at Eurydice, but she had not yet crossed over. As soon as their eyes met, Eurydice turned to dust and scattered in the wind.

Orpheus became inconsolable in his grief and wandered aimlessly. In his journey, he crossed paths with the Thracians, savage women known to seduce bold and intrepid adventurers. Orpheus rebuked their sexual advances, which incensed them greatly. One by one they threw stones and javelins at him, which fell harmlessly at his feet the moment he plucked at his lyre. But then they screamed a ghastly scream that drowned even his music. Alas, the stones and javelins reached him, and no longer impervious, he was gruesomely dismembered. His severed head plunged into the river's currents, where it was consigned to sing a baleful song for all of eternity.

INTRODUCTION

It has been said time and time again that the myth of Orpheus is a testament to the beneficent powers of creativity (McClary, 2007). It can appeal to the conscience of humanity and the "gods" of our civilization. It is a powerful source that can be summoned in the face of loss, a means of retrieving what had been lost. After all, did Orpheus not return from his death-defying journey into the Underworld, with Eurydice in tow? Moreover, creativity can be a protective force against trauma and its attendant turbulent feelings.

But the myth of Orpheus is also illustrative of the *limits* of creativity. While creativity can protect against some of trauma's disastrous consequences, it can also be overwhelmed and rendered impotent *by* trauma. Orpheus's voice and skillful playing could not save him from being torn limb to limb by the Thracians, and his disembodied head would forever sing dismal songs about the fleeting nature of love, recapitulating the traumatic loss of Eurydice, with whom reunion in the afterlife was no longer possible. The myth also shows that creativity cannot be severed from its intersubjective contexts. Its power to heal is inseparable from the human surround, for creativity *is* relationality.

While some creative individuals are redeemed by their craft, some are not. While some find lasting relief in creating, some lose their lives in the process. This is one paradoxical aspect of creativity. Although the stories of Iris Chang and Kevin Carter (previous chapters) and others featured in this book illustrate the power of creativity to traumatize and retraumatize—in short, act as a vector of trauma—it's important to consider the other half of the paradox. Just as important, we must acknowledge that the creative act can encompass both halves in the lifeworld of a person.

In what follows, I present anecdotal and empirical evidence supporting the notion that creativity can be healing. Next, I illustrate several ways through which creativity can traumatize or reactivate past trauma (individual or collective), with suicide being its most tragic outcome. In an attempt to reconcile the two halves of the paradox, I address the relationship between creativity, relationality, and the larger social fabric.

WRITING AND WELL-BEING

Literature on the therapeutic benefits of creative self-expression is overrepresented by studies on written emotional disclosure. Pennebaker and Seagal's (1999) landmark study is a notable example, which found that only a certain kind of writing, one that fuses emotion and description, is associated with healing. Venting one's emotions in writing, or describing one's traumas without emotion, doesn't appear to have lasting psychological benefits, and De Salvo (2000) would concur. Although writing does not resolve conflict directly, says De Salvo, it can be therapeutic when it recounts with honesty and without hypocrisy; when it does not vilify or idealize others; when it transforms rather than controls one's emotions; and when it links concrete experiences with feelings, which can reveal profound insights to one's wounds. Moreover, the writer must realize that the life s/he is presently living may be different from the one s/he is describing on paper. That is, writing that is healing is a *retelling*, not a *reliving*.

The case of James Ellroy, the crime novelist, is illustrative in this regard (Terr, 1994). For many years Ellroy grappled with self-destructive impulses. In each of his novels, he explicitly describes the murder of the victim, sparing no gruesome detail for his horrified readers. In time, Ellroy discovered that his novels concretize a need to unravel the mystery behind *his* own mother's murder. Via writing, he became conscious of the guilt he'd been carrying since he swore, just months before his mother was killed, that she "will never, ever slap me again" (p. 196). Finding the connection between his writings, the trauma of losing his mother, and the magical thinking that somehow, he was responsible for her death, mitigated the rage he'd been directing at himself.

Writing can be especially healing when used *teleologically*, which Henke (1998) calls *scriptotherapy*. And this is exactly what she finds in her study of six women writers, three of whom contemplated or attempted suicide. Sylvia Fraser used writing to safeguard the truth of her abuse at the hands of her incestuous father. For the diarist Anaïs Nin, "The labor of creation is the only thing which makes life bearable" (p. 79), and had it not been for writing, she would have surely perished long ago. Janet Frame imbibed a whole bottle of aspirin after years of curating a false and inauthentic self in her profession as a school teacher. Fortunately, she survived. Writing did not only give her license to be whomever she wanted, it rescued her from future rounds of electroshock treatment. When the hospital received word that Frame was a published author, she was deemed "cured" and released from the mental hospital.

Although Virginia Woolf ultimately succumbed to suicide, we must not discount her personal belief that writing *prolonged* her life by giving her insight into her emotional scars. In "A Sketch of the Past" (1985), she states that writing allowed her to realize connections between present and past, between her shame at seeing herself in the mirror, and the sexual abuse she suffered at the hands of her stepbrothers (she was looking in the mirror when the assault took place). For Woolf, writing also had *exorcising* and *eulogizing* functions. As De Salvo (2000) points out, with her completion of *To the Lighthouse*, she successfully snuffed out the haunting presence of her dead mother and father; and in writing *Jacob's Room*, she finally felt able to mourn the passing of her younger brother Thoby, whom she loved and who bore a striking resemblance to the novel's protagonist. It's not surprising that she called each of her novels an *elegy*, for they rescued from nothingness precious memories of loved ones lost, which she deemed essential to her continuing survival.

HEALING TRAUMA THROUGH ART

As with writing, there is ample support for the idea that various forms of *expressive* creativity can facilitate healing. Jung (1973) himself believed that drawing mandalas can bring to consciousness emotionally laden images that could be harmful to a person's psyche if left unattended. The idea, says Malchiodi (2007), is that creative work can help individuals reach parts of the self that other activities cannot. The healing nature of mandalas has been tested by Henderson, Rosen, and Mascaro (2007), whose participants experienced attenuation of post-traumatic stress symptoms. Rogers (1993) advocates a multimodal approach, one that integrates movements, sounds, images, and written or spoken word, because different parts of the self, says Rogers, yearn for expression in different ways.

The association between symbolic concretization through art and trauma "recovery" is not new, with countless examples throughout time and across cultures. But as a case in point, let's take a quick glimpse at the role of drawing in the life of Elizabeth Layton (Epstein, 1995; Rogers, 1995).

At age 48, Layton was hospitalized for severe depression. She was shocked 13 times and kept on a regimen of lithium; neither were effective in alleviating her dark moods. She described her fierce struggle to stay alive as "fighting cobwebs with no way out" (Epstein, 1995, p. 242), and she felt complete psychosomatic disunity, with her head "completely severed from her body" (ibid.). At age 67, she felt the devastating blow of her son's death to liver disease. Nothing was going right in her life, and at the insistence of her sister, she enrolled in drawing classes to keep her mind off her son's death.

What Layton discovered was a powerful vehicle for coming to terms with the tragic circumstances of her life, and with her aging body. Leyton didn't shy away from the wrinkles on her face or the blemishes on her skin, nor did she recoil from drawing the intensive care unit where her son died. She bared her feelings for all to see; analogous to the subjects of Pennebaker and Seagal's (1999) study, she combined *visual* rhetoric with emotion. Layton received much recognition for her work, but ultimately, what mattered to her was "not whether this is art or not" (Rogers, 1995, p. 249), but that her drawings speak to "other people like me who may be troubled by their feelings" (ibid.). Drawing gave *meaning* to 30 years' worth of suffering; it also imbued the remaining years of her life with purpose and felt connection to others, illustrating post-traumatic growth.

The role of creativity in facilitating group affiliation and community cannot be emphasized enough, especially in tyrannical regimes where the creative act is a luxury. Augusto Pinochet's reign over Chile disappeared many dissident fathers, sons, and grandsons. Unable to remain silent, many Chilean women embroidered stories of torture and political repression into three-dimensional quilts called *arpilleras* (Comas-Diaz, 2008). In these quilts, one will experience, for example, the pained longing of a mother as she waits by the door for a son who would never come home; or an elderly woman's strength and fortitude as she assumes the role of breadwinner for her orphaned grandchildren. Weaving these stories were spiritually uplifting and liberating for the women, whose individual tales became plural when they were woven into collective testimony. Elsewhere, when the box cars of the Warsaw Ghetto were sealed, surviving residents asserted the indomitability of the human spirit through art exhibits, musical recitals, and poetry readings (Feirstein, 2003).

IMPINGEMENT BY COLLECTIVE TRAUMA

It is one thing for individual traumas to be woven into a larger tapestry that affirms collective experience; it is another when collective traumas unleash their full force upon an individual. As the stories of Kevin Carter and Iris Chang illustrate, creative work that confronts the "shadow side" of human history can be as traumatic as it is life-affirming. It is an inversion of creativity's exorcising function, in this case, opening a portal through which countless dead can haunt the living.

Kevin saw with his own eyes the deleterious consequences of the National Party's evil regime. To force whites (and the world at large) to acknowledge the brutal reality of apartheid South Africa, he captured with his viewfinder the carnage of "hostel wars" and township massacres, at great peril to himself. To say that he was traumatized every time the shutters came down would be an understatement; he found no respite from the "dark images of blood and death" (Marinovich & Silva, 2000, p. 53), for they appeared even in his dreams. Iris forced the world to remember the atrocities of Japanese soldiers in the Pacific theater during World War II. Though she herself did not witness the unspeakable fashion in which innocent civilians and POWs were slaughtered in Nanking or Bataan, the stark black-and-white images that confronted her in archives, and the testimonies of elderly survivors that she caught on videotape, bled into the marginal spaces of her life.

In both cases, the psychological price paid for rescuing historical truth from oblivion, so that indignities suffered by marginalized others may finally be recognized in official discourse, was irreparable. Their boundless empathy for their subjects heightened that price. Given that his "reference points" were Black South Africans, it's not surprising that Kevin defended a Black mess-hall waiter during military service, and that he shed tears while paging through a file of negatives. The variant of his dream in which he is being photographed concretizes the merged inner relationship between him and his subjects. Iris broke down in tears after each interview with Bataan veterans, and she was devastated upon seeing the dismal living conditions Nanking survivors had resigned themselves to. One could say that her paranoia also symbolizes empathic identification with her subjects, her hypervigilance to signs of danger and threats to her and her child's safety resembling that of Holocaust survivors and POWs. For Kevin or Iris, neither the frame nor the page could contain decades' worth of human suffering. It exploded in their faces with deadly outcome.

To say that creativity "killed" Kevin Carter and Iris Chang would be too simple, however. It's true that their work forced them into sustained encounter with human nature at its ugliest, and that their willingness to venture into physically and psychologically dangerous terrain was part and parcel of their creativity. Kevin risked danger and death to capture violent yet evocative images. Iris constantly flirted with *contagious* texts, which are texts that capture trauma so powerfully, and so viscerally, that they either reawaken or instill similar traumas in viewers (Berman 1999, 2001). But bear in mind that both felt a great sense of purpose in carrying out their work, which oscillated between traumatizing and life-affirming. This was especially the case for Kevin, who felt so aimless he nearly committed suicide—until he discovered the power of photography, which bifurcated his life but also imbued it with purpose. Death came for them when future avenues of creativity were choked off by circumstances outside their volition: the end of apartheid for Kevin, and for Iris, her son's diagnosis with autism, which she (erroneously) believed she caused.

RECAPITULATION OF PERSONAL TRAUMAS

There are many creative persons who, knowingly or unknowingly, recount their personal traumas in their work. Ernest Hemingway was haunted his entire life by his father's suicide, and he believed that fathers who die by their own hands condemn their sons to a similar tragedy. To shake off his obsession with self-destruction, he wrote what Henke (1998) calls *autofiction*, or autobiography disguised as fiction. This is not to say that Hemingway's works are largely autobiographical, only that they contain fragments of his personal life. For example, in the climax of *For Whom the Bell Tolls*, the protagonist journeys to the top of a mountain and drops the gun his father had used to commit suicide, watching until it faded out of sight. Tragically, unlike his fictional stand-in, Hemingway pulled the trigger on himself. Writing did not exorcise the father's ghost, and the father's proverbial "sin" ultimately visited the son.

Then always bleeds into now, and the traumatized person's past always intrudes upon the present (Herman, 1997), as the case of Hemingway shows. Although trauma is not a necessary precondition of creativity—human beings are symbol-making creatures and are inherently creative (Burke, 1963–1964)—it can be a major impetus to create. Traumatized children, for example, use imaginative play sooner and more frequently than children who have not experienced trauma (Terr, 1994). However, creative work in adulthood runs the risk of retraumatization. To borrow the words of Schultz (2005b): "It sometimes has all the earmarks of wheel spinning, a grim repetition of themes and sequences that never come to any resolution" (p. 138). Hemingway's *autofictions* were not retellings but relivings, and something similar can be said of Phyllis Hyman, Kurt Cobain, and Sylvia Plath, featured in this book in the next several chapters.

Virginia Woolf is relevant here once again. Although writing was life-saving, she also *exploited* her traumas in her writings. As she confesses in her diary: "What seas of horror one dives through to pick up these pearls—however they are worth it" (Woolf, 1979, p. 20). A decade and a half later, she'd come to realize: "The only way I keep afloat is by working . . . Directly I stop working I feel I am sinking down, down. And as usual, I feel that if I sink further I shall reach the truth" (Woolf, 1981, p. 235). Though initially therapeutic, her reactivation of past traumas in creative work, and her total dependence on her craft later in life, as if her being hinged on it completely, could not and did not stave off suicide. She likened writing to submerging in a "great lake of melancholy" (ibid.), one that ultimately drowned her.

CREATIVITY AND RELATIONALITY

In his study of seven extraordinary individuals, Gardner (2003) noticed that the social sphere is not terribly important to creative persons, who are likely to pursue projects at the expense of others. And yet, all seven people profiled in his book benefited from the support of at least one other person during their first major breakthrough. Thus, the midwifery of muses plays an important role in the creative process, and no one can truly forge ahead alone without exacting some terrible price, not when one is wrestling with deeply personal material in one's work. The price, as many examples illustrate, could be as steep as unresolved recapitulation of trauma, and in extreme cases, erosion of the will to continue living.

But it would be naïve to say that the presence of a supportive *other* is foolproof protection against suicide. It is not. As Stolorow (2007) mentions, the feeling of *singularity* is built into the experience of trauma itself, which can render one incapable of feeling the attunement supplied by others. No one will argue that the likes of Iris Chang, Kevin Carter, and Robin Williams had support systems in place, including a close-knit network of family members or friends. In spite of these, however, they were (phenomenologically speaking) unbearably alone in their despair.

Still, the cultivation and maintenance of sustaining ties to others *can* stave off the call of self-destruction. In his study of Henrik Ibsen, the playwright who gave us *The Doll House*, Shulman (1992) observed many biographical similarities to Ernest Hemingway. Both writers wrestled with alcoholism, had thoughts of suicide, and concretized their suicidal impulses via fictional stand-ins who end their lives. And yet Hemingway took his life whereas Ibsen did not. Shulman believes that a supportive marriage that endured for nearly five decades protected Ibsen, whereas Hemingway's difficulty with sustaining lasting relationships placed him at an elevated risk. This is an oversimplification, of course, given the multiplex nature of suicide, but the point stands that the presence of an other can be a breakwater against deep depression.

When the psychological journey is fraught with perils, as it so happens with many creative endeavors, the presence of an *enlightened witness* (Miller, 1991) is vital. Having someone with whom to share our stories, regardless of the form they take, confers benefits that keeping them private does not. I share De Salvo's (2000) sentiment that keeping our pasts locked repeats the lethal pattern of silencing associated with trauma, a pattern that we inadvertently pass down to future generations. But "simply telling the narrative" (Sorsoli, 2004, p. 103) is not enough; listener involvement is crucial, which means having someone walk with us down the unsafe corridors of our hearts, welcoming and encouraging our individualized selfhood in the spirit of *authentic solicitude* (Heidegger, 1996).

This is not to say that one cannot produce great works, come to a discovery of selfhood, and rescue the self from inauthenticity on one's own. But creativity that is a relational act can be healing, while treading the creative act alone comes with myriad risks. Ackerman (1997) once wrote that "each of us has a loaded gun we aim at ourselves" (p. 23). Without a mirroring other, many creative people, in a state of utter despair, fire the proverbial gun at themselves.

Others cry for rescue in their works, but an impersonal audience, no matter how large, is no substitute for one enlightened witness. Hundreds of people were listening to Sylvia Plath when she read "Daddy" (2004) for a BBC radio broadcast, and Kurt Cobain's performance of "Come as You Are" (1991a), which ends with him singing, "No, I don't have a gun," over and over, drew thousands of spectators. Phyllis Hyman, the jazz and blues singer, ends her final song and album (1995a) with the ultimatum: "But I won't leave/ If you give me one good reason to stay." But Sylvia still turned on the gas and put her head inside the oven. Kurt did have a gun, with which he shot himself dead. And Phyllis overdosed on barbiturates on the afternoon of her performance at the Apollo Theatre.

THE LARGER SOCIAL FABRIC

The self does not exist in a vacuum; *Dasein* is always *being-in-the-world* (Heidegger, 1996). From birth onward, the presence of a mirroring other is vital to the postulation of the self's existence (Winnicott, 1989). Sever the person from life-affirming intersubjective contexts and you sever their connection to life. The case of Jeremy Blake and Theresa Duncan, who we will encounter soon, is a chilling example of this. Seven days after the suicide of Theresa, filmmaker and video game designer, Jeremy, her lover and an artist in his own right, was so inconsolable in his grief that he walked into the Atlantic Ocean. In the wake of his muse's death was a depleted self that could not conceive of a life in which she did not exist. Their tragedy is the story of Orpheus and Eurydice set in contemporary times.

Highly creative individuals are often willing to make Faustian bargains (Gardner, 1993). In order to perfect their craft, they may sacrifice their ties to others and/or their psychological well-being. Then there are those who immerse themselves in their work in response to, and as refuge from, an unbearably hostile world. Whichever the case, the work sometimes takes over the life. When one's entire being is staked on one's craft, life appears bleak when the work isn't going so well. It is said that Virginia Woolf wrote 10 pages a day juggling *The Years* and *Roger Fry* (De Salvo, 2000). She wrote to the point of exhaustion and experienced the slightest setback as catastrophic. Similarly, when her most ambitious projects failed to materialize, Theresa Duncan suffered paranoid delusions that the Church of Scientology was sabotaging her forays into the film industry.

The quality of one's creative productions, and the response they elicit from viewers, become linked with feelings of self-worth. That is inevitable. It is when life and work become synonymous that tragedies arise. Sylvia Plath became severely depressed each time a poem was rejected by a magazine. In her diaries, she confessed that publishing in the most prestigious literary journals was essential to her belief in her abilities. With her entire being staked on her writings, every rejection was felt as a vicious attack on her core self. Kevin Carter's already tenuous sense of self-worth diminished with every criticism leveled at his prize-winning photograph. When there was no more work left for him to do, all that remained was a vacuum threatening to implode.

Inspired by the works of Levi-Strauss, the poet Gregory Orr (2002a) would say that the above examples were "monomyths" (p. 197) to the bitter end—tales of suffering experienced by a single person and shared with no other. (This is not to be confused with Joseph Campbell's particular usage of the same term.) Because she believed that her life circumstances were unique, Sylvia, says Orr, created a self in her poems that was not able to "move *through* and *beyond* the trauma" (p. 121) of losing her father. De Salvo (2000) would add that Sylvia's was a *chaos narrative*, which replicates the original trauma and communicates themes of futility and impotence, concretizing a self devastated beyond reconstruction.

Unlike monomyths, "communal myths" are stories shared by groups of people and function as cohesive bonds between members. People who create narratives of healing and recovery, says De Salvo (2000), are more likely to overcome life's myriad crises, for it allows them to integrate (i.e., recover) lost fragments of individual or collective memory and reestablish ties to others based on trust. We see this in the *arpilleras* of Chilean women (Comas-Diaz, 2008); in making "I" plural, they cease to be victims complicit with abuse and become not only *survivors* who "speak up and speak out," but *witnesses* who take responsibility for the telling.

A healing narrative, to borrow the words of McAdams and Bowman (2001), and Tomkins before them, is also a *restitution* narrative that communicates themes of rescue and overcoming adversity. Furthermore, like a *quest* narrative, it conveys recognition of an enduring self despite life's constant flux. Regarding the latter point, the memoirist Brent Runyon comes to mind. Runyon wrote *The Burn Journals* (2005) to come to terms with his past suicide attempt by self-immolation. After months of grueling treatment, reconstructive surgeries, and skin grafts, he decides to pick up where his life left off. He concludes the memoir with this powerful realization: "It doesn't matter if the rest of me looks different. None of that matters. I can still recognize myself. I'm still that person in there. Inside my eyes" (p. 370).

CONCLUDING REMARKS

Gregory Orr wrote his first poem about being alone on a beach by the sea. The poem captures the alienation he felt after he accidentally shot his younger brother dead. Although writing it felt overwhelming, it gave him an incredible sense of release: "I felt as if the passionate and agonized inner world that I really inhabited was suddenly and precisely given form and objective reality" (Orr, 2002b, p. 143). His trauma ceased to be a random, senseless event once put into words. At times, however, poetry "became braided and dry as a rope and I wondered if I were meant to twist it around my neck" (p. 144). Such is one paradox of creativity, which allows us to recreate ourselves anew while threatening to obliterate us.

In response to the question, "Is creative work intrinsically healing?": The answer is obviously no, but if used teleologically, it has the potential to bring about transformation and perspectival change. However, many creative individuals just want to master a medium or create works of superior quality, with some exploiting personal and/or collective traumas (which become their own) for inspiration. But I agree with Rogers (1993) when she warns readers, "Insisting on peeling the scab off a wound is counterproductive. The scab serves as a protection. Allowing it to soften and fall away is more appropriate to healing" (p. 141).

There isn't a single theory that can explain how and why creativity heals in some contexts and not in others (Charet, 2007). Nevertheless, a synthesis (however partial) of what writers on the subject have said has value. To summarize: It is important that we care for ourselves while we create so that the past (ours or others) does not poison our present. That we tread the creative path with an enlightened witness like Eurydice trailing a few steps behind us. That we stay connected to something beyond ourselves and transform rather than control the way we feel. That we retell, not relive, our stories with honesty, honoring the subjective truth of our traumas. That we share our stories with empathetic others, and realize how our personal narratives are part of a larger, communal myth, bound together by our shared humanity.

Chapter 3

"Give Me One Good Reason to Stay"

The Case of Phyllis Hyman

On Thursday, June 29, 1995, the day before her highly anticipated performance at Harlem's Apollo Theater, Phyllis made phone calls to her friends. She wanted to make sure they were going to watch her on stage.

Phyllis Hyman had been touted as the next Billie Holiday by *Black American* magazine and as the world's most exciting Black woman by *Players* (Michael, 2017). Her music, according to David Nathan (1999), the so-called British ambassador of Soul, was a melting pot, an amalgam of jazz, R&B, and pop. Her 1991 album *Prime of My Life* produced three hit singles in "When You Get Right Down To It," "Living in Confusion," and "Don't Wanna Change the World," with the third track climbing to No. 1 in the charts. Though known for her music, she branched out to other media, for instance, playing a lead role in the Duke Ellington Broadway musical *Sophisticated Ladies*, which earned her a Tony nomination as well as the Theater World Award for most promising new talent. In light of her long string of successes, it was truly unfortunate that she fell into deep depression and addiction, which crippled her personally and professionally.

The next number Phyllis dialed was the Barry's, and after a few rings Brenda picked up. Brenda told Phyllis that she got her the vacuum cleaner she wanted for her 46th birthday, which was one week after the show at the Apollo. It was customary for Phyllis to tell loved ones what to buy for her birthday, and she had a gift for every budget, including rolls of toilet paper, so that no one could say they couldn't afford a present. Thus, it was strange that Phyllis told Brenda not to bring anything to the party. After telling Brenda to arrive precisely at 2 o'clock and not a minute later, she said plaintively, "This will probably be the last time that you see me" (Michael, 2017, p. 315).

"We're going to have a good day," Phyllis continued. "I'm going to have balloons for you to take back to Jason. It's going to be a good day. You guys know I love you, and it will probably be the last time I'm going to see you" (p. 315). Brenda didn't know what to make of this ominous statement, and her attempts to probe deeper went nowhere. Whatever Phyllis meant, she would get it out of her after the show.

The topic switched to a wonderful report card Brenda's son Jason brought back home. At the mention of his name, Phyllis began to sob. She repeated how much she loved the Barry's and how much they were like family to her. Then she hung up. Unbeknownst to Brenda, Phyllis had planned to kill herself on her birthday. Only a select few knew, and they were already planning an intervention. This was not the first time Phyllis threatened suicide, and it was not the first time loved ones intervened. But first, the show had to go on.

Friday, June 30, 1995, was going to be a busy day for Phyllis Hyman and her personal assistants. She was due at 3:30 p.m. for a sound check, and she assured everyone that she was going to "rock the house" that night (p. 315). She even reminded the show's publicist to have a menu from Sylvia's, her favorite Harlem soul food restaurant, waiting for her in her dressing room. At 1:00 p.m. she sent her assistants to run a series of errands, saying that she was going to sun for a bit on the roof of her apartment.

Phyllis put on a one-piece, black-and-white bathing suit and a white robe on top, but she didn't climb up to the roof. Instead, she bolted her apartment door shut. She went into her bedroom and locked that door too.

Phyllis never made it to the Apollo Theater in time for the soundcheck. By the time her assistants returned, by the time they forced their way into her apartment, she was already dead from too many sleeping pills. A sleeping mask rested on her forehead, right above her eyes, and on a notepad within arm's reach she had written the following words: "I'm tired. I'm tired. Those of you that I love know who you are. May God bless you" (p. 317). The intervention came too late, for Phyllis had hastened her demise.

"PRIME OF MY LIFE"

Phyllis Hyman was born on July 6, 1949. The oldest of seven children, she and her parents and siblings lived in abject poverty in a small three-bedroom apartment in Pittsburgh, Pennsylvania. Phyllis grew up under the care of a constantly depressed mother who could not attend to the needs of her children and neither showed affection nor dispensed punishment for misbehavior: "My mother never touched me growing up. She didn't hug me. She didn't spank me" (Michael, 2017, p. 12). Her father Philip was a railroad worker who labored long hours, and when he was home, he spent most of it drinking and berating his wife. There was little love and much discord between her parents, and after 20 years of marriage, her father left her mother for another woman.

If indeed both parents reside within their children (Levine & Klein, 2006), then Phyllis clearly teetered between two personas. She could be boisterous and aggressive, "hell bent on pleasing herself at all costs" (Michael, 2017, p. 4), yet very empathetic to others' suffering. It was not out of character for her to give her jacket to a homeless person on a cold winter night or hand over the remaining change in her pockets to a blind man on the streets. But she was also liable to explode with fiery temper at friends and family and humiliate them in public. She was cruelest to the people closest to her while acting as a surrogate mother, sister, daughter, and friend to everyone else. As an adult, she was prone to rage and drank heavily like her father, but like her mother, fell prey to bouts of depression and self-doubt. When her dark moods grew to immense proportions, she started using cocaine.

Devaluation of one parent by the other leaves children feeling devalued themselves. Phyllis displaced her sense of impotence onto those she deemed weaker than herself. She bullied her younger siblings and treated them as if they were her servants, enjoying what she called a free maid and valet service. But it was her mother Louise who bore the brunt of her frustrations and who she saw as undeserving of respect. Phyllis never had to carry a key because Louise never left the house: "I always thought I didn't want to be like that. That woman didn't ask for enough. There was a world out there" (p. 8).

Phyllis thought badly of marriage and vowed never to have children. She thought it was cruel to have kids if they couldn't receive the love and affection they deserved. She criticized mothers who had more children than they could care for, citing the many instances of child neglect and abuse. Phyllis rejected parenthood because she herself did not receive loving parenting. She questioned her own ability to be a parent and feared passing onto future generations her parents' child-rearing practices, a vicious cycle that Alice Miller (1997) called *poisonous pedagogy*. When her father walked out on her family, Phyllis swore that she would become a working woman who didn't need a man in her life. At the same time, however, she feared ending up a broken woman like her mother, a theme that persisted throughout her life and impressed itself upon her songs.

In her quest for independence, Phyllis decided that a career in music was her ticket out of the house. From an early age she had a very special voice. According to her sister Jeannie, "She couldn't have been more than 10, 12 years old and she sounded like an adult singing with another adult" (Michael, 2017, p. 11). She competed in many talent shows in the Pittsburgh school district, and her voice was so mesmerizing that she once stopped traffic while singing Judy Garland's "Somewhere Over the Rainbow" for an audition. In high school, Phyllis was a member of The Sounds of Ebony, a trio that sang what she called "message songs" (p. 15). She attended college for some time but soon dropped out to pursue music seriously. At the age of 20, she joined New Directions, an all-male quartet, and together they went on a six-month tour around the country. When New Directions disbanded, she started her own group, Phyllis Hyman and the P/H Factor. This too disbanded after each member, including Phyllis, received offers from major record companies.

"IN A SENTIMENTAL MOOD"

If there was anyone more true to her craft, it was Phyllis Hyman: "My gimmick, if artists are to have one, is to be me" (Michael, 2017, p. 37). Though she didn't write her own material at the start of her career, she selected songs she could personally relate to and brought them to life. Fans and critics noticed a "tear" in her voice, a well of emotional pain she drew upon during performances. She spoke directly to her audience and was as devoted to her fans as they were to her: "I've been accepted by the general public and feel that they are due good music from me. Once they've accepted me, I have no right to ever slack up" (p. 55). It didn't matter how large or small her fan base was. As one of her friends remarked: "She showed me that no matter how many people are in the room, you should still give it your all. It was the same show for two or 2,000" (p. 26).

Phyllis did not record songs she disliked. A song had to have meaning for her; it had to be visceral and resonant, even painful: "I fought against doing anything that I didn't feel down in my gut and down to my toes. I wanted songs that had storylines, songs that could be visualized in one's mind, not just a bunch of words" (p. 223). Phyllis was singing the story of her life, and efforts to commercialize her material did not only take her away from her jazz roots, but they removed the soulfulness and eclecticism from her work. They were also injurious to her sense of self. She clashed with record moguls over her celebrity persona. They wanted albums that sell, and she wanted albums that captured her true essence—two competing desires that seemed irreconcilable to her.

Phyllis was especially grateful to songwriters who bottled her thoughts and feelings into albums, such as Thom Bell and Linda Creed, who wrote most of her early songs. Linda wrote the first song Phyllis ever recorded, and several more to follow, all of which resonated with the theme of love and loss of love that was at the core of her personal and professional life. One such gift was "I Don't Want to Lose You" (1977), a song about a woman's attempts to hang onto love and seek reassurance that feelings stay even if people grow apart: "Tell me that love will remain/ Though we may change." Phyllis was devastated when Linda died of breast cancer, and as tribute, she sang "Old

Friend" (1986b). Linda was in her thoughts when she recorded the song, and she was reduced to tears each time she performed it live. The narrator of the song reminisces about joyful memories shared with an estranged friend, and she longs for the day they are reunited. Sadly, the line "Welcome back into my life again" was not one Phyllis got to say to any of the lovers who came and went in her life.

"LOVING YOU, LOSING YOU"

As if recapitulating her parents' doomed marriage, all of Phyllis Hyman's relationships ended in failure. A recurring pattern was that she treated her lovers the same way her father treated her mother, especially if they were as sensitive and as mild-mannered as Louise. This was especially the case with Larry Alexander, her first serious boyfriend, manager, and eventually, husband. A friend summarized their relationship as follows: "She would laugh at him. She would beat him up. She would dog him out" (Michael, 2017, p. 28). But the final straw was an aborted pregnancy; Larry wanted children, and Phyllis did not. Again, for Phyllis, parenthood threatened to replicate for future generations the neglect she'd endured as a child. It also meant self-sacrifice, and she refused to live an unfulfilling life like her mother.

After their breakup, Phyllis fired Larry from his manager role. Unfortunately for him, Phyllis's love life always found its way onto the stage. Speaking of Larry, she told an audience: "Well, I married a deaf mute. I mean he wasn't handicapped or nothing. The nigga just couldn't talk!" (p. 123). After the tirade she sang "Give a Little More" (1979), a fitting song given that they'd written it together. The narrator of the song realizes that she and her lover are "now singing out of key," their "sweet love song" no longer so sweet. She implores him to "give a little more," over and over, suggesting (in the context of the performance) that Phyllis placed the blame on Larry.

The cycle repeated with Tad Fennar. As soon as she appointed him road manager their relationship fell apart. She became pregnant with his child but had an abortion once more. This time, to cope with the loss, she started using drugs. Despite her yearning for independence, to be the complete opposite of what her mother represented, she needed another person by her side to sustain her precarious self: "I couldn't think for myself. I had no real sense of self. I became so obsessed that I couldn't really function as an individual" (Michael, 2017, p. 193). Drugs filled the vacuum created by lost love, and the parallels between her need for affection and growing addiction are apparent in "Obsession," a song inspired by "an ended love affair" and laced with "drug addiction terminology and feelings about drugs" (p. 193).

Phyllis flourished professionally when her love affairs were going well, but whenever they turned sour she resumed her drug habits, sabotaging her career prospects along the way. One lost opportunity was the role of Shug Avery in Steven Spielberg's *The Color Purple*. Phyllis came to the audition reeling from drugs she'd consumed the previous night. She was very uncooperative and refused to do what the director asked. However, Phyllis's songs took on a more dramatic quality when she reflected on her failed relationships, and her songwriters took advantage of this by tailoring songs to her situation. For instance, when Nate, another doomed love affair, walked out of her life, she received the title song of her first album with Philadelphia International Records (PIR): *Living All Alone* (1986a). The narrator of the song pines over shattered dreams of their everlasting union, and she finds being "a woman on my own" unbearable: "I can't stand this living all alone." Phyllis felt her lover's absence—and her aloneness—most palpably whenever she returned to her sparsely furnished apartment after a long day in the studio, her lonely existence carved in sharp relief by the hustle and bustle of the city.

During one of her performances overseas, at the Tokyo Blue Note in Japan, Phyllis met Dante James. They felt an immediate attraction to one another and developed a long-distance relationship. Though thousands of miles away, he would occasionally visit her in Philadelphia. For the first time in her life, despite her vow to never have children, Phyllis imagined a home full of kids: "That never, ever crossed my mind, to be in the kitchen cooking food and wiping our baby's nose. That was never on my agenda" (Michael, 2017, p. 236). But with Dante so far away, she fell into a suicidal depression.

One particular night, after hanging up the phone, Phyllis swallowed a handful of sleeping pills. She was rescued in time by personal assistants and friends. Although she fervently believed she had every right to take her life, Phyllis was actually grateful she was saved, and she thanked her rescuers profusely. But over time, her depression combined with her addictions became too much for Dante. He had had enough, and the relationship was called off. Phyllis was devastated, and she blamed no one but herself: "I destroyed it because I was afraid. I just did anything and everything to put him off, to make him not want me anymore. I had never been that happy and it scared me" (p. 236).

She sang her sadness over the breakup in "Walk Away" (1991d), where she pines over "sacrificing those years, in one day" and struggles with saying goodbye "when there's still some love inside." She found uplifting songs especially difficult to perform because she had to pretend. Whereas the narrator of "I Found Love" (1991a) cries "tears of joy" for the happiness her lover brings, Phyllis was crying tears of sorrow. And whereas the narrator of "Meet Me On The Moon" (1991c) feels buoyed by "the everlasting moment of love," the love Phyllis had was not so everlasting; it was short-lived like all the others. Songs like "Living In Confusion" (1991b) more closely approximated her feelings, but as she confessed, the song's narrator was "not being honest with themselves" (Michael, 2017, p. 234), putting the blame on her lover instead of herself. Phyllis was reenacting the drama of her childhood, the mistreatment and abandonment of her mother by her father, in her songs and in her tumultuous love life.

"I REFUSE TO BE LONELY"

The two years leading up to Phyllis's suicide were marked by tragic loss. Many of her close friends died in the AIDS epidemic, a beloved grandmother passed away, and most significantly, she suffered the loss of her own mother. Prior to her mother's death, during a brief stint in a drug rehab facility, Phyllis wrote a letter expressing remorse over the way she'd been treating Louise. She felt ashamed of her mother's lack of aspirations, for treating her with disgust, and for belittling her every decision in life—from having too many kids to not wanting more for herself. She acknowledged the pain she caused Louise, including replicating her father's abusive behavior, and she was grateful that in spite of her cruelty, Louise remained patient and understanding. Phyllis ends the letter with, "I love you mommy" (Michael, 2017, p. 211), casting herself in the role of loving daughter.

Sadly, Phyllis never got to send the letter to her mother, shattering all her hopes for reconciliation. The fear that she, too, would die alone was visceral, and Phyllis strongly felt her mother's pain when her father walked out, for several men in her own life had done the same. Only two days after her mother's death, she performed the song "This Too Shall Pass" (1995c) at a school for troubled teens. The song is about two people whom love "always passed over," who are always "close to weeping" during long, sleepless nights. But their plaintive cries remain unheard because the people they trust are "strangely unkind." Hearing this song, one can't help but feel that Phyllis is singing the story of her *and* her mother's life, with Phyllis assuming the dual role of jilted lover and "unkind" daughter. Although this daughter only heard her mother's cries when it was too late to mend their rift, the song does end on a hopeful note, with the narrator realizing that even "the longest night becomes a day."

Phyllis's final album, *I Refuse To Be Lonely* (1995), was a heartfelt attempt to exorcise the loneliness that had been the core of her life, and she contributed greatly to the creation of its songs. She credited her recent losses as inspiration and cried a lot through the writing process, saying that the "pain brought out some of my best work" (Michael, 2017, p. 269). The title song (Hyman, 1995b) itself captures her newfound determination. Though the narrator admits to feeling “alone,” “afraid,” and “on my own,” and despite the many heartaches that await, she refuses to surrender to these feelings. “Lonely is the place I used to be, but I’m closing the door,” Phyllis sings resoundingly. “Yes I’m gonna ache, but I will not break.”

During an interview, Phyllis remarked: “I’m my problem and I have to work on me. That’s the kind of songs I’m writing now” (Michael, 2017, p. 264). When asked if she would live her life differently if she could do it all over again, her response was an emphatic no. But despite her efforts to project an image of strength, it did not represent the life she was living during those final two years. She found love once again, this time with a woman, Martha David, her personal assistant and valet of seven years. Phyllis never had such intense feelings for anyone that long, but due to miscommunication and a series of heated arguments, the relationship—the best in her life, by her own admission—ended on a bitter note. The falling out was confirmation that all good things come to an end, sabotaged by her own hands. In “Why Not Me” (1995d), the narrator laments her inability to find happiness when others seem able to effortlessly. Having “traveled down this road before,” she wonders if it’s worth believing that “there’s someone there for me.” “Doesn’t everyone deserve to find their dream,” Phyllis asks of her listeners.

Her career was also sliding downhill. She ballooned to over 300 pounds, crushing her self-esteem further. She resented the music industry’s rapt focus on younger and more glamorous looking women, even those of lesser talents. To add to her frustrations, PIR was taking too long to release her albums. Her will to live sapped, she confined herself to her apartment and resorted to drugs to numb the pain: “I’m going to get fucking high. It just makes me not feel” (Michael, 2017, p. 206). Her drug abuse ruined many of her performances. Once, she sang with her back turned to her audience. “Turn around. You sing to us. We paid to see you,” yelled a spectator, to which she replied, “Well, I got your money already, so ain’t nothin’ you can do about it” (p. 296). This Phyllis was a far cry from the woman who gave it her all whether she was singing for two or two thousand. That she sang with her back turned is a clear refusal of the connection her viewers once provided her. It was a refusal of life.

Phyllis concluded that “the only answer to life is really death” (p. 292): “The only bright light is to die . . . I have no personal life and no energy” (p. 3). She insisted on her right to self-determination, talking openly of suicide with loved ones and getting angry when they tried to talk her out of it. When boxed into a corner, she howled with desperation: “I don’t want to live . . . I’m all alone. I ain’t got nobody” (pp. 3–4). Her final song, “Give Me One Good Reason To Stay” (1995a), is an ultimatum. On the surface, it is about a woman who’s had enough with her lover. Her “bags are at the door,” and she doesn’t want to “go through this anymore,” seeing as “there’s no way we can make up." Unlike her previous sad songs, which finds the narrator "passed over" or jilted by lovers, here there is a shift in agency, with the narrator *choosing* to leave unless she is given a good reason to stay.

But Phyllis Hyman chose not to stay. Her latest suicide attempt would be her last, and instead of dying on her 46th birthday, when others were set to intervene, she died on the day of her lifetime's most anticipated performance, suggesting that she deliberately misled loved ones. Her show at the Apollo Theater in Harlem was supposed to revive her flailing career, and her latest album was supposed to be called *Strength of a Woman*, but not even the title song made it into the final cut.

Chapter 4

"A Dry Place to Call Their Home"

The Case of Kurt Cobain

On April 8, 1994, Kurt Cobain, the lead singer and songwriter of Nirvana, was found dead by an electrician inside the greenhouse of his Seattle home. He had been missing for days. After two days at a Los Angeles drug rehab facility for celebrities, he escaped. But now the search was over, and so was his life, terminated by what appeared to be a self-inflicted shotgun wound to the mouth. Autopsy and toxicology reports later showed that he had lethal amounts of heroin in his system. Kurt is survived by his wife Courtney Love and their daughter Frances Bean, then only 20 months.

Kurt Cobain was a key figure in the grunge scene of the 1990s, which had its roots in the Pacific Northwest before it swept the rest of the world. Grunge was rebellious, transgressive, and antiauthoritarian. For Kurt, it was the embodiment of "musical liberation . . . freedom from pain and suffering in the external world" (Cobain, 2002, p. 156). Nirvana, the celebrated epicenter of grunge, captured the hearts of many dispirited youth, echoing their angst, their dissatisfaction with authority, and their frustrated search for meaning and identity. Kurt was timid offstage but played with intensity in front of audiences. For instance, during a performance of "Love Buzz" at Evergreen State College in Olympia, Washington, Kurt smashed a guitar and people scrambled to put pieces of it in their pockets (Cross, 2001).

Upon hearing news of Kurt's suicide, many adolescents and teenagers became suicidal themselves—a classic example of media contagion. Calls to crisis hotlines in the greater Seattle area skyrocketed, but fortunately, the rate of *actual* suicides did not. His death placed him in the Forever 27 Club alongside Robert Johnson, Brian Jones, Jimi Hendrix, Janis Joplin, Jim Morrison, and more recently, Amy Winehouse—all musicians, and all dead by age 27.

Even today, much speculation surrounds the death of Kurt Cobain. Some say that it wasn't suicide but foul play, a murder scheme orchestrated by

Courtney Love herself. For those who aren't swayed by conspiracy theories, Kurt's death was another sad tale of the emptiness of stardom and the addictions that plague celebrities, who cannot seem to cope with the entertainment industry's demands. While these factors certainly contributed to Kurt's suicide, his self-destruction—and his creativity—have roots that extend further back into the past.

According Schultz (2003), every life narrative contains a *prototypical scene*, a singular event that draws webs of meaning together; in short, the leitmotif of a life. The prototypical scene is organized around unresolved conflict, typically with members of the family. It exhibits repetition and possesses developmental gravity, exerting influence even in adulthood. For Kurt, the prototypical scene is none other than his parents' divorce, whose impact, as I illustrate in this chapter, he narrated with his "belly-aching," his search for a "dry place" to call home, his furious music, his drug use and abuse, and his threats and attempts at suicide. The loss of the nuclear family was catastrophic, and this traumatic loss was concretized in his art and music. Though he would go on to create a new family of his own, the specter of the past continued to haunt the present. Fearing further loss, and realizing the painful contrast between what his life had once been, and what it had become, Kurt took his own life.

"THAT LEGENDARY DIVORCE IS SUCH A BORE"

Kurt Cobain was born in Aberdeen, Washington, on February 20, 1967. He was a "happy, smiling baby" (Cross, 2001, p. 8) with remarkable blue eyes, and as the first grandchild of both family trees, he was pampered like a prince. Everything he did, from beating a toy drum his aunt Mari had given him, to taping his conversations with his imaginary friend Boddah, was showered lavishly with praise.

Kurt's creativity was apparent from an early age, and his teachers remarked that he was very inquisitive. He could replay tunes he'd heard on the radio on the piano, and as his family liked to joke, he started playing the drums before he'd even learned how to walk. But as a child, music came only second, after art. Kurt dreamed of becoming a visual artist, not a musician, and he especially liked drawing. He wanted to be an illustrator for Disney someday. He designed birthday and holiday greeting cards with his own logo, his bedroom wall was a gallery of crayon creations, and he took on many multidimensional projects, including a dollhouse for his grandmother.

He would always remember the first eight years of his life as "amazing, incredible, realistic, and an absolute grateful joy" (Cobain, 2002, p. 18). Tragically, his picture-perfect childhood did not last. His mother and father quarreled often, and financial strains kindled heated arguments. Kurt and his younger sister Kim witnessed the love between their parents diminish with each passing day, and when he was nine, his parents finally divorced.

To say that Kurt was left scarred by the divorce is an understatement. No one seemed able to help him work through the physical and emotional reactions of shock and grief that accompany parental separation, nor explain to him that parents divorce adults, not children. He somatized his grief, which initially manifested as involuntary twitching of the eyes, backaches, gastrointestinal pains, and other complaints for which no doctor could find an underlying physiological cause. And like many children of divorce, he blamed himself and would forever link the event to many of his problems in adulthood.

Of the divorce, Kurt wrote on his bedroom wall: "I hate Mom, I hate Dad, Dad hates Mom, Mom hates Dad, it simply makes you want to be so sad" (Cross, 2001, p. 21). It's not surprising that its impact was transposed onto lyrics he would later write. "Paper Cuts" (1993c), for example, evokes the helplessness he felt upon seeing his nuclear family dissolve: "They come with a flash of light/ And take my family away."

Each parent held onto one child, so Kurt lived with his father Donald ("Don") in a trailer for some time after the divorce. Upon reaching puberty, he began to seriously consider life as a musician or artist. He would compete, quite successfully, in school and local art competitions, but Don wanted him to be an athlete. Kurt joined his school's wrestling team in an act of compliance, but purposely lost matches, taking every blow without retaliating just to spite his father: "I waited for the whistle to blow, just staring straight into his face, and then I instantly clammed up—I put my arms together, and let the guy pin me" (Cross, 2001, p. 36). His repudiation of Don inevitably found expression in his songs. In "Serve the Servants" (1993d), Kurt laments: "I tried to have a father/ But instead I had a Dad." According to a draft of the liner notes, the song is about Don's inability to communicate "at the level of affection in which I have always expected" (Cobain, 2002, p. 222). What Kurt received instead of affection were public slaps to the face for being a clumsy adolescent. At home, Don sometimes struck him on the temple or chest, causing him to flee to his room out of pain and humiliation. The damage to Kurt's self-esteem was lasting, extending to adulthood. During an interview, he said of his mistreatment: "That's a weird psychological thing to play on a child. I still put myself down and cuss myself out for knocking things over . . . Fuck him for that" (Schnack, 2006).

His repudiation of Don is most damning in "Mr. Moustache," a comic strip he created (Cobain, 2002, p. 24). In the comic, a bigoted father eagerly anticipates the birth of his son, who he hopes will become a football player, "a Jew, Spic, Nigger, and Faggot hatin 100% pure beef AMERICAN MALE!"

He puts his head against his pregnant wife's belly to listen for a kick inside the womb. A kick is exactly what the unborn does, impaling the father with its "strong little legs."

When Don remarried and started a new family, Kurt packed his bags and left. For Kurt, the second marriage was confirmation that he was "one of the last things of importance in [Don's] list" (Schnack, 2006). He soon moved in with his mother, Wendy, and his younger sister Kim, but this was not without its share of problems. Kurt didn't approve of the men Wendy dated. One was physically and verbally abusive; another was a mere seven years Kurt's senior, young enough to be an older brother instead of a stepfather. To complicate matters, Wendy seemed to encourage the overtures of Kurt's male friends. The tension between mother and son reached its peak when she caught him in bed with one of his classmates, resulting in her kicking him out of her house. During this time, he started contemplating suicide and pictured himself leaping off of rooftops. One cannot help but feel that "Paper Cuts" (1993c) also alludes to his mother's crushing rejection: "The lady whom I feel maternal love for/ Cannot look me in the eyes."

"FOR YEARS AND YEARS I ROAMED"

Between the ages of 15 and 19, Kurt lived as a vagabond in 10 different homes with 10 different families. He lived with his paternal grandparents but tested his grandfather's limits. He was then taken in by a Christian family but was asked to leave after he'd convinced the pastor's son to skip school and smoke weed. When he didn't have the generosity of others to rely on, he lived in makeshift homes, among them, a cardboard refrigerator box on a stranger's porch, the hallways of centrally heated apartments (he would sneak in at night and sneak out at dawn), and the waiting room of a community hospital. There, he pretended to be the bereaved relative of one patient after another, scoring free meals in the cafeteria by charging them to made-up rooms. It's worth noting that Kurt was born in this same community hospital. That he would return to his birthplace when he had no place to call home, suggests an unconscious yearning to return to the way things were before the divorce.

Kurt wished he were an alien from outer space so that he could pretend there was a reason for him to be on Earth. Aliens symbolized his lack of belonging, his being far away from home. In high school, he told everyone he was gay even though he was straight (his only friend at the time was gay), and he was harassed in gym class because of it. He then gravitated toward punk, which reverberated with his outcast status. By then, songwriting had become his way of being. He dropped out of school and devoted himself full-time to finding structure to his songs, and an original sound for Nirvana when he finally assembled the band.

Contrary to popular belief, Nirvana was not an overnight success. Kurt sent hundreds of query letters to record companies and received as many rejections. He became so desperate that he offered to *pay* for the release of a single album, which proved to be futile. He wrote song lyrics relentlessly and toured for years without seeing a dime. In order to survive he worked a handful of odd jobs, among them, a janitor in his former high school. Kurt finally achieved success with the release of his SubPop album *Bleach* (1989), which reached Top Ten in the U.K. independent label charts. This was soon followed by *Nevermind* (1991), which reached No. 35 in the Billboard Top 200 within a month of its release, and then No. 1 upon reaching Gold status. *Nevermind* would ultimately sell over eight million copies, propelling Kurt to cult status and international acclaim. But no matter how highly he soared, the specter of Kurt's past loomed ever so closely.

When recounting his story later in life, Kurt told people that he'd lived "underneath a bridge"—curiously, the first line of "Something in the Way" (1991d). This was an exaggeration, of course, but one that contained an emotional truth: Kurt felt like such a vagabond that he might as well have lived under a bridge. His music is confessional, rendering autobiographical life as symbolic expression. He also covered songs that resonated with his vagrant status, including David Bowie's "The Man Who Sold the World" (1994c) ("I searched for form and land/ For years and years I roamed"), and Leadbelly's cover of the American folk song, "In the Pines" (1994a) ("I will shiver the whole night through"). For Kurt, home was everywhere and nowhere. It was where his feet landed next.

"REMIND ME TO STAY A CHILD"

Kurt's wish to relive the first eight years of his life lasted a lifetime, and he did many things, both consciously and unconsciously, "to remind me to stay a child" (Schnack, 2006). When he received his first record deal, he giddily spent one-third of the check in Toys "R" Us (Cross, 2001). He continued to draw his parents living happily together, with stepsiblings and stepparents conspicuously missing, a habit common among children of divorce (Bowlby, 1980; Levine & Kline, 2006). In one of his many journals (he was a prolific diarist), Kurt drew a small child flanked on each side by an adult male and female, representing his mother and father (Cobain, 2002, p. 112). But the figures are ghostlike, mere outlines with zero details filled in. The drawing encapsulates his wish to restore the original nuclear family, and the simultaneous recognition that what once was could never again be.

Kurt's artwork is full of imagery related to the womb, expressing a deep desire to rewind the hands of time, to the beginning of life. In "Heart-Shaped Box" (1993b), he pleads with the listener to "Throw down your umbilical noose/ So I can climb right back." Interestingly, Kurt insisted that the cover art of *Nevermind* feature a woman giving birth underwater. Because such an image would have been too controversial, executives rejected the idea. As a compromise, the parties agreed on a naked baby chasing after a dollar bill underwater. The cover art of *Lithium* (a single) does feature a sonogram on the back, and on the front, alien-looking dolls Kurt himself had carved. Whereas the fetal imagery is serene—a luminescent blue figure against a black amniotic background, the seed of life pulsating from nothingness—the dolls are horrifying and grotesque, as if they'd been skinned alive. The juxtaposition is a haunting portrait of Kurt's emotional life: peace and tranquility in early childhood, turbulence in adolescence and adulthood.

But perhaps the most profound manifestation of Kurt's womb fantasy is this fictionalized account of his birth in his diary:

> My first memory was a light aqua green tile floor and a very strong hand holding me by my ankles. This force made it clear to me that I'm no longer in water and I cannot go back. I tried to kick and squirm, back to the hole, but he just held me there, suspended in my mother's vagina. It was like he was teasing me, and I could feel the liquid and blood evaporating and tightening my skin. Reality was oxygen consuming me, and the sterile smell of never going back into the hole, a terror that could never be repeated again. (Cobain, 2002, p. 341)

For the neonate of Kurt's imagining, the current of expulsion was abject terror, and the evaporation of liquid and blood from his skin was a sure sign that he'd reached the point of no return.

For Kurt, maternal warmth is synonymous with home. In "Sliver" (1992), he recounts a time when his mother and father dropped him off at his grandparents' house so that they could watch a show. "Grandma take me home," the narrator begs. The separation anxiety is mitigated at the song's end. After dinner, after ice cream, and after late night TV, the child falls asleep and wakes up "in my mother's arms."

As an adult, Kurt could not soothe himself and depended on others for succor. In Winnicott's (1955) parlance, Kurt never attained mastery over the *depressive position*. He suffered recurrent nightmares where he was pursued by bloodsucking vampires, assailants with baseball hats, and shadowy figures with knives, and he'd wake up sweating profusely and in tears. The only people able to pacify him were the mother surrogates of his adulthood: his string of girlfriends, and his eventual wife Courtney Love. They would stroke his hair and whisper in hushed tones, as a mother would for a terrified child.

"HEAL A MILLION, KILL A MILLION"

Kurt's resentment over his childhood spawned further resentment in adulthood. During an interview, he said matter-of-factly: "I had this hatred towards a lot of people . . . I'm a firm believer in revenge. I think there's a time and place for violence, in every situation" (Schnack, 2006). However, he added that while alienation could lead to violence, he would rather kill himself than harm another living thing. Still, he felt rage toward those who'd abandoned him; typical of children of divorce, he oscillated between love for and hatred of the lost "other," an ambivalence that sought expression in his fantasies and art.

He had a morbid fascination with the Virgin Mary. In his late teens, he and his ex-girlfriend Tracey stole a sculpture of the Virgin from a cemetery and painted tears of blood underneath her eyes. One of his artworks even features a shattered Mary inside a briefcase (Cross, 2008, p. 152). He had dreams of the Holy Mother in a dilapidated church, surrounded by candles, with meat hooks through her back (Cobain, 2002, p. 77). From a psychoanalytic standpoint, these profane images suggest disavowed hatred of his mother, who (figuratively speaking) had sent him packing with his own briefcase. But rather than admit to such intense feelings and risk irreparable rupture between mother and self, the child transposes them onto something or someone else—in this case, a mother yet not one's mother, the mother of Christ.

Equally horrific are the drawings in his journals: "Dali-esque" landscapes with dissolving clocks, headless creatures, severed limbs, and pornographic body parts, melded together like a scene from Dante's circles of hell. In one page, a grotesque monster with pustulant skin and razor sharp teeth has torn an egg in half, spilling its contents, which are revealed to be gastrointestinal parts of the human body (Cobain, 2002, p. 4). His songs also serve as portals to the shadow side of his psyche. The addicted narrator of "Lithium" (1991b), for example, struggles to contain his violent impulses: "I love you, I'm not gonna crack/ I kill you, I'm not gonna crack." Here, the narrator's object of desire becomes the target of his murderous rage, and this dialectic of love and hate surfaces again in the chorus of "Scoff" (1989): "Heal a million/ Kill a million." Meanwhile, "Polly" (1991c) recounts the true story of a girl who'd been kidnapped, raped, and tortured with a blowtorch. Told from the point of view of the assailant, "Polly" has a surprisingly soothing melody, which makes the disturbing lyrics stand out in even greater relief. "Polly wants a cracker/ I think I should get off her first," the song begins, suggesting lovers engaged in intercourse, until the details of the girl's torture and captivity are laid bare.

But the most chilling are Kurt's treatment of children and infants—not in real life, of course, but in his journals and artistic creations. For some time, he was obsessed with "flipper babies," infants born with defective limbs due to the mother taking thalidomide (a sleep aid and antiemetic) during pregnancy. Then at age 23, he started making dolls that looked like child corpses. The music video for "Heart-Shaped Box" (2009) features a human fetus hanging from a tree, which reappears in the next scene, inside an IV drip hooked to the veins of a recuperating Jesus. And in a comic strip titled "Crybaby Jerkins Fouls It Up Again" (Cobain, 2002, p. 90), a monstrous chef at a "Benny Hanna" restaurant serves the day's special, "fried babies on toast with juice," as his severed arm bleeds profusely. Splattered across the page: the decapitated heads, limbs, and torsos of infants. Several pages after this drawing, a diary entry reads: "I like to make incisions into the belly of infants then fuck the incisions until the child dies" (p. 99).

What do these horrific images mean within the context of Kurt's emotional life? Do they represent his loathing of children and the innocence they stand for? Or do they suggest condemnation of life itself? To answer these questions, we must consider that Kurt behaved in ways diametrically opposed to his violent imaginings. He never acted on such impulses in real life, even when fantasizing about kicking 50-year-old men's rubber underwear until "the brown stuff soaks into their beige slacks" (Cross, 2001, p. 165). He never inflicted physical pain on anyone but himself, and even as a child, he'd been very empathetic toward human and animal suffering. Once, after finding a broken-winged bird, Kurt knocked on a veterinarian's door in the middle of the night, refusing to leave until he was sure the bird was going to receive proper care. When he became a father, the sight of innocent children dying on television, and the testimonies of parents who'd lost sons and daughters to illness or accident, never failed to move him to tears. One might say that his compassion was greatest for those who were as helpless as he had been.

Kurt's gruesome portrayals of conception, birth, and the mother archetype can thus be seen as manifestations of his inner turmoil. He was the child ripped out of the womb too soon, the child upon whom (emotional) violence had been inflicted, the same child who was "fucked" repeatedly as he meandered from one home to the next. (As we will see shortly, the infant belly he wanted to "fuck" was also the site of his somatized psychic distress.) He staged and restaged the details of his childhood to preserve the truth of his past and to "shore up an imperiled subjective world" (Atwood & Stolorow, 1993, p. 92).

"HELP ME INHALE AND MEND IT WITH YOU"

The stomach pains that emerged in Kurt's childhood persisted until adulthood, tormenting him to the point of wanting to die: "I wanted to kill myself everyday. I came very close many times. This is no way to live a life. So

I decided to medicate myself" (Schnack, 2006). And so, in order for the excruciating pains to abate, Kurt medicated himself with drugs. Although he started experimenting with drugs in eighth grade, he did not become a habitual user until after his musical career flourished.

Kurt had uncanny insight into the origins of his gastrointestinal problems. In an interview with his band's biographer, he remarked offhand: "I have just been brooding and *belly-aching* about something I couldn't have, which is a family, a solid family unit, for too long" (Schnack, 2006). When asked why he resorted to opiates, heroin, and a gamut of other drugs, his response was, "to feel the security I wanted to feel" (ibid.). Kurt belly-ached until the very end because he denied himself the truth his body had been trying to tell him. His was a sad story in need of mourning, but instead, he told himself repeatedly, "it's not my story anymore" (ibid.). Even the following line from "Serve the Servants" (1993d) downplays the enduring impact of his parents' separation on his life: "That legendary divorce is such a bore." Thus, like many children of hurtful parenting (Miller, 2006, 2008), Kurt silenced his story and his true self with substances, which his body pushed back against.

Kurt was fascinated with excreta, going so far as to call his first band Fecal Matter (they never got to play in public). He found conventional pornography sexist and objectifying of women, but he was delighted by what he called "shit love," or sex acts involving defecation and the smearing of feces. Very little has been written about *coprophilia*, or the fascination with excrement. It has been theorized by Abraham (1924) that coprophilia is indicative of childhood loss, characterized by intense ambivalence toward the lost object, typically the mother. As the theory goes, the coprophilic person oscillates between expulsion and retention of the lost maternal object. Whatever one makes of this theory, it does apply to Kurt Cobain, who felt ambivalence toward his own mother. He loved her dearly yet hated her for repudiating him. But because the hatred must be denied, kept from spilling onto conscious awareness in order to maintain emotional ties to the mother, it sought expression in other ways, as disavowed feelings tend to do. Hence the shit love.

But an equally plausible explanation, one consistent with an intersubjective systems approach, is that Kurt's obsession with fecal matter symbolizes *his* own feelings of expulsion. After all, he'd been ejected from no less than 10 different homes. To put it crudely, he himself felt like other people's shit, and seeing others debase themselves so gave expression to his subjective feelings of homelessness.

Kurt's drug addiction manifested in his art in similar ways. "Dumb" (1993a), for example, addresses his self-medication with drugs—his "glue" for his "broke" heart—treating it as a solution to his interpersonal and marital problems: "Help me inhale/ Mend it with you." The outcome, of course, was euphoria, but Kurt couldn't stay at the zenith for long. Following the rapid ascent into the clouds was an equally violent descent, as in "Very Ape" (1993e): "Out of the sky/ Into the dirt." "Very Ape" captures the highs and lows of drug abuse, but it is also a metaphor for Kurt's rise to and fall from stardom.

He overdosed on heroin on numerous occasions but was resuscitated by Courtney Love each time. But once she started using heroin herself, a game of see-saw ensued: when one entered rehab, the other relapsed. Fortunately, she was afraid of needles, which enabled her to exert some gating control over her and Kurt's use. His friends called him Rapunzel because he rarely left his room when his withdrawal symptoms worsened. During these times, only Courtney and his mother Wendy were permitted to see him.

"NO I DON'T HAVE A GUN"

Kurt Cobain was preoccupied with suicide for much of his life. This is not to say he was clinically suicidal throughout life, but it had been an obsession since his parents' divorce. He made Super 8 films in which he pretended to cut his throat and wrists with a can lid, spilling blood made of Kool-Aid, ketchup, or tomato sauce. He fantasized about lying flat on train tracks so that a train would run him over. In his journals, he drew a stick figure with a smiley face chopping its legs off, as well as a man hanging from a noose (Cobain, 2002, p. 106). Kurt told classmates that he had "suicide genes," and that he was going to turn himself into Helen Keller by "puncturing my ears with a knife, then cutting my voice box out" (p. 115). Jokingly, he also told friends that "I'm going to be a superstar musician, kill myself, and go out in a flame of glory" (Cross, 2001, p. 23). Taken together, we have the chilling portrait of a child who felt as if his life ended when his family fell apart.

He had a fatalistic outlook of what adulthood was going to be like, cryptically stating that he was never going to make it past age 30. When asked why, he said: "You know what life is like after thirty. I don't want that" (p. 76). His vision of adulthood was that of familial and relational rupture, of squabbles over money and responsibility, of heated arguments followed by separation and abandonment. But fatalism and hope are two sides of the same coin. Despite his childhood yearnings, the adult Kurt *knew* that there was no reclaiming the original family he'd lost. But that did not mean he couldn't start his own family, on which he could pin new hope.

As the story goes, Kurt fell in love with Courtney Love, lead singer of Hole, with whom he felt a deep connection because she too experienced a turbulent childhood. Together, they thought they could overcome their pasts. They then had a child named Frances Bean—the same child whose sonogram appeared on the cover of *Lithium*. Her birth made him feel so alive that he experienced a resurgence in his creativity, fueling his art. He even considered giving up his musical career so that he could paint for the rest of his life. At that point, he was so rich that he would have been able to afford a humbler lifestyle, free from the demands, expectations, and constraints of the music industry.

Kurt continued to oscillate between fatalism and hope, however. He constantly worried that his marriage would end. In an interview, he said: "I'd rather die than go through *another* divorce" (Cross, 2001, p. 312). He'd never been married prior to Courtney, so when he said "another divorce," he was clearly referring to his parents. Even before Frances was born, Kurt watched her ultrasound as frequently as he watched bootlegged copies of Pennsylvania state official R. Budd Dwyer's suicide on live TV. Here, the juxtaposition of life and death speaks to the past haunting the present, to the threat of the original loss being replicated. The day *after* Frances was born, Kurt went to the hospital and brought a loaded .39 pistol, reminding Courtney of the pact they'd made: that they were going to end their lives together should they lose their daughter. Fearing traffic accidents, he was reluctant to take baby Frances into his car. If his child were to die, he would see to it that he himself died. Death was preferable to the dissolution of another family.

A profile of the couple in *Vanity Fair* fueled Kurt's fears. The article was very candid about the couple's drug abuse history, which led courts to doubt the legitimacy of their parenting abilities. Kurt and Courtney lost custody of Frances, albeit temporarily, until they fulfilled the court mandate of seeking rehabilitation. While they ultimately regained custody of their daughter, the impact on Kurt was catastrophic, and he became acutely suicidal. Furthermore, this episode rekindled his long-standing belief that adulthood was nothing more than a string of disappointments, that all good things must come to an end, that family is impermanent.

His drug habits did not help. What once was a means of pain management and relief, had at this point become a full-blown addiction. On one occasion, he locked himself inside his bedroom with a gun, forcing the police to break into his house and seize every substance and firearm they could find.

DENOUEMENT

A few months before his suicide, during his *Unplugged* concert in New York, Kurt requested that the stage be made to look like a funeral. It was decorated with candles, chandelier lamps, and stargazer lilies, creating a somber atmosphere. "Lake of Fire" (1994b), played by Nirvana at the event, powerfully captures his life as a vagrant and his everlasting search for "a dry place to call their home." But the song is haunted by a sense of impending doom, with angels and devils fighting over the vagabond narrator's soul. Alas, despite Kurt's repeated pleas in "Come As You Are" (1991a), "No, I don't have a gun," he ultimately did have a gun.

Kurt's suicide note (Cross, 2001, pp. 337–339) was addressed to "Boddah," the imaginary childhood friend that only he could see, and thus, the only real witness to the dramas of his life. The note is a recapitulation of all the troubles plaguing him. He admits that he has not felt "the excitement of listening to as well as creating music . . . for too many years now," and that he experienced guilt whenever he stepped on stage, "pretending as if I'm having 100% fun." "I'm too sensitive," he writes. "I need to be slightly numb in order to regain the enthusiasms I once had as a child."

Like many victims of suicide, Kurt believed that the world would be a better place with him gone. He writes that his daughter "will be so much happier without me" and that he is undeserving of his "goddess of a wife who sweats ambition and empathy." He worries that Frances Bean, "who reminds me too much of what I used to be, full of love and joy, kissing every person she meets," will become like him: a "miserable, self-destructive, death rocker" who, "since the age of seven," had become "hateful towards all humans." His letter ends with words of gratitude "from the pit of my burning, nauseous stomach," and with the iconic line: "it's better to burn out than to fade away."

Chapter 5

Individuation through Poetry and Death

The Case of Sylvia Plath

One winter night, Sylvia Plath, the confessional poet, tucked Frieda and Nicholas in bed. She had just read them a bedtime story. It hadn't been long since her separation from Ted Hughes following his affairs with Asia Wevill. For months, she struggled to make ends meet for herself and her children, generating meager income through her writing. Though she was a well-known poet, poetry was not very lucrative.

Soon enough, the children were asleep. Sylvia opened the windows, blew the lit candle, and exited the room, but in the event they woke up hungry and thirsty, she returned with a plate of cookies and two glasses of milk, leaving the items in plain sight. Once outside, she locked their room and sealed the edges of the door with thick adhesive. As an added measure, she tucked a towel in the gap between the door and the wooden floor.

Just before dawn, Sylvia scribbled a note and placed it on the kitchen counter. When she was certain that all the doors and windows in the kitchen were shut, she turned on the gas and put her head inside the oven.

The *au pair* girl arrived on schedule. She rang the bell several times. No response, from Ms. Plath or her downstairs neighbor. She then dialed the number for the Plath residence from a nearby phone booth. Still no response; the line was dead. The door would remain shut for several more hours until the arrival of painters who had keys to the flat.

The children were safe and sound in their room; their mother was not. Sylvia was dead by the time she was found; her death on February 11, 1963, ruled a suicide. She was only 30 years of age.

INTRODUCTION

Sylvia Plath is considered one of the greatest female poets of the twentieth century, and following her death, her place in the literary canon began to approach that of the nineteenth-century poetess Emily Dickinson. Sylvia had an early start to her career. She published her first poem at the age of nine—shortly after her father's death—in *The Boston Herald*, and she became only more prolific with the passing of time (Alexander, 1991). Her poems generated interest because of their raw expression of female subjectivity, whose contents were drawn from the vicissitudes of her inner life. The *Ariel* collection of poems, considered to be the best she had ever written, emerged during a burst of creativity in the four months leading to her death (Kirk, 2004).

It is undeniable that Sylvia tapped into the currents of her emotions to power her work. In the Foreword to the restored edition of *Ariel*, her daughter Frieda wrote:

> She used every emotional experience as if it were a scrap of material that could be pieced together to make a wonderful dress; she wasted nothing of what she felt, and when in control of those tumultuous feelings she was able to focus and direct her incredible poetic energy to great effect. (Plath, 2004, xix–xx)

Her poems are thus windows to her subjective world, illuminating not only her suicide but the nuclear crises of her life, which emerged during childhood and became thematized, and concretized, in her adult life and work.

An examination of her biographical life, and the lines and stanzas that comprise her work, reveal two inextricable themes. The first is a struggle for freedom and individuation; the second, ownership of her life through death and rebirth. The first theme is twofold. One one side is an ambivalent escape from a father who continued to haunt her long after his death. Despite her wish to reunite with him, she knew that reunion meant death, so she used poetry to symbolically resurrect, and later, exorcise his ghost. On the other side is fierce resistance against a suffocating mother, whose failure to become a writer turned into vested interest in the success of her poet daughter. Within this symbiotic relationship, Sylvia felt not her mother's love but its absence. Writing was originally an act of compliance, but later turned into rebellion against this mother.

Both reunion with father and engulfment by mother threatened to erase Sylvia's self, and she attempted to thwart the pull of these forces through poetry. Whenever writing failed the project of emancipation, she engaged in the ritual of suicide to lay claims to a life and existence of her own making. Throughout her life, Sylvia attempted suicide three times. The first attempt was disguised as fiction in her only novel, *The Bell Jar* (1996). The second is recounted by Alvarez (1973) in his study of suicide, *The Savage God*. The third and final attempt resulted in her untimely death at age 30. The deep meaning of these suicide attempts unravel when considered in light of her creativity and the aforementioned forces.

A VOICE FROM THE GRAVE

Arrested Mourning and Grief

The death of her father Otto was a traumatic experience for the eight-year-old Sylvia, and being unable to mourn his passing had a profound effect that lasted throughout her life. It wasn't until she was 27 that she finally had the chance to visit his grave, to see where he laid buried with her own eyes (Alexander, 1991).

Otto Plath was a university professor who was heavily invested in his research. So as to not disturb his work, the man and his wife Aurelia arranged it so that the children were confined to one section of the household and he in another. Thus, there was a limit to how frequently Sylvia and her younger brother Warren could visit him. Whenever they received the green light, they would entertain him in his chambers with theatrical acts and performances. For Sylvia, poetry was the way to her father's heart. She would dedicate hours to crafting poems that would win Daddy's approval, and in diaries she kept as a child, she recounted the joy of sitting on her father's lap, being held and kissed on the cheeks for her fine performances (Kirk, 2004). These moments were important for Sylvia, because they were the only times she felt recognized by a man she deeply loved yet was absent from most of her waking life. One could say that his scarcity only made her heart swell with longing.

Otto's death denied Sylvia her transient yet irreplaceable source of happiness. As she recounts in *The Bell Jar* through Esther Green, her fictional counterpart: "I thought how strange it had never occurred to me before that I was only purely happy until I was nine years old" (Plath, 1996, p. 75). The death was sudden; unbeknownst to Otto, he was suffering from diabetes, which came to light when a stubbed toe turned into a gangrenous leg that required amputation. Shortly after the procedure, he died of an embolism to the lung.

Sylvia and her brother were not permitted to attend the funeral. Aurelia feared that allowing the children to witness the burial would have been too painful, and for years after, they were denied the chance to visit his grave. When Sylvia turned 10, the family moved to Wellesley, leaving their home by the ocean in Winthrop, Massachusetts. Her memories of her father were left there as well, the facticity of his death—and his life—denied: "And this is how it stiffens, my vision of that seaside childhood . . . . My father died, we moved inland. Whereon my first nine years of life sealed themselves off like a ship in a bottle" (Alexander, 1991, p. 32).

Resurrection and Reunion through Poetry

The poet in Sylvia surfaced to win Otto's approval, but with his death, his love became forever unreachable. She longed to reunite with him, which meant keeping him symbolically alive, and to that end, she resurrected him in and through her poetry. In many of her poems, Otto is imbued with godlike and larger-than-life significance. In "Full Fathom Five" (1973), for example, she likens him to Neptune, Roman god and powerful patron of the seas, whose appearance, though seldom, heralds "the tide's coming" (p. 46). To tread too closely to his waves is to risk being pulled in, and Sylvia knew that reunion with Otto required a price, one paid in blood. She would breathe air that is "thick" and "murderous"; she would "breathe water" (p. 48). To stay alive, she must stay on dry land and "walk on your dry kingdom's border" (p. 48), whereas Otto must remain in the seaside home of days past, from which she was "exiled" when the Plath family relocated. Interestingly, the denial system erected by Aurelia Plath is referenced when the narrator speaks of the "muddy rumors" of father's burial, which she finds "shallow" (p. 47). For eight-year-old Sylvia, father was never buried; he continued to beckon because he was not given a proper send-off.

The deification of father is apparent as well in "The Colossus" (1973), where Otto is compared to the historical Roman Forum, the majestic heart of ancient Rome, one that boasted architectural wonders like "fluted" columns with "acanthine" ornaments (p. 21). But it now lays in ruin, a dead civilization like the dead man that was Otto. Sylvia's invocation of the Oresteia in "The Colossus" is also worth noting. The Oresteia is a trilogy of tragedies penned by the Greek dramatist Aeschylus, and each installment ends with murder. Sylvia herself would undergo three symbolic "murders" (i.e., three suicide attempts), so the linkage between father and these murders was no mere accident. The narrator is by her own admission "married to a shadow" (p. 21)—the shadow of father, the shadow of death.

In "The Colossus" just as in "Full Fathom Five," the narrator is aware that father can never be truly resurrected: "I shall never get you put together entirely" (p. 20). Nonetheless, the daughter continued to "piece" and "glue" father back together, however tenuously, and for decades at that: "Thirty years now I have labored/ To dredge the silt from your throat" (p. 20). To keep Otto alive in her poetry was to tap into a source of pain and anguish that would eventually destroy her. As Alvarez (1973) notes, "Because this impossible payment involved also the fantasy of joining or regaining her beloved dead father, it was a passionate act, instinct as much as with love as with hatred and despair" (p. 18). The love she felt for her father, and the hate she felt toward his abandonment and her inability to join him, transformed into love and hate toward living itself. Sylvia had to break free from her dead father's haunting if she were to live a creative and authentic life that was fully her own.

A Man Named Ted

Lovers came and went in Sylvia's life, and their exit recapitulated father's abandonment, nurturing her abhorrence toward men. As she confesses in her diary: "I hated men because they didn't stay around and love me like a father: I could prick holes in them and show they were no father-material. I made them propose and showed them they hadn't a chance" (Plath, 2000, p. 431). Throughout her adult life, Sylvia searched for a man to fill the shoes left by Otto Plath, only to realize that none could ever rival the Colossus, that is, until Ted Hughes, writer and novelist, and future husband and father of her children, entered the picture.

Sylvia's engagement to Ted is analogous to the Freudian resolution of the Electra complex via marriage to a father substitute (Lester, 1998b). She herself "identify him with my father at certain times" (Plath, 2000, p. 447), and if Ted could provide Sylvia with love comparable to that provided by Otto, then the curse of father's haunting could be lifted. But Ted had wandering eyes, and any sign of infidelity was obliterating to Sylvia. For instance, on the day of their wedding anniversary, she found him courting one of his students at the University of Massachusetts Amherst, where he was teaching creative writing at the time. Writing in her journals:

> I found him not-there on the special day and with another woman. I had a furious access of rage. He knew how I love him and felt, and yet wasn't there. Isn't this an image of what I feel my father did to me? I think it may be. (p. 447)

Ted's absence on their very "special day" conjured, in full force, the attendant feelings of father's absence.

But this episode pales in comparison to Ted's extramarital affairs with another writer named Asia Wevill. Sylvia's discovery and Ted's confession reawakened the devastating trauma of losing her father. By then they were already living in England, and after they separated, she and their two children lived in a flat formerly inhabited by W. B. Yeats (Alexander, 1991). She and Ted spoke of reuniting and reconciling their differences, which only incited ambivalence in Sylvia. She loved Ted but hated him for loving another woman. Such ambivalence mirrored what she felt toward Otto, and the separation brought back his beckoning voice of death.

"Daddy"

The horizons of past, present, and future converge in Sylvia's gripping poem, "Daddy" (2004). It recounts the original crisis of losing her father—"I was ten when they buried you" (p. 76)—and then jumps 10 years ahead to her suicide attempt at age 20 after her summer internship at *Mademoiselle* magazine: "At twenty I tried to die" (p. 76). The juxtaposition of the two lines suggests an eerie causality, with the father's death begetting his daughter's own death. Sylvia genuinely wanted to die, to "get back, back, back" to daddy and join him in the casket. Every sleeping pill she popped into her mouth brought her closer to a reunion, but her mother found her in time in the cellar of their Wellesley home. She was pulled "out of the sack" and sent to McLean Hospital, where she was pieced "together with glue" and one shock treatment after the next.

To hang onto her new lease on life, she had to exorcise her father's ghost and assert her own agency. Toward this end, she found a living father substitute: Ted Hughes. By marrying Ted, Otto Plath's voice was silenced. Sylvia found a "model" of Otto that she could embrace while alive, to whom she said "I do, I do" at the altar. However, daddy's "black telephone" did not stay off the hook too long. After Ted's betrayal seven years into their marriage, daddy rang his daughter again, his voice worming through this time.

To break free from the men who caused her anguish, Sylvia must attempt suicide and survive once more. Only in doing so could she assert agency over life. Daddy promised reunion in exchange for death; Sylvia would teeter close to that death, but survive. The poem ends with the line, "Daddy, daddy, you bastard. I'm through" (p. 76). She was indeed through with daddy, but her final attempt at exorcism cost her her life.

INTERMISSION

Sylvia's second suicide attempt powerfully encapsulates the theme of overcoming death to claim ownership of an agentic life. One stormy night in England, her car swerved off the road and crashed into a tree. She sustained a few injuries and was sent to a hospital (Kirk, 2004). Though the collision was ruled an accident, Alvarez (1973) claims otherwise.

Alvarez had known Sylvia during her years in England. He too was a suicide-attempt survivor, and because of their shared experience, Sylvia confessed to him that the car incident had been no accident. "She had gone off the road deliberately," Alvarez writes in *The Savage God*, "seriously wanting to die . . . it was something to be felt in the nerve ends and fought against, an initiation rite qualifying her for a life of her own" (p. 18). Therein lies a paradox: to stay alive as a woman, mother, poet, Sylvia had to pay with her own life and blood. Death was an obstacle to be surmounted, and what lies waiting on the other side was life.

Thus, when she stepped on the accelerator, when her car was nearing collision, and when the hood of the car impacted the tree, Sylvia was striving for individuation. She sought to free herself from forces of negation by bringing herself to the edge of annihilation and resurfacing a liberated woman. We have already established that one of these forces is the haunting presence of Otto Plath. The death of one parent need not be a death sentence for the child, however, provided that empathic attunement is supplied by the surviving parent. But such attunement was neither supplied by Aurelia nor felt by Sylvia.

HATRED FOR MOTHER

An Absence of Love

Sylvia's mother had once aspired to become a writer, but this dream ended when she married Otto Plath. She was the ghostwriter of Otto's book, *Insect Societies*, but received no acknowledgment for it. Over time, she resigned herself fully to the role of wife and mother, abandoning her dream of writing a novel that would earn her recognition and success. Aurelia saw Sylvia's potential as a writer and began to nourish this talent early in childhood. Sylvia would lead the life she could not. From Sylvia's point of view, however, what she received was not nourishment but suffocation.

Sylvia felt only her mother's vested interest in rearing a poet daughter. The love she was seeking, and especially needed because her father was no longer alive to provide it, was painfully absent. Recounting a session with her female psychotherapist, she writes in her journal:

> Why do I cry with her and only with her? I am experiencing a grief reaction for something I have only recently begun to admit isn't there: a mother's love. Nothing I can do . . . can change her way of being with me which I experience as a total absence of love. What, then, do I expect in the way of love? (Plath, 2000, p. 446)

Besides grief, there was also anger and resentment, which she subdued in the presence of her mother and in their letter correspondences (Plath, 1992), affectionately (and ironically) called "sunshine letters" by Aurelia. Wrote Sylvia:

> One reason I could keep up a satisfactory letter-relationship with her in England was we could both verbalize our desired image of ourselves in relation to each

> other: interest and sincere love, and never feel the emotional currents at war with these verbally expressed feelings. (Plath, 2000, p. 449)

Symbiosis with Mother

Aurelia's attempts to live vicariously through her daughter's successes were suffocating. The relationship was far from symbiotic; it was parasitic. Over time, Sylvia felt strongly opposed to her mother overrunning her life:

> What to do with her, with the hostility, undying, which I feel for her? I want as ever, to grab my life from out under her hot itchy hands. My life, my writing, my husband, my unconceived baby. She's a killer. Watch out. She's deadly as a cobra under that shiny greengold hood. (p. 433)

The extent of Aurelia's involvement in various facets of Sylvia's life is apparent from this diary entry. It was a symbiosis that Sylvia feared would swallow her whole, and desperate to seize her life from her mother's clutches, she sought individuation through poetry. I agree with Axelrod (1990) when he writes, "Being unable to achieve 'separateness and individuation' in life . . . [Sylvia Plath] increasingly sought to achieve them in her art" (p. 95).

The fierce struggle for separation is palpable in "The Disquieting Muses" (1973). In Greek mythology, the muses were minor goddesses who breathed creative inspiration into their beloved charges. The poem is Sylvia's reproach to the idea that her creativity was the product of Aurelia's midwifery. Try as she might to "hire" muses for her daughter—dance, piano, and voice teachers—the daughter sought, and found, muses on her own: "I learned, I learned, I learned elsewhere" (p. 59). She discovered them within.

The mother is castigated again in "Medusa" (2004), where she is objectified as an "old barnacled umbilicus" that keeps itself in a perpetual "state of miraculous repair" (p. 60). This is a mother who cannot seem to cut the umbilical cord linking her to her daughter, a mother who looms over and follows her child across great distances, despite the child's protests: "I didn't call you at all" (p. 60). Among the other images invoked by the poem is a "fat and red" placenta, symbolic of children's life-sustaining dependence on their mother, only in this case, the roles are reversed, and it is the unwanted mother who needs the sustenance. For the daughter, the unbreakable bond was asphyxiating. The narrator then refers to "kicking lovers," a reference to Sylvia and Ted's marital difficulties, which prompted Aurelia to travel to Devon on a steamship to play the role of mediator. But as the poem's penultimate line makes clear, the disgusted daughter wants nothing to do with her mother: "Off, off eely tentacle!" (p. 61).

Individuation through Death

If individuation from mother could not be accomplished through poetry, then death was another avenue. As Sylvia writes in her diary:

> I lay in bed when I thought my mind was going blank forever and thought what a luxury it would be to kill her, to strangle her skinny veined throat which was never big enough to protect me from the world. But I was too nice for murder. I tried to murder myself, to keep from being an embarrassment to the ones I loved and from living myself in a mindless hell. How thoughtful: Do unto yourself as you would do to others. I'd kill her, so I killed myself. (Plath, 2000, p. 433)

The entry looks back to Sylvia's first suicide attempt. It was August 1953, the summer of her junior year at Smith College. She had just returned from an internship at the fashion magazine *Mademoiselle*, when she learned from her mother that Harvard rejected her application to a prestigious writing seminar.

The rejection was radical invalidation of her being, of her means of separating from forces that threatened to engulf her, including her mother. Because she could not kill this destructive force, she opted to kill herself instead, to "free herself from the emotional 'clutch' of her mother and become her 'real' self" (Firestone & Catlett, 1988, p. 677). Although she survived this suicide attempt, the point stands that creativity and suicide both took on an authenticating function for her.

CONCLUDING REMARKS

Sylvia Plath's suicide attempt on February 11, 1963, 10 years after her first one, was not supposed to have ended in her death. She wanted to be resuscitated. She knew that the *au pair* girl would arrive by the time she lost consciousness. She also knew that her downstairs neighbor would not yet have left for work. A few days ahead of the attempt, she had sent a letter to her psychotherapist in which she pleaded for help. Minutes before the attempt, she wrote a note for the *au pair* girl, instructing the girl to call her physician. The note was left in plain sight on the kitchen counter.

Tragically, Sylvia's desperate cries for help, and her struggle to resist the call of self-destruction once and for all—by tethering close to the edge of death, but emerging from the precipice renewed—were stymied by unforeseen twists. The letter to the psychotherapist was inadvertently delivered to the wrong address. Plath's downstairs neighbor was knocked unconscious by carbon monoxide that seeped into his unit through the floorboards. By the time the *au pair* girl arrived, there was no one to open the door in time for her to find Sylvia's near lifeless, but still breathing, body. There was no coming back from this near-death experience.

As Sylvia writes in "Kindness" (1998), "The blood jet is poetry / There is no stopping it" (p. 269). She struggled to achieve individuation through the dark magic of her poetry, and through the cycle of death and rebirth she felt herself undergo once every 10 years. Her poetry was talismanic in that it thwarted the engulfment she feared would nullify her agency and authenticity. However, to participate in the creative act meant reexperiencing the trauma of father's death and abandonment as well as mother's constant invalidation and absence: "All my life I have been 'stood up' emotionally by the people I loved most: daddy dying and leaving me, mother somehow not there" (Plath, 2000, p. 455).

It is tragic that Sylvia Plath felt she had to risk death in order for her self to remain intact. The final lines of "Edge" (1996), one of her last poems, speak of a woman "perfected" by death, her dead body wearing "the smile of accomplishment" (p. 272).

Interlude II

Creativity and Temporality

One popular idea about creativity is that loss, in all its manifestations, is a major impetus behind creative human endeavor (e.g., Brink, 1982). It is an idea rooted in Freud's repetition-compulsion principle, which states that unresolved conflict lies beneath perseverative thoughts and behaviors. I personally do not espouse the idea that loss is a necessary precondition to lifelong creativity, as humans are intrinsically creative beings. Having said that, one may indeed find trauma and loss compressed in the symbolic language of art and other creative productions, a point eloquently made by Alice Miller in *The Untouched Key* (1991). It may do so directly via *explicit imagery*, or indirectly via *implicit imagery* (Ceglia & Pfeffer, 1999).

We have already seen individual traumas recapitulated in the songs of Phyllis Hyman (chapter 3) and Kurt Cobain (chapter 4) and in the poems of Sylvia Plath (chapter 5). We have also seen *collective* human suffering and memory authenticated by the writings of Iris Chang (chapter 1) and the photographs of Kevin Carter (chapter 2). But what is truly remarkable about creativity, I think, is its ability to fold the dimensions of time. Let us take time's first dimension: the past.

CONCRETIZATIONS OF PAST TRAUMA

According to Miller (1991), suffering that is repressed in childhood can find its way into art, imbuing the work with intensity and expressiveness without the artist realizing it. As an example, she cites the charcoal drawings of Käthe Kollwitz, which reflect both her antiwar stance and her shattered childhood. Käthe's childhood was one of constant invalidation. Two older siblings and a younger brother lost their lives, and they were idealized by the mother at the expense of Käthe, the only surviving child. Unable to measure up, she believed that her own death—psychic death, that is—was a prerequisite to mother's love. Miller (1991) is not surprised that her drawings are preoccupied with Death himself snatching terrified children from their mothers. The children are Käthe, wondering if her mother will love her back if she were to reach directly for the grim reaper's outstretched hand. Politically, the drawings illustrate the catastrophic impact of the war in Vienna on children's physical and psychological well-being. Phenomenologically, they articulate Käthe's frustration with and anguish over her mother's never-ending sorrow.

The suffering that was experienced in childhood and later encoded in art need not have been repressed, however. Similar to Kollwitz, Arshile Gorky's abstract expressionism takes as its subject matter his devastated childhood. Growing up, he lived in the humble village of Khorkom under the Ottoman Empire's rule and bore witness to the Armenian genocide. One of its many casualties was his mother, who gave up the sustenance her own body needed so that her children did not die of starvation. To escape persecution, Gorky and his sister eventually fled to the United States, where he began to paint with fervor, his works of art reflecting a longing for his mother and motherland (Akiskal & Akiskal, 1996). In his case, however, the trauma is consciously addressed. In his own words, his paintings "duplicate the colors of Armenia" (p. 223) and conjure memories of his mother's embroidery, a protective force that kept the horrors of the past from spilling onto and contaminating the present. Sadly, in the final years of his life, Gorky's painting arm was paralyzed during a car accident. When his wife left him and took their two children with her, he slashed his last unfinished painting and hanged himself.

Sometimes, art does not point to a singular trauma, but implicates multiple traumas simultaneously. Miller (1991) provides yet another compelling example: Pablo Picasso's *La Guernica*. Though a political statement, *La Guernica* is also an attempt to make sense of an earthquake Pablo experienced at age three, an emotion memory sublimated into art. The contorted faces, the female nudes writhing as if in agony, create a visual portrait of people in panic when an earthquake struck the artist's hometown of Malaga. But Miller (1991) complicates any notion of a one-to-one correspondence between trauma and art by adding that yet another experience was encoded in the painting, and that is young Pablo witnessing his sister's birth a mere three days after the earthquake. Thus, the prototypical nude of *La Guernica* is also Mrs. Picasso screaming in labor. Two unique if not traumatic experiences are folded into a singular work of art.

But we can take this even further by considering that at age 16, Pablo witnessed an eerie dissection (Gardner, 1993). A young girl and an elderly woman were struck dead by lightning, and for some inexplicable reason, a dissection was performed on the girl's face, revealing her brain. The split heads and double profiles that feature prominently in his paintings are therefore part of a larger symbolic repertoire that addresses not one but multiple instances of trauma.

ART AS FINAL COMMUNICATION

Freud (1965) postulated that dreams, the royal road to the unconscious, are purely retrospective, whereas Jung (1968) believed that dreams are not always oriented to the past, but can be prospective as well. Creative productions possess the same logic; they can point to past experiences but also anticipate future occurrences. When interpreting the works of creative suicides, we must be careful not to confuse the outcome of a life with the intention behind the work. Having said that, such an interpretive activity has much to teach us about the notion of art as final communication.

Heiman's (1976) treatment of Vincent van Gogh's *Crows Over the Wheat Field* as a de facto suicide note is illustrative. Arguably van Gogh's last painting, it deviates from his previous works in that the perspective here is inverted. The vanishing point is not located in the horizon; instead, three lines converge violently toward the painter/spectator, as if "the vanishing point is the point of death" (p. 75). The wheat field seems to stretch infinitely in all directions, threatening to swallow the spectator whole, while crows, "ominous in their blackness" (p. 78) and symbolic of violent death, dart across the blue sky toward the viewer. The idea that the vanishing point telegraphs impending suicide has been observed in various media forms (Aaron, 2015) and has purchase here as well. Van Gogh was said to have been working on this painting in a wheat field when he shot himself in the stomach, and the affective significance of the place is apparent in the following letter to his brother Theo: "They are vast fields of wheat under troubled skies, and I did not need to go out of my way to express sadness and extreme loneliness" (quoted in Heiman, 1976, p. 76). The wheat field represented the inescapability of loneliness, with death as the only foreseeable way out.

Mark Rothko's abstract paintings have also been described as pictorial suicide notes—massive canvases composed of rectangles that appear to float against a contrasting background. Rothko himself said that "only tragic and timeless subject matter is worthy of painting," that he paints "to project a tragic vision," and that "a clear preoccupation with death" was essential to his art (quoted in Ravin, Hartman, & Fried, 1978, p. 78). His paintings supposedly correlate with suicidal patients' descriptions of Rorschach inkblots in "terms that indicate transparency or translucency," through which other objects are visible (p. 78). His canvases look like translucent clouds, after all, and his colors shade into instead of confronting one another.

But what's more telling is Rothko's description of his paintings as containing "all my feelings about life" (p. 79), the darkening of his canvas mirroring his descent into the abyss of suicidal depression. In the early years of his career (1950s), black was merely a contrasting background, with orange, yellow, red, and blue occupying the foreground. These colors eventually gave way to brown, black, and maroon as the decade came to a close—a period of relative despondency—and when he was commissioned to paint the walls of the Houston chapel (1964–1966), he depended heavily on pigments as red as coagulated blood, representing a resurgence in his creative vitality. However, the last three years of his life, a period marked by separation from his wife and children, saw only black, gray, and brown.

THE ECSTASIS OF TEMPORALITY

Ultimately, all three dimensions of time are linked. Past and future are implicated in all present moments. We have come from somewhere, and we are going somewhere. Our construction of the past is indelibly influenced by the present, which in turn colors our anticipation of the future. This is relevant to our discussion because the *ecstasis of temporality* (Heidegger, 1996; Stolorow, 2007) is apparent as well in creative productions and works of art, such that a single work can be bound to more than one dimension of time, and for that matter, multiple iterations of a single dimension.

Let us take the example of Frida Kahlo, a gifted artist who was overshadowed by her husband, the Mexican muralist Diego Rivera, and who deserved more recognition in her lifetime than she received. Even to this day the cause of Frida's death is shrouded in mystery. Some say she died of a pulmonary embolism (the official cause), while friends and family members suspected suicide. The night before her death, she gave her husband a ring in anticipation of their 25th wedding anniversary. The anniversary was 17 days away, and when he asked why she was giving it to him early, she replied, "Because I feel I am going to leave you very soon" (Herrera, 1983, p. 431). The last entry in her diary is a drawing of an angel rising into the sky, with the following message underneath: "I hope the exit is joyful—and I hope never to come back" (Kahlo, 1995, p. 287). The combination of text and image expresses longing for a peaceful demise (a joyful exit), but it is also a powerful condemnation of what was being left behind: a lifetime of pain and agony. Thus, past and future interweave in the present, that moment in time the diary entry was created.

If the previous example is too abstract, then let us take a more concrete one. A closer inspection of Frida's diary reveals a preoccupation with a severed human leg. This image is nontrivial, for it encapsulates a lifetime of physical and psychological pain as powerfully as her self-portraits, for which she was better known. Specifically, the image concretizes lifelong assaults on her bodily integrity. When Frida was six years old, she was confined to bed for nine grueling months with polio of the right leg. Twelve years later, at age 18, she was severely injured in an accident (a foreign object impaled her through the hip and vagina), and for the remainder of her life underwent 35 surgical procedures to correct the disfigurement. A year before she died, she developed gangrene in one leg, which had to be amputated. She attempted suicide shortly after the procedure and wrote candidly about wanting to kill herself in her diary. The image of the severed leg surfaced during this time.

This singular image concretizes the helplessness and immobility Frida experienced in the distant past, when she was but a child, as well as the pain of having her body violently penetrated in her teenage years. It also expresses her fractured self-image resulting from the amputation in *her* present (now our past), and arguably, her pained longing for psychosomatic unity and cohesion, a future that would never come to be. Again, past, present, and future coalesce, giving temporal unity to the artist's subjective history, whose meanings are, of course, indiscernible in the absence of biographical context.

Chapter 6

"The Soul We Have Loved, the Soul that Has Left Us"

The Case of Jeremy Blake and Theresa Duncan

Jeremy sat motionless in the living room while the coroner took Theresa's body away, but once she was finally gone, he began "sobbing, pounding the walls with his fist, screaming, 'Dammit, fuck, no, this can't be happening'" (Sales, 2008). It was he who found Theresa unconscious in their bedroom, a bowl of Benadryl pills, a bottle of Tylenol PM, and an empty champagne glass on the nightstand. Her face seemed to be wearing a smile. There was a note nearby, expressing how deeply she loved Jeremy and that she was at peace with her decision.

Theresa's suicide on July 10, 2007, was as surprising as it was devastating for Jeremy, her lover of 12 years. They met for lunch earlier that day; he'd just gotten the approval to direct a film adaptation of the George Pelecanos novel, *Nick's Trip*, which she was to write and coproduce. He then resumed his busy workday at Rockstar Games while she returned to their apartment in Manhattan's East Village. But on that day, she had posted an ominous entry in her blog, *The Wit of the Staircase*: "A need to tell and hear stories is essential to the species Homo sapiens—second in necessity apparently after nourishment and before love and shelter. Millions survive without love or home, almost none in silence" (Duncan, 2007h). The passage, lifted from the Reynolds Price novel *A Palpable God*, is accompanied by the photo of a blonde woman in a gray suit, her face covered by a black lace mask.

Following her suicide, Jeremy assured friends that he wasn't "going down that rabbit hole. No way am I going to follow Theresa" (Amsden, 2007), but then one evening, he said, "I get it. She won" (Sales, 2008). He told them he needed to make a decision; about what, he did not say. Jeremy and three of his friends were supposed to drive to Theresa's funeral on July 17, but he never showed up. Instead, he rode the A train to Rockaway Beach in Queens.

He took off his clothes and wrote on the back of a business card, "I am going to join the lovely Theresa" (ibid.), which he left on the sand before walking into the Atlantic Ocean. His body was found in Sea Girt, New Jersey five days later.

INTRODUCTION

Theresa Duncan was a respected filmmaker, blogger, and video game designer. Formerly a secretary at Magnet Interactive, her reputation for transforming video games into a legitimate medium of storytelling began when she walked into the CEO's office and pitched an idea about a game tailored exclusively for girls. In 1995 she codesigned *Chop Suey*, "a child's game that had an edge, that lacked condescension" and was named *Entertainment Weekly*'s "CD-rom of the Year" (Amsden, 2007). The previous year, she met Jeremy Blake, an aspiring artist who at the time was working on his Masters degree at the California Institute of the Arts. The introverted Jeremy, 23 at the time, fell in love with the charismatic Theresa, five years his senior. They worked as partners on numerous projects and were each other's inspiration. She designed two other narrative video games with Jeremy as illustrator: *Smarty* in 1996 and *Zero Zero* in 1997. Two years later, she wrote and directed and he illustrated *The History of Glamour*, an animated film about the corrupting influence of ambition and emptiness of the celebrity life. The film was featured in the 2000 Whitney Biennial and ironically got her noticed by Hollywood. Theresa was also the producer, and Jeremy the designer, behind the animated *Closet Cases*, "real audio fashion testimonies" that appeared in the Oxygen Network show *x-chromosome*.

In many respects, it was Theresa who nurtured Jeremy's artistic prowess, going so far as to make friends with New York City gallerists so that she could promote his artwork. But to his own credit, he came into vogue with chromogenic prints that appear like paintings and photographs but are neither. Soon he would use an electronic drawing tablet to create continuously looping sequences of images that were neither painting nor film. His "moving paintings," which were shown in three Whitney Biennials between 2000 and 2004, and in a solo exhibit at the San Francisco Museum of Modern Art in 2005, blurred the line between representation and abstraction, on one hand, and between object and time-based art, on the other. Each came in three installations, the slowly looping videos playing simultaneously in three adjacent plasma screens.

Jeremy's time-based paintings address myriad subjects, "from violence and terrorism to glamour and decadence, from metaphors of architectural spaces to profiles of cultural personifications" (Tillou Fine Art, n.d.). For instance,

Guccinam (2000), the title an amalgam of Gucci and Vietnam, used "the same brightly tinted smoke and droning mechanical noise" that were commonplace in films that dealt with the Vietnam War, while *Station to Station* (2001) took as its subject "chemical weaponry, global warming gasses, and mysterious technologies." Jeremy also created the hallucinatory, dreamlike sequences that marked turning points in the Paul Thomas Anderson movie, *Punch Drunk Love* (2002), as well as a series of covers for Beck Hansen's 2002 album *Sea Change*. But the *Winchester* trilogy (2002–2004), based on the true story of Sarah Winchester, whose psyche was devastated by profound trauma, was arguably Jeremy's crowning achievement. It chronicles with uncanny precision the paranoid mind of its subject, and that of its creator *and* his lover. Each installment took Jeremy one year to complete.

Over time, the couple came to believe that they were being persecuted by the Church of Scientology. Convinced that members of the Church were trying to defame her, Theresa sent accusatory letters to friends and colleagues and mounted confrontational posts on her blog. No matter how outrageous her claims, Jeremy defended her. He went so far as to prepare a 27-page document that he planned to use in a lawsuit against the Church. Presumably, Hollywood was also under a right-wing invasion by religious extremists and the Bush administration, with the "devil incarnate" Dick Cheney pulling the strings. The couple left their cottage in Venice Beach, California and sought refuge at St. Mark's rectory in the East Village, but the demon of paranoia followed them there. Rather than surrender to these forces, Theresa ended her life. Cleft in twain, the bereaved Jeremy walked into the ocean to reunite with the lost half of his soul.

In this joint case study, I address the developmental roots of the dyad's creativity and how the dominant themes of their childhood are replicated in their respective artworks. I then shift the focus to Theresa's growing paranoia and its infection of Jeremy via their symbiotic union, which is concretized by his time-based paintings. Finally, I consider their suicide in light of their quest for agency, emancipation, and reunion.

THE WELLSPRINGS OF CREATIVITY

Jeremy Blake was born on October 4, 1971, in Fort Sill, Oklahoma, but spent much of his childhood in Takoma Park, MD. He started drawing at a very young age. According to his mother:

> He drew "Star Wars," starship things for the longest time. And when he was little, he went through a phase of drawing mazes, and then he created his own comic book characters. And then he just filled notebooks with drawings when he was in high school. (Blair, 2007)

His art took on a more self-referential quality following the death of his father to AIDS when he was 17. He attended the Art Institute of Chicago for college, and then Cal-Arts for graduate school, where his father was the subject of several paintings and a sculpture (Phillips, n.d.; Kennedy, 2007).

Because his time-based paintings can be more abstract than representational, it can be difficult to apprehend the story being told, but "in his head, at least, there are underlying narratives," many quite personal (Valdez, 2002). For example, *Reading Ossie Clark* (2003b) was created in memory of the Swinging London fashion designer who from 1966 to 1974 outfitted celebrities around the globe, and whose published diaries inspired the script for the artwork. The cinematic portrait includes footage of the floral and geometric patterns Ossie used in his dresses. On the surface, it is a tale about the fashion designer's life on the proverbial fast lane, culminating in "a digitized reminder that Clark was murdered by his lover" (Leffingwell, 2004, p. 119). But as Jeremy confessed in an accompanying artist statement:

> My personal investment in that subject matter was in tracking the trajectory of someone who reminded me of a close relative of mine who had also lived fast during that era, and who, like Mr. Clark, had also died prematurely.

It's unclear who exactly he was referring to, but regardless, just like some of his earlier works, *Reading Ossie Clark* is at its core an elegy, a lamentation for the dead.

Choosing Sarah Winchester as the subject of his highly acclaimed trilogy is telling, in light of the fact that the heiress to the Winchester Repeating Arms Company started her lifelong construction project following the death of her husband, who was struck by pulmonary tuberculosis shortly after their only child died at infancy. Jeremy noted that "Winchester's powerful compulsion to build is an instance of psychological 'haunting'—a frustrated effort to deal with trauma" (Weil, Schwarzer, & Blake, 2005, p. 31). In many respects, this statement was also self-referential, for he chose to document the labyrinthine mind of the widow and the architectural wonder it gave rise to out of empathy for her loss, with which he himself could identify.

Theresa Duncan was born on October 26, 1966, in Lapeer, Michigan. Like Jeremy, she too experienced traumatic loss, but of a different kind. The exact nature of this trauma was one she dared not share with others. According to the scant sources available, she lived through "a dark childhood" under the care of a father who "had serious mental health problems and was notorious around town for doing bizarre things" (Coe, 2007). Again, the nature of this bizarre behavior is left to the reader's imagination, but such an upbringing could set the precedent for a general distrust in men. Meanwhile, her mother worked two jobs, "one stocking shelves in a grocery store at night, often having to leave them all alone in a freezing house with not enough to eat" (ibid.). The traumatic loss she endured, in other words, was that of a safe and secure childhood where the basic conditions for human survival were guaranteed.

Theresa sought refuge and "learned to swim in the Lapeer library" (Duncan, 2007c), reading books in a "desperate attempt to romanticize the Michigan forest that spread out for miles around me" (Duncan, 2007a). She truly wanted "to be in New York City, where all the big glam ladies were," but anywhere else was preferable to her oppressive home (Duncan, 2007c). But because she could not physically escape, she used her imagination to transform her surroundings into something magical, swimming her way through written words to faraway lands.

As an adult, Theresa meandered from one odd job to another in Detroit, then to a family friend's antiques store in Washington, D.C., where she met Jeremy for the first time. They moved to Manhattan separately, she to pursue a job at Nicholson Interactive, but their paths intertwined once more backstage during a concert at the Knitting Factory. The narrative video games Theresa designed whisk enthusiastic gamers away from the here and now, as if they were on a magic carpet. *Chop Suey* tells the story of Lily and June Bugg, who hop on clouds that change "from teapots into tennis shoes into Aunt Vera—a character who acts as a window into another world" (Coe, 2007). *Smarty* drops its viewers off at the rooftop of a French cathedral on New Year's eve at the turn of the nineteenth century. Her animated film *The History of Glamour* and the script for *Alice Underground*, a project that never materialized, also reveal themes central to her childhood, namely, the longing to escape and become captive in a world of her own making. *Glamour* follows the androgynous Charles Valentine, who bears a striking resemblance to Theresa, and who leaves her hometown of Antler, Ohio, to become a rock star and cultural icon. At the end of the film, it is revealed that it was Valentine who burned down the nail salon where she worked. This "accident" served as the catalyst for her journey away from home; it also concretized Theresa's desire to break away from her past. *Alice Underground* follows yet another rock star, who unwittingly gets kidnapped by schoolgirls during a tour in the Big Apple, the place Theresa yearned to be as a child.

THE GERMINATING SEEDS OF PARANOIA

Theresa Duncan began to think that Scientologists were conspiring to defame her when her efforts to turn the script for *Alice Underground* into a film languished. She originally had a two-picture deal with Fox Searchlight, but her projects were shelved due to budgetary considerations. The proposal she wrote for another film, *You Got the Look*, also hit a dead end, as did *Left of the Dial*, a VH1 television series whose pilot episode she was supposed to write and direct. When it became known that musician Beck Hansen, whose album *Sea Change* featured Jeremy's artwork, was a Scientologist, she was convinced that his membership was connected to her doomed projects. Hansen denied allegations that he'd agreed to play the lead role in *Alice*, yet during a previous interview he spoke excitedly about starring in a movie that sounded too much like *Alice* (Brown & Graham, 2007). Further undermining his credibility and compounding Theresa's paranoia, he referred to her as a passing acquaintance when numerous pictures of him and his wife having a splendid time at the beach with Jeremy and Theresa can attest to the contrary. Ultimately, she held Tom Cruise responsible for killing Alice because "his profound loyalty to Scientology" (Amsden, 2007) clashed with the script, making her "priority No. 1 for *their* paranoid and dangerous security wing" (Dokoupil, 2007).

Theresa was soon creating mountains out of molehills. She accused friends and neighbors of eavesdropping on her phone conversations and sending locks of hair from her hairbrush to the Church. Strange occurrences only strengthened her beliefs. She was especially terrified when she and Jeremy found a dead cat on the roof of their Venice Beach apartment, and when a man approached her while she was walking her dog Tuesday and said, "Hey, what a sweet dog. It would be too bad if something happened to it" (Sales, 2007). She took hundreds of photos of out-of-state license plates in a desperate but futile attempt to monitor her neighborhood for suspicious activities. She sent accusatory e-mails to friends and colleagues and posted incendiary entries on her blog. Her obsession with domestic surveillance, conspiracy theories, mind-control programs, overseas assassination attempts under the Nixon administration, and the wiretapping of dissidents between the 1950s and 1970s, found its way into her delusions as well. In one blog entry, she alleged that she and Jeremy "experienced theft, intimidation, illegal wiretapping, a 1950s-style smear campaign based on utter psychological projection, damage to our property, verbal and physical harassment and death threats" from his ex-girlfriend and the girl's family (Duncan, 2007f).

Writings on the developmental origins of paranoia are especially relevant to Theresa. A cardinal feature of paranoia, a basic lack of trust, stems from the absence of a loving relationship with primary caregivers (Kantor, 2008). Parental behavior that leads children to believe that adults can't be trusted contributes heavily to the development of persecutory delusions. As children, they are hypervigilant to signs of betrayal. As adults, they feel that the world is hostile to their needs because they expect from strangers in life the same treatment they'd received from their caregivers.

Theresa felt neglected by a mother who, out of necessity, worked two jobs and left her in the care of an unstable father. As if communicating the subjective truth of her experiences, Theresa herself became notorious in Venice Beach for her strange and frightening conduct, just as her father had been for *his* "bizarre behavior." One neighbor was caught off guard by this daring proposition: "Jeremy and I started a club where we've found a bunch of old men and we're letting them fuck us in the ass, and we wanted to know if you wanted to be part of it" (Sales, 2008). Others observed her body jerk and her hands and face twitch when she repeatedly called a neighbor, whom she suspected of being part of the Scientology conspiracy, "cult whore" and "cult hooker." Here we see, encoded bodily, the proverbial sins of the parent visit the child in a dangerous cycle of generational transmission of trauma that Miller (1997) called poisonous pedagogy. Theresa claimed that "some really bad things happened to her" with men and thought that "every man was out to get her" (Sales, 2008). The only men she trusted were Jeremy and her psychoanalyst of five years, whom she considered "a huge source of strength" (Duncan, 2007d).

The psychodynamic perspective on paranoid ideation is also relevant here. According to this line of thought, paranoia is a defense against, or disavowal of, unacceptable feelings that are projected onto others, real or imagined, which in turn makes oneself the target of such feelings (Kantor, 2008). Projection makes one feel the self-importance that was missing from one's childhood. Theresa herself admitted to disavowing the hatred she felt toward her mother and father. Only in adulthood did she finally come to realize the feelings she'd renounced, which she candidly posted in her blog:

> And yes, I pretty much hate my parents, and it took me five years of psychoanalysis and nearly $100,000 to grow the nuts to admit it to myself. And now I am blissfully unafraid to challenge even the biggest, meanest, mightiest bad authority. (Duncan, 2007b)

Decades of pent-up anger were projected onto the Church of Scientology, one of the "meanest" and "mightiest" patriarchal authorities, notorious for forcing its members to submit to the questioning of auditors and for threatening defectors by making their past indiscretions known to the public. Theresa meted out her anger at the Church, but never directly at the rightful targets of this anger.

At their heart, Theresa's paranoid delusions can be seen as the product of radical invalidation, with the child being forced to surrender her needs to meet parental agendas (Orange, Atwood, & Stolorow, 1997). Circumstances in adulthood that are harsh in and of themselves, especially those that revive childhood traumata, can contribute to the development of persecutory delusions, like water to germinating seeds (Siegel, 1996). What tidbits Theresa revealed about herself to her blog followers suggest that telling stories was essential to *her* survival. It was crucial for her to continue making films, just as it had been crucial for her to immerse herself in stories as a child. Sadly, her most ambitious projects since *Glamour* failed to materialize, echoing the silencing and repudiation of her past. Against this backdrop, it is unsurprising that the seeds of her paranoia sprouted when her seven-year wave of success came to a grinding halt.

A SYMBIOTIC RELATIONSHIP

Jeremy Blake was not immune to the persecutory beliefs that took hold of Theresa, evidenced by his 27-page indictment of the Church. Among other things, he was convinced that subliminal ads recruiting people to be in the C.I.A. were running on the Cartoon Network. He tossed urine onto the barbecue of a neighbor whom he suspected was a Scientologist and nearly got into a fight with a friend Theresa had accused of wiretapping. To defend themselves against sinister forces sent by the Church, Jeremy purchased a gun. Their shared delusion was so strong that during a fundraising event to repair the entrance to St. Mark's rectory, where they lived, the couple experienced a "collective vision" that the grill was going to explode and harm Theresa (Amsden, 2007). Jeremy held her firmly, stroking her hair and speaking in his usual soft voice, as if singing a lullaby to a terrified little girl.

Shared delusions, or folie à deux, is a rare phenomenon that involves two closely related persons, especially those who live together in relative isolation. The delusions typically originate with the more dominant personality, referred to as the *inducer* or *primary case* in clinical literature (e.g., Siegel, 1996). Theresa neatly fits the profile of the inducer: bold, assertive, confrontational, and confident. Similarly, Jeremy fits the profile of the secondary case. Friends described him as "funny, brooding, and gentle" (Phillips, n.d.), with "a sweet and fragile personality" (Dyer, n.d.). Taxonomies aside, their lives were so intertwined that one depended heavily on the other. Theresa felt safest in the presence of Jeremy, and she was not comfortable seeing him work with anyone else. He likewise thrived on her exuberance, and their symbiotic relationship is evident in a number of his time-based paintings.

For instance, Theresa is personified as the *Sodium Fox* (2005), and Jeremy as the protagonist, in his eponymous cinematic portrait. The protagonist, says Jeremy in his artist statement, combs the "lonesome internalized American landscape 'just looking for a lifelong conversation with one person.'" In his journey, he meets a mysterious woman, shown wielding a blade, who rescues him from unbearable aloneness and confers upon him bravery, "not in external violence, but rather in an internal struggle against intimidation."

Ueland (1987), paraphrasing Tolstoi, once wrote: "Art is *infection*. The artist has a feeling and he expresses it and at once this feeling infects other people and they have it too. And the infection must be immediate or it isn't art" (p. 116). In other words, an artist who has experienced something intensely may need to instill similar feelings in his viewers. Jeremy's time-based paintings were designed to evoke "a sense of instability and unease," and he hoped that "viewing my work will leave one in a quietly contemplative, but also somewhat disoriented state" (quoted in Tillou Fine Art, n.d.). Although some are elegies that encapsulate his grief over a loved one lost, others mirror the intense paranoia he and Theresa shared and experienced together. In other words, the intense feelings he sought to express were not solely his but Theresa's as well.

Sodium Fox (2005) is about "an evil regime which threatens to devalue individual experience" as much as it is about love. Jeremy cites as inspiration for his cinematic portrait Jean Luc Godard's 1965 film *Alphaville*, an intergalactic tale about a technocratic dictatorship that "seeks to wipe out both individual memory and *evocative language*." The "negative authority" in *Sodium Fox*, and the sentient computer in *Alphaville*, are stand-ins for the Church of Scientology, which in turn represented the forces that were silencing Theresa.

The couple's shared delusions are captured most poignantly by Jeremy's critically acclaimed series, *The Winchester House of Mystery* (2002–2004). On the surface it follows the story of Sarah Winchester, heiress to the company that manufactured "the gun that won the West" (Weil, Schwarzer, & Blake, 2005). Following the deaths of her husband and child, she sought the advice of a medium and moved to California, where for 38 years she undertook a lifelong construction project to appease the ghosts of the rifle victims. When she died of old age, the mansion she commissioned had 160 rooms, 40 staircases, 467 doorways, and over 10,000 windows. Today, it stands today as a monument to the troubled psyche of a woman who sought expiation for a crime that preceded her, through a name that she received in marriage. But the *Winchester* series is also about two other individuals who were persecuted by forces larger than themselves.

The first installment, *Winchester* (2002), begins and ends with a view of the mansion's exterior and the silhouette of a man aiming his rifle. The phantom represents the haunting Sarah Winchester experienced, but it also symbolizes the threats that lurked in every corner of Jeremy and Theresa's world, like the strange men who allegedly stood outside their Venice Beach home, watching them through the windows. Bullet holes then blossom into colorful Rorschach ink blots that engulf the entire screen, suggesting that the ghosts of rifle victim would forever haunt Winchester. Like gas to a vacuum or ink to a white piece of cloth, paranoia is all-consuming, and Jeremy exquisitely captures this state of mind with his skillful manipulation of color.

Viewers are offered access to the mansion's interior in *1906* (2003a), the second installment, but what they find are parts damaged by the earthquake that Sarah Winchester chose not to repair. According to Jeremy, the ruptured interior symbolizes refused mourning, which is transposed onto staircases with missing steps, chandelier lights dangling precariously, and shattered windows next to crumbling walls. Disavowal of loss led to the mansion's construction, just as disavowal of anger over her childhood became the foundation of Theresa's persecutory beliefs. Just when viewers think they've escaped the suffocating confines of the mansion, "the sun is eclipsed, becoming a gloomy, pulsating, spectral presence" (Weil, Schwarzer, & Blake, 2005, p. 31). The haunting, it would appear, stretches beyond the mansion's perimeters.

Century 21 (2004), the third and final installment, switches magnification to zoom out of the mansion and focus on the wider American landscape. It is on the surface an examination of how the "myth of regeneration through violence," upon which this nation was founded, "has been repackaged and broadcast since the end of the Victorian era" (Monk, 2005, p. 108). Simultaneously, it can also be read in terms of the diffuse nature of trauma, infectious and all-enveloping.

AUTHENTICATIONS OF THE SELF

On a blog entry dated May 28, 2007, Theresa posted the following quote from Romain Rolland:

> The more we create, the more we love and lose those whom we love, the more we *escape from death.* With every new work we round and finish, we escape into the work we have created, the soul we have loved, the soul that has left us. (Duncan, 2007e)

The entry is titled "The Creative Process," and it espouses the philosophy that in creating—in her case, making films and telling stories—one opts for life instead of death. It follows that the blockage of creativity brings one *closer* to death, and when projects like *Alice Underground* and *You Got the Look* failed to materialize, self-destruction seemed to be a viable pathway.

Intersubjective systems theory posits that delusions are attempts to hold onto a reality that is slipping away fast, contrary to Freud's view that they're an escape from a reality that has become unbearably painful (Orange, Atwood & Stolorow, 1997). Viewed in this light, Theresa's persecutory delusions may symbolize her struggle to forestall self-negation when creative avenues in her life were stifled. They were her means of preserving her agency, which was in danger of being usurped. Delusions revolve around influencing machines, real or imagined persons, and nefarious organizations to give the delusional person *illusory* control over the threat. If it can be located in physical space, then it can be confronted or averted. But in a strange twist of irony, to remain autonomous and preserve her agency was to die: "The CoS is going to have to kill us before we will give up *any* of our free will or any of our constitutional rights to do and say what we please" (Dokoupil, 2007). In other words, she'd rather die than succumb to these oppressive forces.

But did she not also kill herself to liberate Jeremy, whom she loved deeply? According to Siegel (1996), the *secondary case* is relieved of paranoia when the *inducer* is dead or gone. Perhaps there is some truth to speculation that Theresa committed suicide after realizing how damaging her delusions had been to Jeremy's career. According to Bradford Schlei, head of production for Muse Productions:

> Jeremy was her creation. And she was killing the thing she created, this great, terrific artist. She realized what she had done. To let him live, she had to go. But in a symbiotic relationship, one couldn't last without the other. (quoted in Lee, 2007)

Theresa fulfilled Jeremy's search for "a lifelong conversation with one person" and her untimely death meant his death as well.

Jeremy took his life seven days after Theresa took hers. His reasons are clear from what he wrote on a business card before he walked into the ocean: "I am going to join the lovely Theresa." But one might wonder why he chose to die the way he did. Someone remarked that Jeremy's life imitated art, arguing that in one of his favorite movies, Robert Altman's remake of *The Long Goodbye*, a heartbroken character kills himself in the same fashion (Lee, 2007). But this simplistic explanation overlooks the fact that Jeremy's C-prints and time-based paintings contain within them co-occurring images of death and the sea.

The chromogenic print *Planet Waves* (2003c), based on *Reading Ossie Clark*, is bracketed by vertical strips of the moon, which are made to appear like human skulls. *Sodium Fox* (2005) begins with the image of a skull on a makeshift flag, which "seems to mark a site where burdens are both acknowledged and laid to rest," and there is filmed footage of the ocean before the skull's reappearance at the end. Furthermore, says Jeremy, the cinematic portrait is "an abstract reinvention of a well-worn literary trope, such as the sailor who returns to his beloved after many years at sea." Although the ending of his story is an inversion of the trope, the sea represented the channel he must traverse to reunite with a loved one lost, even if that meant death. By ending his life in such a manner, he joined "the lovely Theresa" and authenticated his beautiful and haunting art.

SUMMARY AND CONCLUSIONS

Jeremy Blake and Theresa Duncan both exhibited creative promise in childhood and adolescence. Though Jeremy's talents were evident from an early age, his works took on a more self-referential quality following the death of his father. His earlier works can be read as elegies, enshrining memories of loved ones lost. As for Theresa, she lived through a tumultuous childhood under the care of a "mentally unstable" father and a mother who worked long hours, often leaving her freezing and starving. She became captive in a world of her own making and immersed herself in stories in order to escape from an oppressive surround. As an artist, she took her audience away from the here and now with narrative video games tailored for girls, which prioritized exploration over action.

Raised by parents she deemed untrustworthy, Theresa became hypervigilant to signs of betrayal and grew up believing the world was hostile and cutthroat. But the anger she felt toward her mother and father was disavowed and projected onto a larger threat, in turn making *her* the target of such unacceptable feelings. When her most ambitious projects failed to materialize, putting an end to her seven-year wave of success, she blamed the Church of Scientology for orchestrating a conspiracy to silence and defame her. Psychoanalysis helped her uncover deep-seated emotions, but it did not stop the onslaught from within. Jeremy and Theresa loved each other deeply, and whatever emotions they felt found their way into his moving paintings. However, the dissolution of boundaries separating two human beings, and their merged inner relationship, rendered him susceptible to her paranoia, leaving indelible traces in his highly acclaimed *Winchester* series. Whereas Theresa's madness exploded when her creativity was stymied, Jeremy's creativity was fueled by this madness. Theresa committed suicide in order to preserve the last remnants of her agency and set Jeremy free. Unable to live without her, he walked into the ocean so that they can be reunited.

Chapter 7

A Lifelong Project of Resurrection

The Case of Alan Turing

Alan Mathison Turing was a British mathematician and logician who is universally recognized as the father of the modern computer, a title long held by John von Neumann. He helped secure victory for the Allied Powers during World War II by creating a machine that cracked Nazi Germany's Enigma code. With his theoretical work on computability and intelligent machinery, he boldly challenged the era's assumptions about human consciousness. One could say that Alan Turing changed the world twice, but despite his accomplishments, he was unfairly persecuted for his homosexuality in postwar Britain, a factor that contributed to his suicide on June 7, 1954.

Turing remains more salient in popular consciousness today than he was during his lifetime. His life and work has been the subject of several films and theatrical adaptations. For instance, Hugh Whitemore's stage play *Breaking the Code*, based on Andrew Hodges's biography, *Alan Turing: The Enigma*, has seen many productions domestically and internationally and was adapted for the screen by director Herbert Wise in 1997. *Codebreaker*, a 2011 drama documentary directed by Claire Bevan, aired on British Channel 4 and screened at select theaters and film festivals, amassing two million viewers worldwide. More recently in 2014, *The Imitation Game*, directed by Morten Tyldum and starring Benedict Cumberbatch of the BBC TV series *Sherlock*, premiered at the Telluride Film Festival in Colorado and released theatrically across the United States and the United Kingdom.

Turing has also been honored with a Google doodle of his so-called universal machine (more on this ahead), and a blue plaque at his childhood home in St. Leonard's at Sussex on June 23, 2012, the 100th anniversary of his birth. Rumor has it that the Apple logo is a nod to the means of Turing's demise (an apple laced with cyanide), though spokespersons for Apple continue to deny this, claiming that the logo is a homage to Isaac Newton.

The story of Alan Turing is so gripping to the cultural imaginary because it is a story in which creative ingenuity, queer identity, and self-destruction coalesce in a Gordian knot. As I illustrate in this chapter, Alan's creativity found expression in his scientific pursuits, which were encouraged in adolescence by an older boy for whom he felt deep love and affection. Tragically, the boy died unexpectedly, but he was kept symbolically alive over the years by Alan's attempts to become the brilliant mathematician his friend could have been, and by his project to materialize a body for his friend's spirit—an intelligent machine that could think, feel, learn, and love. However, his attempts to build such a machine—to link the theoretical with the concrete, the mystical with the terrestrial, the spiritual with the earthbound—were undercut by the prejudices of his time. He was prosecuted for the crime of loving another man, which prevented him from carrying out his lifelong project. With his agency, creativity, and bodily integrity undermined, Alan terminated his own life in a way that suggested everlasting union with his dearly departed friend. If creativity could no longer guarantee symbolic reunion, then death by suicide would.

CHILDHOOD CREATIVITY AND GAY IDENTITY

Alan Turing was born on June 23, 1912, to Julius and Ethel Turing. He was the younger of two boys, his older brother, John, four years his senior. He was described as a rather strange and idiosyncratic child. He didn't know that Christmas landed on the same day every year, and during walks with his mother stopped at every lamp post to examine the serial number, a habit she found infuriating. He walked a fine line between initiative and disobedience, experimentation and naughtiness. He once planted toy soldiers in the ground, expecting them to grow like trees. In light of his achievements in life, it may seem surprising that he was not at all an exemplary student. He had difficulty learning how to write, he could not tell left from right, and he received mediocre grades.

But he was *unconventionally* bright. He came up with unorthodox solutions to problems, for instance, at age six, locating beehives by observing the flight patterns of bees. He was not a rote learner but an empiricist, to say the least. Mixing compounds and solutions gave him much satisfaction, and to perform household experiments, he manually extracted elements from common substances, such as iodine from seaweed. Instead of reading books required by his school curriculum, he pursued books about the basic building blocks of nature, the human body, and the human brain, his favorite being E. T. Brewster's *Natural Wonders Every Child Should Know*.

During adolescence, Alan discovered his attraction to other boys. At Sherborne, one of the original public schools in the UK, he fell in love with

Christopher Morcom, whom he described as "brilliant," "charming," and "unconceited" (Hodges, 2012, p. 46). Christopher was very popular and exceptional at math and science, and Alan worshipped the ground the older boy walked on. Alan's heart swooned whenever Christopher smiled at him sideways. He aspired to improve his marks and become as intelligent as Christopher, taking as many classes with him as he could and sitting next to him in every class. The two became good friends over their shared love for math, chemistry, and astronomy, and when Christopher won a scholarship to Trinity College, Alan vowed to follow him, which the older boy encouraged.

Sadly, Christopher never got the chance to attend Trinity. He contracted bovine tuberculosis from drinking infected cow's milk, and despite many life-saving operations, he ultimately succumbed to the illness. Alan was devastated. He once believed that human bodies and spirits existed in separate universes; when the body died, the spirit went elsewhere. In the wake of Christopher's death, Alan discarded this belief. In a letter to Mrs. Morcom, he writes:

> I consider that the body by reason of being a living body can "attract" and hold on to a "spirit" whilst the body is alive and awake the two are firmly connected. When the body is asleep I cannot guess what happens but when the body dies the "mechanism" of the body, holding the spirit is gone and the spirit finds a new body sooner or later perhaps immediately. (Hodges, 2012, p. 64)

In other words, Alan very much wanted to believe that the dead remained with the living—that Christopher remained with him. Every night before going to bed, Alan would look at a photograph of Christopher Mrs. Morcom had given him. He would also treasure "with the tenderness of a woman the pencils and the beautiful star map and other souvenirs" (p. 50) that once belonged to Christopher but now belonged to him.

Alan sought to be deserving of Christopher. If Christopher could no longer fulfill his own dreams, then Alan would fulfill them for him. In a letter to Mrs. Turing:

> I feel sure that I shall meet Morcom again somewhere and that there will be some work for us to do together, and as I believed there was for us to do here. Now that I am left to do it alone I must not let him down but put as much energy into it, if not as much interest, as if he were still here. If I succeed I shall be more fit to enjoy his company than I am now. (p. 47)

As a first step toward becoming "fit to enjoy" Christopher's company, he would win a prize Mrs. Morcom had founded in her late son's memory. In the ensuing years, he would become the brilliant mathematician and scientist his friend was poised to be, effectively keeping Christopher alive.

RISE TO INTELLECTUAL PROMINENCE

Leonard Shlain (2007), in his comparison of Isaac Newton with Leonardo Da Vinci, highlights several notable similarities between the scientist and the artist. Both exhibit high degrees of abstract and symbolic thinking. Both pursue their vocation with relentless passion and have a penchant for decoding secrets and unraveling mysteries. Both seek to prove what has yet to be proven and challenge what to them are untenable ways of seeing the world. Though Alan Turing was more of a scientist than an artist in conventional terms, he exhibited the aforementioned qualities, blurring the line between Apollonian and Dionysian notions of creativity.

After Sherborne, Alan attended King's College in Cambridge, where he was named a Fellow. During his time at King, he tackled the *Entscheidungsproblem* in mathematics, also known as the decidability problem. Simply put, he disproved (independently of Alonzo Church, who is often credited) the idea that one can devise a method that could ascertain whether any given mathematical assertion is true. Some mathematical assertions are true, concurred Turing, but the proof does not always exist, nor could one prove the impossibility of a proof. The important point is that he undermined the notion that mathematics was unassailable and complete. For him, mathematics was less complete, more disorderly, and more chaotic than his contemporaries believed. Mathematics was more like life, equally beset by unpredictability, its ontological status not always secure. His discoveries had serious ramifications for the state of mathematics at the time; one could even say they had an unbalancing effect.

Like many creative people, Alan preferred to work in isolation, though he could be very sociable. His obliviousness to others' works proved humorous, if not problematic, whenever he discovered something that had already been discovered. For instance, his dissertation furnished proof for the central limit theorem, 16 years after it had already been proven by Finnish mathematician Jarl Waldemar Lindeberg. Nevertheless, his committee passed him with flying colors for his bold and novel approach, earning him a PhD from Princeton in 1938.

Shortly after receiving his PhD, he was called upon by the British government to work at Bletchley Park, Britain's code-breaking center. The fuse of World War II had just been lit, and Alan would spend the next several years doing cryptanalysis—specifically, decoding Nazi Germany's Enigma encipherment machine. This was a matter of vital importance because the

Enigma enabled unimpeded communication between German U-boats, allowing them to perform concerted attacks against Allied forces, down ships, and interrupt supply lines to Europe. It was impossible to decode the Enigma by hand because the machine's electrical rotors made over one hundred *billion* permutations possible.

How does one combat such a small but terrifying machine? By building another machine, of course. Alan was thrilled by his work in cryptanalysis because it allowed him to link the abstract with the concrete, to apply mathematical principles to the creation of an actual machine. He himself oversaw the machine's construction, installation, and application. The resulting product—six-and-a-half feet tall, seven feet wide, and weighing one ton—came to be known as the Turing bombe, so named for the noises it made. It simulated the activities of 30 Enigma machines working simultaneously, and its use led to a rapid decline in the number of Allied ships sunk by German U-boats, and consequently, to the preservation of Allied supply lines. It goes without saying that the Turing bombe played no small part in securing victory for the Allied Powers during World War II.

CREATION OF A LIFELIKE MACHINE

The Turing bombe was designed for one purpose only, and that purpose had been met. After the war, Alan proposed to work on a universal machine that can take on *any* function, and he received a small grant in order to build a small prototype.

Alan believed that thinking machines were inevitable. He believed that such machines would be able to converse in a language that is as meaningful to them as the languages spoken by humans to one another. They would be capable of deception, and like humans, make mistakes, but that fallibility would not be due to lack of intelligence. Most importantly, Alan believed that they could be taught like children. Embedded in his excitement to build such a machine was a deep desire to create a mechanical body to house Christopher's spirit. Christopher had been dead for over a decade at this point, but according to Alan's childhood metaphysical beliefs, the boy continued to exist in this realm.

This set of beliefs, which was as mystical as it was scientific, paved the path for what was arguably his most enduring contribution to society: the "universal" machine, also known as the Turing machine. Prior to the war, "computers" were humans—typically, female operators who were relegated to performing largely rote computational tasks. Basic computing machines eventually freed human operators from the drudgery of this labor, but unlike modern-day computers, they required modifications to the hardware itself in order to carry out other functions. They had neither storage nor software. The Turing machine, a theoretical machine that laid the foundations for today's computers, envisioned a way through which computers can be altered from within. Specifically, through the 0s and 1s of the binary system, a computer could perform virtually any task, hence the appellation of "universal."

Turing explicated the workings of his universal machine in the paper, "Computing Machinery and Intelligence," published in 1950 in the scientific journal *Mind.* It was considered his "most perverse paper" (Leavitt, 2006, p. 240), criticized as antihuman by critics who espoused humanist values and feared machine takeover—a fear that persists today in talks about the "coming singularity" (Kurtzweil, 2006). The anthropomorphism of a machine as a child also left a sour taste in critics' palates.

In a tongue-in-cheek response to his detractors, Alan attributed the following characteristics to machines of the future:

> kind, resourceful, beautiful, friendly; have initiative, have a sense of humour, tell right from wrong, make mistakes; fall in love, enjoy strawberries and cream; make some one fall in love with it, learn from experience; use words properly, be the subject of its own thought; have as much diversity of behavior as a man, do something really new. (Leavitt, 2006, p. 251)

Though delivered with wit and sarcasm, his response evocatively captures his vision of a lifelike machine that is indistinguishable from living, breathing humans, a machine that could ponder its own ontology. Alan would never have the chance to build this machine, however.

POSTWAR PERSECUTION

A mere two years after publication of his hotly contested paper, Alan would be branded a criminal and sexual deviant for engaging in sex acts with a 19-year-old boy. It was 1952, and at the time, sex between men was illegal in the UK. The offense, called "gross indecency," was punishable by imprisonment. The law had been in existence long before Turing was born; in fact, Oscar Wilde had been sentenced to prison half a century earlier because of it. Strangely, the House of Lords voted against extending the law to women out of fear that breaching the subject would give them *ideas*. Like many Englishmen, Alan traveled to other parts of Europe for sexual fulfillment, such as Norway and France, where gay sex was not criminalized. But Manchester, too, offered the occasional tryst, and it was here that Alan met Arnold Murray, a working-class boy 20 years his junior.

Alan had been pretending to look at posters outside the Regal Cinema when he caught Arnold's eyes. The boy didn't have much cash in his pockets or food in his stomach; like many working-class youth of his time, he traded sexual favors for money and material goods. The two went out for lunch, and Alan invited Arnold over to his house for the weekend. The boy never showed up. The two met again the following week, and this time, Alan suggested that Arnold come home with him immediately.

It wouldn't be a stretch to say that Alan saw in Arnold some semblance of his childhood love. Like Christopher, Arnold was fragile—not physically but situationally, as in the background of domestic violence from which Alan sought to rescue him. He was also very intelligent—not academically, but pragmatically. Arnold didn't want rescuing, however, nor did he want to be treated as a prostitute. He turned down Alan's offers of cash, though he did enjoy the older man's company.

Alan's unraveling began when Arnold boasted of their affair to a boy named Harry. Harry proposed to rob Alan's house, but Arnold wanted nothing to do with the heist. Harry robbed Alan's house anyway; when Alan returned home, he found 50 pounds' worth of items missing, which he reported to the police. But instead of arresting the thief the police arrested the victim. Apparently, Harry had tipped them off to the nature of Alan's relationship with Arnold. To complicate matters, Alan was oblivious to the law and utterly averse to dishonesty (white lies included). He'd assumed sex between men would be legalized, and when questioned by the police, he told them the entire story of his romantic affairs. He even played the violin and served them wine while doing so.

Until its abolition in 2005, nearly one hundred thousand men were charged with gross indecency, and it has been estimated that 10 times that number lived in fear of conviction. Typically, the convicted person was sent directly to prison, but because others pleaded on Alan's behalf, he was given a choice between imprisonment and chemical castration. He chose the latter. Arnold was also found guilty, but being the younger of the two parties, he was released.

Unlike surgical castration, which entailed removal of the testicles or ovaries, chemical castration, as the name implies, depended on chemical means. But unlike sterilization, which is irreversible, the effects of chemical castration are reversible once treatment has been discontinued. The logic behind chemical castration during postwar Britain was that it would reduce sex drive, arousal, and compulsive sexual fantasies. It had been used to curb the behaviors of child molesters and so-called paraphilics, and by applying the same punitive measure to Turing, a categorical fallacy was committed, which can be summarized by the following set of propositions: (a) Turing has been sentenced to chemical castration; (b) Chemical castration is for child molesters and paraphilics; (c) Therefore, Turing is a child molester or paraphilic.

But an even bigger atrocity was being committed; periodic injections of estrogen undermined his bodily integrity. He grew breasts, gained weight, lost bone and muscle mass, and lost body hair. He became a bloated shade of his former self. He'd been a marathon runner and took pride in his athletic ability. As a child, when rail services were suspended due to the general strike, Alan biked the 60 miles from Southampton to Sherborne to make it in time for the first day of the summer term. The feat was so astonishing it was covered by the local press. In adulthood, he was a contender for a spot in the British Olympics, had it not been for an injury that marred his performance during tryouts. But following treatment, Alan did not dare show himself in public; the physical changes caused him great humiliation.

Alan was not only castrated, he was also denied his freedom to wander physically and intellectually. He was stripped of his security clearance, preventing him from doing any more work in cryptanalysis. At the time, the myth of the homosexual traitor was salient in British consciousness. A year prior to Alan's conviction, it had been discovered that Guy Burgess, a radio producer and Foreign Office official, was a member of the Cambridge Five, a spy ring that passed Western secrets onto the Soviet Union. Because Burgess was a homosexual, the British government became wary of homosexuals, fearing that they could be seduced into giving classified information to enemies of the state.

Alan worried that his conviction would discredit his wartime contributions, as well as his work on intelligent machinery and AI. In hindsight, this fear was not unfounded given that John von Neumann, rather than Alan Turing, was for decades recognized as the father of computer science. The following limerick he wrote to a friend and colleague concretized his concerns: "Turing believes machines think/ Turing lies with men/ Therefore machines do not think" (Leavitt, 2006, p. 269). Alan was punished with castration and discreditation for the crime of loving another man. He had worked so hard over the decades to be worthy of Christopher's company, to tread the path his beloved would have walked, only to have his efforts undercut. He was offered a five-year position in the theory of computing at the University of Manchester, but this consolation prize would not give him the satisfaction of linking the realm of the intangible with that of the concrete. The Turing machine—the machine that could be taught like a child, the machine that could be loved and love back, the vessel that could house the spirit of Christopher Morcom—would remain in theoretical form.

THE DEATH OF ALAN TURING

On June 7, 1954, two weeks short of his 42nd birthday, Alan was found frothing in the mouth by his housekeeper. On the side of his bed stood half an apple from which several bites had been taken. Elsewhere in the house, a jar of potassium cyanide and a jam jar of cyanide solution were found. The death came as a shock to those closest to him, for he seemed to have been in good spirits in the days leading up to his suicide. Mrs. Turing was unconvinced; since Alan used cyanide for gold-plating, she argued that her son's death was the result of an electrolytic experiment gone awry.

But the good spirits Alan exhibited were those of a person who'd secretly made peace with the decision to die, for whom death offered release from shame and suffering (Atwood, 1972). This is corroborated by the fact that he'd made a new will months prior to his death, by the state in which he was found (in bed, peacefully asleep), and by the way he enacted his suicide. To understand the deep symbolism of his suicide, one would need to travel back in time to 1938.

The animated Disney film *Snow White and the Seven Dwarves* had just premiered in Britain, and Alan Turing, 26 at the time, was smitten. For weeks after its theatrical release, he chanted this line from the film: "Dip the apple in the brew/ Let the seeping death seep through." He was enamored by the idea that a sleeping princess, on the doorstep of death, could be woken to life by the kiss of a handsome prince, that love could rescue her from the poison apple's curse.

I concur with Alan's biographers (Hodges, 1983/2012; Leavitt, 2006) that his symbolic invocation of Snow White at the moment of his death is not without significance. One could say it brought him back to the innocent times of childhood, when love was pure and unblemished by society's prejudice. Consistent with his childhood metaphysical belief—that there is an essence that lives outside the human body, as he'd assured Mrs. Morcom in his letter—the apple also brought him back to Christopher. But whereas Snow White was reunited with her prince in life, Alan Turing was reunited with his prince in death. There would be no waking Alan from his poison-induced sleep.

CONCLUDING REMARKS

Alan Turing's work in artificial intelligence was prescient. He laid the foundation for the binary system, and without him, we might not have software, only hardware. Without him, a game of chess with an AI opponent might still be the stuff of science fiction. The outcome of World War II might have also been different had it not been for his scientific and mathematical acumen, since his work on the Enigma machine (i.e., Turing bombe) helped turn the tides of war in the Allied Powers' favor.

These advances were made possible by his infusion of creativity, originality, and playfulness into his work, which allowed him to see the workings of the world in ways never before envisioned. Even among his contemporaries, Alan stood on the margins, deemed by many to be too unconventional. He was, after all, the strange but gifted boy who checked out the serial numbers on streetlamps, who planted toy soldiers in the soil to make them grow. It would be a mistake, however, to attribute his revolutionary accomplishments solely to his unorthodoxy. His rise to prominence, and his conception of the universal machine, were driven in no small part by a deep yearning to keep alive and resurrect an idealized, lost other.

It is ironic that a facet of his identity that placed him on the path to becoming a great mathematician and scientist would also eventuate in the undoing of that path. Despite his contributions to wartime victory, he was unjustly persecuted for being homosexual. Discredited, chemically castrated, and unable to materialize an intelligent, artificial body for the spirit of Christopher, Alan Turing bit into a poison apple.

In 2003, nearly 50 years after Alan was tried and found guilty of gross indecency, homosexual acts between men in the UK were decriminalized. Six years later, three hundred thousand people signed a Downing Street petition seeking a posthumous apology from then British prime minister Gordon Brown, who went on record to say: "The debt of gratitude [Alan Turing] is owed makes it all the more horrifying, therefore, that he was treated so inhumanely" (quoted in Wockner, 2009). But an apology from the prime minister does not constitute an official pardon, which was finally granted on December 24, 2013, by Queen Elizabeth II under the Royal Prerogative of Mercy (Davis, 2013). The pardon doubled as a symbolic apology to the tens of thousands of gay men who had been convicted and to the million others who lived in fear of conviction. Finally, as part of the Lesbian and Gay Foundation's "Homo Heroes Awards," the Alan Turing Award was launched in Manchester to recognize individuals who champion the rights of sexual minorities.

Interlude III

Suicide as Authentication of the Self

The Greek origins of the word "authenticity" is a curious thing. One of its roots, *authenteo*, is a verb that means "to have full power over; also, to commit a murder" (Noyes, 2000, p. 210). But more relevant to our discussion is *authentes*, a noun, "not only a master and a doer, but also a perpetrator, a murderer, even a self-murderer, a suicide" (ibid.). The association of self-destruction with agency and mastery is no mere coincidence, because the willful termination of one's life can signify the farthest (and darkest) reach of free will, hence our notion of suicide as self-authentication.

But what is *authenticity*? It is a loaded term indeed, and as a starting point, let's invoke Heidegger's (1996) definition. For Heidegger, the human being is governed by two modes of existence: the authentic and the inauthentic. Inauthentic existence refers to humankind's inescapable embeddedness in a normative system of social customs and practices. We are constantly *falling* into inauthenticity in our identification with "the they" (*das Man*), which is in part motivated by our flight from *anxiety*. Anxiety—or *anguish*, in Sartre's (2001, 2007) parlance—is caused by the burden of our responsibility to determine ourselves at every instant. By fleeing from *anxiety*, we escape from holding ourselves responsible for our own actions, becoming thinglike in the process. Individuality is thus replaced by the collective identity of "the they," a symbolic self-cessation. To live without *anxiety* is tantamount to *nonbeing*, to not being alive at all.

Authentic existence, on the other hand, is *Being-toward-death*. Aware of our own finitude, we seize upon the possibilities to which we have been delivered, and in our pursuit of transcendent liberation, we realize ourselves as truly existent and human. But such pursuit brings us closer and closer to *anxiety*, and in the midst of this anxiety we might encounter *the nothing*, from which one distinguishes all things that are. Many private wars have been waged against *the nothing*'s threat of *nonbeing*, with suicide as both a weapon and an outcome.

Heidegger's conceptualization of *authenticity* is not without drawbacks, of course. It is deeply steeped in ethnocentrism, precluding the possibility that suicide can also authenticate the collective self, as we see in Durkheim's (1897) *altruistic* suicide. Still, there is much value in Heidegger's definition, particularly the attention he draws to loss of self and nonbeing. As I illustrate throughout, suicide can authenticate by forestalling the complete dissolution of self or facilitating its emergence. Let us now turn to the many variants of self-loss and their bearing on suicide.

THE THREE ANXIETIES

The threat of self-loss is not unidimensional, and in his study of persons with so-called schizophrenia, Laing (1959) identified three variants encountered by the ontologically insecure person—for whom one's presence in the world is never felt as continuous or real, and whose identity and autonomy are always in question. In *engulfment*, the first of Laing's three anxieties, every human relationship threatens to dissolve the ontologically insecure person's self with absorption into an other, such that being loved or understood is felt as catastrophic. *Implosion*, the second anxiety, is experienced by the person who feels himself to be as empty as a vacuum. Any contact with the objective world is terrifying because it threatens to obliterate the identity the person supposes himself to have, which is that of nothingness. Finally, *petrification* (or *depersonalization*) is the dread of being turned into an inanimate or dead thing by an other. One's subjectivity drains away in the face of being treated like an *it*, some *thing* that one is not.

I mention Laing here because his three anxieties are not exclusively limited to the existential study of schizophrenia; they are equally applicable to our notion of self-destruction as self-authentication. Laing added that threats to the ontologically insecure person's selfhood can be encompassed to forestall their occurrence:

> Thus, to forgo one's autonomy becomes the means of secretly safeguarding it; to play possum, to feign death, becomes a means of preserving one's aliveness. To turn oneself into a stone becomes a way of not being turned into a stone by someone else. (p. 51)

It follows that suicide can be mobilized in the struggle against the negation or erasure of self: "I kill myself, therefore I am."

We have seen many examples of this already. For instance, Kevin Carter (chapter 2) is someone who felt himself to be nothing, a person utterly lacking in worth. It's no wonder that he hermetically sealed himself off after the vicious attack of critics, after the death of his "good twin" Ken, and after years and years of photographing township massacres, which assailed even his dreams. Further contact with the outside world was annihilating, and he annihilated himself when his attempts to venture out into the world only confirmed his sense of inherent worthlessness. In forsaking biological life, he preserved what few shreds of his self remained, averting total negation by implosion.

Sylvia Plath (chapter 5) would be a classic example of the threat of engulfment averted via suicide. As mentioned, suicide was her means of exorcising forces that stood in the way of her emancipation: "for her, death was a debt to be met once every decade: in order to stay alive as a grown woman, a mother and a poet, she had to pay—in some partial, magical way—with her life" (Alvarez, 1973, p. 18). These forces, of course, were a suffocating mother whose love she never felt and who expressed only vested interest in her success as a writer, and the haunting specter of her father, whose dangerous love she yearned for but threatened to pull her into his casket. She could not kill her mother, she could not kill her already dead father, and so, to remain agentic, she had to attempt to kill herself and survive.

Another curious case of implosion can be seen in the life and death of the photographer Diane Arbus. Since childhood, Diane suffered from a pervasive feeling of nonexistence:

> I felt confirmed in a sense of unreality which I could feel as unreality, and the sense of being immune was, ludicrous as it seems, a painful one . . . the world seemed to belong to the world. I could learn things, but they never seemed to be my own experience. (Bosworth, 1984, p. 30)

Growing up, she was struck by the duplicity and inauthenticity she saw in others, especially her mother, "who always seemed to be cultivating an air of indifference" (p. 278), and her father, who she described as a "frontal person" (p. 10). Seeing others cleft in twain bred an image of her own self as fragmented, incomplete, and yet to come into being.

Diane struggled to overcome her sense of unreality through photography, her means of authentication. She took photos of people on the fringes of society—giants, midgets, prostitutes, transvestites, circus performers, and in her final years, the so-called mentally retarded—because "freaks," she believed, possessed the authenticity she coveted: "Freaks were born with their trauma. They've already passed their test in life. They're aristocrats" (Arbus, 1972, p. 3). At the same time, she stripped "ordinary" people of their masks, exposing the ugly visage underneath the inauthentic façade. She once declined a friend's request to have his picture taken, saying, "It would take five hundred exposures before I'd get you without your mask" (Bosworth, 1984, p. 178). Talk about a damning indictment.

I share the sentiment that for Arbus, photography was both a shield against and a means of contact with the outside world (Sass, 2005). Camera in hand, she entered into situations that she normally avoided. She had sexual intercourse with several of her subjects, achieving merger-like closeness that, however tenuously, rendered her existent. But most importantly, she saw fragments of her self (and her fragmentation) in her subjects, which came together with the press of the shutter. For instance, *Triplets in the Bedroom* reminded Diane of what she used to be: "Lined up in three images: daughter, sister, bad girl, with secret lusting fantasies, each with a tiny difference" (Bosworth, 1984, p. 217). By pressing the shutter, she fulfilled her ontological need for integration and wholeness, albeit shakily; photography was her (partial) antidote to the derealization she was prone to experiencing.

But the camera lost its power to authenticate, to render herself existent, when she shifted her focus to the so-called mentally retarded for her *Untitled* (1995) series. These subjects did not ratify her existence, "they didn't look her in the eye, they didn't acknowledge her presence or tell her their stories, nor were they charmed or seduced by her" (Bosworth, 1984, p. 312). She saw only the maw of the abyss, for there was absolutely nothing for her to integrate. Their world was one "she could never know, could never enter, and this angered and frustrated her, depressed her" (p. 318). Two weeks after she was heard crying, "My work doesn't do it for me anymore" (ibid.), she committed suicide. Her newfound subjects threatened her with implosion, and her ultimate response was self-destruction.

VARIETIES OF PERSONAL ANNIHILATION

There are many dimensions of self-experience that are called into question, or even annihilated, when one is in the grips of madness. Laing (1959) identified a few such dimensions; Orange, Atwood, and Stolorow (2001) offer several others. Such anomalies in self-experience (or varieties of personal annihilation), which emerge within the context of intersubjective catastrophes, include: inertness, or taking on the properties of a physical object; temporal fragmentation or discontinuity; loss of inner cohesion, in which mind and body are irrevocably separated; boundary dissolution, or the inability to demarcate self from nonself; artificiality, the sense that one is fictional, lacking substance, or unreal; usurpation of agency, by forces perceived to be external to oneself; and loss of affectivity, or psychic deadness. As the authors gently remind readers, human subjectivity "always overflows the category systems with which we try to capture it" (p. 50), and so, this conceptual scheme (pictured as spokes on a wheel) is not meant to be exhaustive.

Although these anomalies are observed in psychotic states, they also have relevance for the phenomenological study of suicide. Just as the sensorimotor symbols of concretization may encapsulate both threats to self and efforts at self-restoration (Atwood & Stolorow, 1993), these experiences may encapsulate the catastrophes that the very act of suicide seeks to overcome. We have seen an imperiled sense of agency in both Iris Chang (chapter 1) and Theresa Duncan (chapter 6), who felt as if they were under attack by sinister forces (Japanese ultranationalists and the Church of Scientology, respectively) that sought to undermine their credibility and prevent them from speaking the truth of their experiences. We have also seen the threat of depersonalization and inertness in Kevin Carter (chapter 2) and Alan Turing (chapter 7). Kevin's prize-winning photo was twisted by critics into a signifier of his failure to be human, effectively turning him into the vulture he'd photographed. Alan's bodily integrity was assailed by the British government for the crime of sexual contact with another male body.

Interestingly, suicidal depression may also express itself in the language of these anomalous self-experiences, as the memoirs of suicide attempt survivors illustrate. The loss of inner cohesion is evident in William Styron's experience of disembodiment on the night he intended to kill himself. In his memoir, *Darkness Visible* (1992), he speaks of "a melodrama in which I, the victim-to-be of self-murder, was both the solitary actor and lone member of the audience" (p. 64). The audience, a disembodied specter, was "a wraith-like observer who, not sharing the dementia of his double, is able to watch with dispassionate curiosity as his companion struggles against the oncoming disaster, or decided to embrace it" (p. 65).

Susanna Kaysen writes about aberrations in her experience of time in *Girl, Interrupted* (1993)—specifically, the two sources of inexplicable torment she calls *viscosity* and *velocity* of the mind. Viscosity is "cellular coma": "Experience is thick. Perceptions are thickened and dulled. Time is slow, dripping slowly through the clogged filter of thickened perception" (p. 75). On the other hand, velocity is warp speed: "There is too much perception, and beyond the plethora of perceptions, a plethora of thoughts about the perceptions and about the fact of having perception" (ibid.). Both states are maddening.

But it was loss of affectivity and artificiality that Kaysen fiercely struggled against. A sudden loss of feelings prompted Kaysen to swallow a bottle of painkillers, which resulted not in death but in years of confinement inside McLean Hospital. There, she engaged in self-injurious acts to assert her continuing aliveness. Using her fingernails, she scraped away at her skin until she bled, hoping to see the bones underneath. She needed to know that she wasn't hollow, that she was a living, feeling human being: "I got a gruesome satisfaction from my sufferings. They proved my existence" (p. 42).

CONCLUDING REMARKS

One of the symbolic functions and meanings of suicide is self-authentication, with threats to the integrity of self assuming a variety of forms. Self-destruction can avert a single threat, or it can avert a constellation of threats; they are not mutually exclusive. The threats can even encode themselves in the language of suicidal depression. Suicide can also authenticate the truth and facticity of one's lived experiences—for instance, Phyllis Hyman's lifelong loneliness (chapter 3), and the destruction of Kurt Cobain's original nuclear family (chapter 4)—making intersubjective catastrophes visible, with physical death serving as testimony to psychic death.

Of course, as the examples I provide throughout show, suicide is a last resort. It preserves the integrity of the self and forestalls threats to selfhood when the creative act no longer could. Phrased another way, impediments to creativity are conduits to suicide. But in some cases, creativity does not prevent suicide but builds the momentum for it. For someone like Yukio Mishima, who we now turn to, suicide is the final chord in a lifelong project to materialize the self and render it existent.

Chapter 8

Existence through Annihilation

The Case of Yukio Mishima

On November 25, 1970, Yukio Mishima, the postwar author and playwright, infiltrated the Imperial Palace, headquarters of the Jietai, Japan's Special Defense Forces. He took hostage an Armed Forces general, whom he threatened to kill if law enforcement did not comply with his demand for an audience of ambassadors and officials from across the capital of Tokyo. The breach was broadcast nationwide, and once the palace was surrounded by the police, Mishima stepped out onto the terrace of the top floor. The crowd was utterly confused; Mishima was among the most patriotic of Japan's esteemed writers, and his actions were anything but.

Mishima began to speak. He reproached his countrymen for allowing the "Green Snake," the Western promise of modernization, to ensnare Japan. It had only been two decades since the land of the rising sun lost World War II, and yet traditions of old were quickly fading into oblivion. He expressed feeling betrayed by the Jietai, once loyal subjects of the emperor that now were upholding a Constitution imposed by the West. The preservation of Japan's sanctity was at stake, and it was his avowed duty to reel his people back to their senses, to avert the complete erasure of Japan's authenticity.

But they were unconvinced of the need to restore Japan to former glory. Madman. Insane. Fanatic. Such were the words of the people gathered below him. The Green Snake's grip was strong indeed, and he alone remained disillusioned.

Mishima decided it was time to show Japan and Her people the depths of his sincerity. He returned to the office of the general, who was held captive by four members of his own private militia, the Tatenokai. He undressed himself down to a loin cloth and sat cross-legged in front of the general with a knife in his right hand. Among the Japanese, it is said that sincerity resided in the guts. Mishima laid bare his sincerity by striking the side of his stomach with the knife, and with ruthless endurance, he ran the blade across his abdomen, forming a crescent through which blood and intestines spilled. With his dying gasps he exclaimed: "Long live the Emperor!" A member of the Tatenokai unsheathed a sword, and with one downward swing decapitated Mishima's almost lifeless body.

The ritual suicide of *seppuku*—self-disembowelment followed by decapitation—was practiced by the samurai during the Edo Period as a final expression of allegiance to their feudal lords. Bushido, the way of the samurai, was abolished during the Meiji Restoration, which overthrew Japan's feudal system. The general and the Tatenokai were moved to tears by Mishima's unequivocal display of sincerity. In unison, the grown men cried softly, "Long live the Emperor."

INTRODUCTION

The Meiji Restoration during the late nineteenth century was a period of social unrest and instability, because for the first time Japan opened its gates to the Western frontier (Scott-Stokes, 1974). But a century later, with the Japanese economy booming after World War II, stability was achieved. The way of the sword, epitomizing Japan's dark half, faded to memory and lost its luster to both Westerners and the Japanese. The soft side of Japan became the centerpiece of Western fascination. The patriotic Mishima wanted to preserve this duality for those who had misunderstood Japan's tragedy, and toward that end, he sought to revive the samurai spirit. But at its core, the idea of reviving the samurai was entangled with his personal struggle to materialize the self—a human drama he transposed onto the fabric of history.

This chapter is divided into two parts. In the first half, I examine the nuclear crises that dominated Mishima's childhood and adolescence—specifically, how the lack of a facilitative intersubjective context cultivated in him a pervasive sense of nonbeing. Feeling immaterial and incorporeal, young Mishima began to crave flesh, and he fulfilled this craving by imagining the death and suffering of others, sometimes taking on the role of executioner in his fantasies. In vicariously experiencing the finality of others' lives, Mishima himself flickered into being.

In the second half, I trace the concretization of these themes in his adult life and work—from his glorification of death in *Patriotism* (1953), to his modernization of classic Noh plays, to the cycle of death and rebirth to which he subjects characters in his magnum opus, *The Sea of Fertility* tetralogy. However, a literary death was not enough; Mishima rendered himself corporeal by practicing various forms of martial arts. Only upon attaining the flesh he long coveted did he become worthy of a glorious death—a philosophy he espoused in *Sun and Steel* (1968), rehearsed in various cinematic and theatrical productions, and actualized in the Imperial Palace.

CHILDHOOD YEARS AND LIFELONG THEMES

The Roots of Incorporeality

Born on January 14, 1925, as Kimitake Hiraoka, Yukio Mishima was a child who felt eternally excluded from life. He was raised by a domineering grandmother (Natsu) who was so dismayed by the failures of her husband (Jotaro) and son (Azusa) that she vowed to instill in her grandson the strict discipline and crude ways of her samurai lineage (Scott-Stokes, 1974). For the first 12 years of his life, Mishima was denied the maternal warmth and compassion of his mother Shizue, and contact with his parents was limited to periodic visits. Shizue was forbidden from speaking her mind when it concerned the boy's well-being, and Azusa was unsuccessful in his attempts to convince Natsu to grant his son some freedom. Feeling resigned, they accepted Natsu's rule without protest. Looking back, "Shizue says bitterly that her son's dark fate was sealed by the time he was twelve, and adds that she longed for years to leave the house and take him with her" (Nathan, 1974, p. 10).

Natsu was devoid of empathic concern for the boy. During an unfortunate household accident, Mishima was severely injured. Natsu was not there to witness it, but upon learning from the housemaids she asked point-blank, without a trace of worry, "Is he dead?" (Mishima, 1949, p. 6). A facilitative intersubjective context during the formative years is a necessary precondition for the symbolic articulation of affect, and this is blocked in the absence of validating responses in the familial surround (Stolorow & Atwood, 2002). Against this backdrop, it is perhaps unsurprising that young Mishima could not express any emotion in the presence of others. For instance, when he was five, Azusa held him close to a steam engine at a railroad crossing. The man was astonished at the absence of fear or delight on the boy's face; it was simply blank.

Mishima's inseparability from Natsu cultivated in him an intimacy with death. He was confined to her presence during waking hours and in sleep: "My bed was placed in my grandmother's sickroom, perpetually closed and stifling with odors of sickness and old age, and I was raised there beside her sickbed" (Mishima, 1949, p. 6). Because Natsu suffered from sciatica, stomach ulcers, and kidney disease, she was under her grandson's care at all times. Her pain was so overwhelming that at one point she held a knife to her throat and threatened to kill herself in front of the boy.

According to Lacan (1949), the absence of the paternal figure and function (*le non du pere*) renders problematic the seeking of erotic pleasures and thwarts entry into the social and linguistic order. Without this paternal figure to triangulate the relationship between the child and the maternal figure, the latter becomes a dangerous and hostile force. The effect is psychologically destructive, and in Mishima's case, being raised by a suffocating grandmother propelled him face to face with the ubiquitous nature of death. The following fantasy of the passageway to Natsu's sick chamber is very telling:

> And at every turning point I met at least one "disease." They are in a great hurry too. They are much taller than I. Some have no faces, and some do. One who had a face—he was smiling innocently. He must have been a "disease" not intimate with "death" yet. He must have been taking news to a "disease" more intimate with "death." One day the little finger on my right hand just brushed that slimy, invisible presence. (Nathan, 1974, p. 21)

The "disease" Mishima writes about came in different shapes and forms. Some were human size; others were bacterial, like the "disease" that lurked in the bottle of medicine for Natsu's neuralgic spasms, a dwarf "totally unaware of the sea of medicine washing his body" (p. 21). Disease "would occupy the house as if it were the owner" (p. 20), crawling in every nook and cranny, dripping from the ceiling, and wedged between floorboards. They threatened to contaminate anyone who dared to come close, but alas, Mishima himself had already been contaminated.

Mishima felt unable to share in the joys and sorrows of the world. In his autobiographical *Confessions of a Mask* (1949), he recalls his delight upon seeing from behind the gates of the Hiraoka household a bustling town festival filled with streetcar operators, portable shrine carriers, colorful toy and food stands, and costumed participants. The sight of something so novel yet alien to himself filled him with yearning and sadness, for he was a prisoner of his own dwelling, a detached observer barred from participation in the world:

> Existences and events occurring without any relationship to myself, occurring at places that not only appealed to my senses but moreover denied to me. . . . It seemed that my grief at being eternally excluded was always transformed in my dreaming into grief for those persons and their ways of life, and that solely through my own grief I was trying to share in their existence. (Mishima, 1949, p. 10)

If he could not experience the ebb and flow of life directly, then he'd do so vicariously by sharing in the sorrows of other. But the sorrow he was imputing to them belonged to no one but himself.

Phenomenologically, Mishima was a boy who never existed, and Lacan (1949) is once again relevant here. According to Lacan, identity begins with the mirror stage, which gives "I" its meaning and function. An infant is able to recognize himself in the mirror before he can exercise coordinated control over his movements. But unlike his image in the mirror, which is whole, his bodily movements are uncoordinated. Consequently, the infant realizes his own fragmentation, which must be overcome by identifying with the seamless image and by turning to an adult caregiver, the "big Other," who validates the infant's mastery over the image. Only then is the infant able to bask in his wholeness and corporeality.

But Mishima never felt whole and corporeal. Again, he lacked the facilitative intersubjective context necessary for a cohesive selfhood, undermining his developing sense of embodiment and *indwelling* (Stolorow & Atwood, 2002). Nothingness was his natural state of being, which expressed itself through a disconnect between his feelings and their outward expression, and was reinforced by his exclusion from the world of humanity and constant exposure to the visage of death. Sharing in the experiences of others was Mishima's first step to affirming his own flickering existence, but it would not be sufficient in giving him a taste of the life he earnestly coveted. So began his bloodlust, which he satiated through the imagined death of idealized others.

A Longing for Death

In childhood and adolescence, Mishima felt "a sensuous craving for such things as the destiny of soldiers, the tragic nature of their calling, the distant countries they would see, the ways they would die" (Mishima, 1949, p. 14). He was "all the fonder of princes murdered or princes fated for death. I was completely in love with any youth who was killed" (p. 20). Death is life's endpoint, and its arrival renders the life that preceded it complete; something that dies must have therefore lived. For Mishima, life reaches its apex at the climactic moment it is extinguished. If his self could flicker into being through empathic identification with suffering others, then it stands to reason that identification with deathbound figures could make that self ignite.

Mishima didn't like tales in which male protagonists escape from danger with their lives intact. He once read a Hungarian fairy tale of a handsome prince sent to a distant land to slay a dragon. The prince was devoured, his flesh torn asunder, but to the boy's dismay, he came back to life unscathed and smote the fearsome dragon. Mishima quickly rewrote the ending of the tale to his satisfaction:

> Without a moment's delay, the dragon chewed the prince greedily into bits. It was almost more than he could stand, but the prince summoned all his courage

> and bore the torture steadfastly until he was finally chewed completely into shreds. Then, in a flash, he sank to the ground and died on the spot. (p. 23)

The prince was valiant in his resolve to slay the dragon, and in Mishima's eyes, it was the futility of his struggle that endowed his life with meaning.

"Correcting" tales became somewhat of a habit for Mishima. He collected magazine clippings of men engaged in some type of activity and made the necessary alterations. Detectives are shot by the objects of their pursuit. Valiant knights are slayed. Tight rope walkers plummet to their doom, their skulls split open to the horror of spectators. The list goes on. One could read in these acts of correction idealization of, and simultaneously, unconscious hostility toward those who possessed what he lacked: wholeness and corporeality. And with the stroke of a pen he was able to carry out a narcissistic form of revenge and assert his dominion over these signifiers of male beauty. This act of "correcting" would persist into adulthood (more on this ahead) in his modernization and transfiguration of traditional Japanese Noh plays.

The thought of his own death entranced young Mishima. Recalling his defeat in gunplay, he writes: "I was enraptured with the vision of my own form lying there, twisted and fallen. There was an unspeakable delight in having been shot and being on the point of death" (p. 28). His yearning for death is equally palpable in his childhood writings. In one such story, "A Forest in Full Flower," a six-year-old boy (Akihiko) escapes from home and ventures into the heart of a forest despite warnings from his mother that an escaped convict lurks there. Of course, the boy encounters the convict, and their chance meeting unfolds as follows:

> *Convict:* "I had a child. A pretty boy like you."
> *Akihiko:* "Where is he now?"
> *Convict:* "Now he is a seagull flying above the vast sea. And when he spies the silver glitter of scales among the waves he thrusts his neck into the water and he says, 'I was murdered on the gray evening sea. My murderer sank to the dark, dark bottom.' But the devil who killed that poor poor seagull has found his way up to the surface. And you know who showed him the way—it was you." (quoted in Nathan, 1974, pp. 29–30)

The association between being young and "pretty" and being marked for death is clear from the outset, as is the transformation from one state of being (child) to another (seagull) that death brings. Like Akihiko, his fictional stand-in, Mishima was denied by a maternal figure the chance to set foot in the outside world, and he longed to venture into that world even if (or especially because) it meant courting death, which promised to infuse life with fullness.

Perhaps the most striking example of Mishima's embrace of death was his first ejaculation, which he experienced at the sight of Guido Reni's painting of St. Sebastian. As the martyr's tale goes, St. Sebastian was the captain of the Praetorian Guard during the benevolent reign of Diocletian, but when power over the Roman Empire fell into Maximian's hands, conversion to Christianity became punishable by death. St. Sebastian was one such convert, and charged with treason, he was bound to a tree, shot with arrows, and left for dead. Mishima found the sight of arrows piercing St. Sebastian's body titillating: "His blood was coursing with an even fiercer pace than usual within his white flesh, watching for an opening from which to spurt forth when that flesh would be torn asunder" (Mishima, 1949, p. 45). In his tense anticipation of the moment life escapes the martyr's body, Mishima reached climax.

A Sensuous Craving for Flesh

Mishima's first love, as he disclosed in *Confessions of a Mask*, was a boy several years his senior named "Omi." It was a love that emerged from Mishima's feeling of incorporeality, for he coveted what he did not possess: "If such a blunt way of speaking be forgiven, it was a love closely connected with desires of the flesh" (p. 61). He writes further: "What I derive from him was a precise definition of the perfection of life and manhood" (p. 64). In Lacan's terms, Omi was the *ideal love-object*, his exuberant strength both respected and feared by his peers. But this "ideal love-object lives on the brink of death, [his] life itself is overshadowed by imminent death" (Zizek, 1991, p. 85). After all, Omi was "Infected with this violent power, his flesh had been put on this earth for no other reason than to become an insane human-sacrifice" (Mishima, 1949, p. 78).

Omi's rule over the meek was absolute. One afternoon, balancing himself on top of a log, the boy challenged his classmates to topple him to the ground; one by one they marched toward defeat. Mishima felt a sudden compulsion to accept the challenge, but within him resided a struggle:

> And this instability was made even more precarious by the fact that within it two contrary forces were pulling at me, contending for supremacy. One was the instinct for self-preservation. The second force—which was bent, even more profoundly, more intensely, upon the complete disintegration of my inner balance—was a compulsion toward suicide, that subtle and secret impulse to which a person often unconsciously surrenders himself. (p. 68)

Mishima hopped on the log and tackled the hulking boy. The challenge ended in a stalemate, with both boys on the floor. It was neither a victory nor a defeat.

The attainment of the ideal love-object is impossible, or rather, strips it of all its luster. In the case of Mishima, attaining the qualities that made Omi so desirable would strip Omi himself of his sublime allure. But there's more.

Because the ideal love-object "is marked by some hidden curse or suicidal madness" (Zizek, 1991, p. 85), Mishima's assimilation of Omi's characteristics would consign him to an eventual, tragic death. For Mishima, the materiality of flesh was a prerequisite for existence, but for existence to be fully realized, the body must eventually and totally be destroyed. A stalemate with Omi was a symbolic endorsement of that flesh. As was the growth of hair in his own armpits, for Omi's abundant growth, which he envied, fascinated him to the point of erection. But these by themselves weren't enough.

Mishima arrived at school one morning to find that Omi was gone; he'd transferred to a different school. The fantasies of beautiful young men dying tragic deaths persisted, with one important elaboration: Mishima was now the executioner of these men. His "victims" included Grecian soldiers, Arabian slaves, army officers and their cadets, hotel elevator boys, and his own peers. In one such fantasy, Mishima knocked a classmate unconscious, stripped him naked, and bound him to a sacrificial altar (a fixture in his fantasies). The classmate was then served as the main course at a dinner party, and as host, Mishima had the honor of the first bite. He thrust a knife into the boy's heart and kissed the boy's lips while the body moved spasmodically. Of the experience, he writes:

> The sacrificial victim must send up long-drawn-out, mournful, pathetic cries, making the hearer feel the unutterable loneliness of existence. Thereupon my joy of life, blazing up from some secret place deep within me, would finally give its own shout of exultation, answering the victim cry for cry. (Mishima, 1949, p. 93)

For Mishima, biological life is not synonymous with *being*, but its mere precondition. The "unutterable loneliness of existence" is satiated by death, which fully endorses the life of whomever it touches. However, feeling bereft of flesh, Mishima was unable to die because he was not existent to begin with. Through sadistic fantasies of sacrificial victims, he was able to imagine possession of flesh and the existential implications of its destruction. The "pathetic cries" of his victims, and his "exultation," were one and the same: a yearning to be material and whole.

REHEARSING AND ACTUALIZING DEATH

Rendering the Self Corporeal

Under his father's orders, Mishima entered the Imperial University to study German law, but his studies were interrupted by draft summons during World

War II. The specter of death loomed large over the battlefield, and the prospect of dying filled Mishima with delight. He "found myself deeply immersed in a desire for death. It was in death that I discovered my real life's aim" (Nathan, 1974, p. 57). But following routine medical examinations, he was deemed unfit for military service because of his poor health and frail constitution. Shortly after, the emperor himself announced Japan's defeat. Being deprived of the chance to participate in battle frustrated Mishima greatly, and he blamed his unfit body, a body undeserving of a glorious death.

Mishima's idealization of the male physique, his personal philosophy of authentication through death, and his postwar plea for war to return—so that he may once again have the chance to die in battle—coalesce in his novella, *Patriotism* (1953). *Patriotism* follows Lt. Takeyama, a young army officer who takes his own life rather than execute friends who'd become insurgents. What is perhaps most noteworthy about this work is the author's painstaking attention to the details of the lieutenant's demise, from its preparation to its actualization.

Lt. Takeyama shaves his face with great care as he readies himself for his end: "There was a certain elegance, he even felt, in the association of death with this radiantly healthy face" (p. 22). The frail body is undeserving of a tragic and violent death; such a death is reserved only for the robust and healthy body, and so the face must be expunged of any trace of sickness. In a subsequent scene, he makes love to his wife Reiko. He savors the sexual act as if it were his own death:

> Was it death he was now waiting for? Or a wild ecstasy of the senses? The two seemed to overlap, almost as if the object of this bodily desire was death itself. But, however that might be, it was certain that never before had the lieutenant tasted such total freedom. (p. 25)

The healthy body is a virile body, and thus, the virile body is also poised for death, hence the conflation of sex with death. In the final scene, the lieutenant commits ritual suicide. Reiko bears witness to the emergence of her husband's existence while hers lies in wait: "But now, while her husband's existence in pain was a vivid reality, Reiko could find in this grief of hers no certain proof at all of her own existence." (p. 47) To render herself existent, she, too, ends her life by slitting her own throat.

Following the publication of *Patriotism*, Mishima ventured to Greece to cure himself of "a sick mind," that is, his obsession with dying (Nathan, 1974). Without a war to give him the salvation he was seeking, he felt an urgency to shake off his decades-long intimacy with death. However, what he found was inspiration for the eventual solidification of his flesh, a means to satiate his unquenched thirst for his own blood. Mishima was captivated by the splendor of classical Greek antiquity, by the statues of Olympian youth and Grecian gods and their perfect bodies. Upon his return to Japan, he engaged in a daily regimen of martial arts and excursions to the gym (Scott-Stokes, 1974). Because death was no longer ubiquitous in his surroundings, he made it ubiquitous in every inch of his flesh. The muscle he attained became an equivalent substitute for war.

The transformation of Mishima's body from pale and sickly to one coursing with vitality was immediately noticed by the public. Also noticeable was the change in tone of his writings. Shortly after his return from Greece, he published *The Sound of Waves* (1954), arguably his only happy novel, one that strays from the pattern of protagonists fated to die or languish in misery. But underneath the joyful front of his brand-new life and work was death's telltale heart, which would soon overwhelm the precarious façade.

Transfiguration of Noh Plays

Some time after publication of *The Sound of Waves*, Mishima began to adapt classic Noh plays for modern audiences. Noh plays faced the threat of extinction when the Shogunate was overthrown in 1868 during the Meiji Restoration (Mishima, 1956). The Shogunate was the originator of Noh plays, and following its abolition, everything symbolic of the old regime was held in contempt by its usurpers. But by some strange twist of fate the plays survived and became classics. Mishima reinvented these classics by infusing them with the themes that haunted him, namely, the ubiquity of death, incorporeality in life, and existence through one's end. One can say that his adaptations bear the stamp of his childhood habit of "correcting" fairy tales and magazine cutouts. Two such plays are exemplary: "The Damask Drum" (1956) and "Hanjo" (1956).

In the classic version of "The Damask Drum," a palace gardener (Iwakichi) falls in love with the princess who resides there (Hanako). Mishima's remake simply swapped the roles for a janitor and a fashion couturiere's client. In both versions, Hanako promises to return Iwakichi's affections if he could beat a drum loud enough for her to hear—a drum covered in damask, and therefore, soundless. Iwakichi fails this impossible task and ends his own life. Here is where the classic and the adaptation diverge. The classic finds Iwakichi returning as a ghost to torment Hanako with the damask drum's beating for the cruelty she had inflicted on him. In the adaptation, Iwakichi does indeed return as a ghost, but not to seek retribution; he beats the drum with the same hope of winning Hanako's love—if not in life, then in death. He tells the audience: "I'm not a phantom anymore. While I was alive I was a phantom. Now all that remains is what I used to dream about. Nobody can disappoint me anymore" (p. 70). Through Iwakichi, Mishima equates a phantomlike existence (i.e., incorporeality) with life, an association nullified by death. What's more, he tells audiences that what cannot be fulfilled in life can be fulfilled in death.

In "Hanjo," a young woman (also named Hanako) loses her sanity after years of waiting for her lover (Yoshio) to return. Day by day she sits on a train station bench, eyeing the faces of the men who pass her by. On their faces she sees only death:

> I don't think anyone has a living face except Yoshio. The faces of all the other men in the world are dead. They are all skeletons. Many, many people with skulls instead of heads and brief cases in their hands got off at the station. (p. 178)

There is an eerie parallel between Hanako's vision of skeletal men and young Mishima's fantasy of "diseases" lurking in his grandmother's home: both evoke the omnipresence of death.

In both the classic and the remake, Yoshio returns to Hanako with a keepsake she had entrusted to him. The classic concludes with a joyful reunion, which restores Hanako to sanity, but Mishima's adaptation ends in tragedy. Yoshio is no longer recognizable to Hanako; she sees him as one of the dead: "The faces of all the men in the world are dead, and only Yoshio's face was alive. You are not Yoshio. Your face is dead" (p. 194). An aghast Yoshio responds: "What! You too are a skeleton. Your face is only bones. Why do you look at me that way with your hollow eyes of bone" (p. 195). At the story's conclusion, Hanako bids Yoshio farewell: "I am alive. I can tell a dead man's face as soon as I see one" (p. 195). In the adaptation, life is envisaged as death, and death is envisaged as life. The living are the walking dead, and Hanako, who in the eyes of Yoshio has ceased to live, feels herself pulsing with life.

Rehearsing the Final Act

The last decade of Mishima's life was a rehearsal of his own annihilation. During this time, he played characters fated for death in both cinematic and theatrical productions, some of which he himself directed. Three examples are notable: *Karakkaze Yarō* (Afraid to Die), *Yūkoku* (Patriotism), and *Hitokiri* (Human Slayer).

In *Karakkaze Yarō* (Masamura, 1960), Mishima stars as Takeo, a *yakuza* (Japanese gangster). The film starts with Takeo being released from jail, only to find himself fleeing from an assassination plot orchestrated by a rival gang. He kidnaps the son of the rival gang's boss, but is shot to death amid a crowd at the film's conclusion.

Yūkoku (Masaki & Mishima, 1966) is based on none other than the aforementioned novella, with Mishima himself playing the role of Lt. Takeyama.

With Mishima codirecting and writing the screenplay, the adaptation hews closely to the original source material. Recall that the novella was written before Mishima's involvement in martial arts; with his renewed physique, one can read his insistence on playing the lieutenant (who commits the ritual suicide of *seppuku*) as rightful claim to a tragic death.

Hitokiri (Gosha, 1969) follows four elite samurai who are striving for Imperial restoration during the Bakumatsu era of Japan—the final years of the Edo period, and thus, the twilight years of Bushido and the samurai identity. Mishima plays Tanaka Shimbe, one of the four *hitokiri*. Like Lt. Takeyama, Shimbe dies by self-disembowelment, making this the second time Mishima practiced *seppuku*.

The Sea of Fertility

The themes that have dominated Mishima's life since his formative years impress themselves upon his final work, *The Sea of Fertility* tetralogy. The four novels follow protagonist Shigekuni Honda from 1912 to 1975—from the time he is a law student in *Spring Snow*, the first installment, to his years as a retired judge in *The Decay of the Angel*, the final installment. In each work, Honda races against time to save successive reincarnations of his friend, Kiyoaki Matsugae, but fails to avert the karmic cycle each time. Although the author himself did not believe in transmigration, the horizons of Mishima's past, present, and future converge in these novels and their characters.

Spring Snow (1966) concludes with Kiyoaki succumbing to a life-threatening illness, his compromised health representing Mishima's blood lust and lack of blood. His death at age 20 is significant because it was the author's age when Emperor Hirohito admitted defeat in World War II. Recall that this was a period of great frustration for Mishima; deemed unfit for military service, he was denied the opportunity to die a glorious death on the battlefield.

In *Runaway Horses* (1968a), Honda meets right-wing terrorist Isao Iinuma, whose extremist politics calls for the restoration of the emperor to the throne. Isao's politics represents Mishima's desire to bring back traditions of old, and with them, the ubiquitous nature of death. Isao dies by *seppuku*—again, the same method employed by Mishima. He is reborn as the Thai princess Ying Chan in *The Temple of Dawn* (1969), who bears the same three moles in the midriff as Kiyoaki and Isao. She dies a horrible death in a fire.

In the final installment of the tetralogy, *The Decay of the Angel* (1970), Honda finds Kiyoaki in Tōru Yasunaga, a sadistic teenager whom he adopts so that he could stave off the boy's death. Tōru attempts suicide by drinking methanol; he is blinded but survives. That he does not die on the appointed day makes Honda question the existence of Kiyoaki in the first place. Something that is genuine is fated to die; if it does not die, it was not genuine to begin with. *The Decay of the Angel* was completed on November 25, 1970, the day Mishima took his own life to assert his authentic existence.

Sun and Steel

Mishima's personal philosophy of corporeality followed by death as a prerequisite to *being* is made fully explicit in his semiautobiographical essay, *Sun and Steel* (1968b). In it he recalls his childhood yearning for "Death and Night and Blood," a yearning that remained insatiate throughout much of adulthood. It was indeed revelatory to Mishima "that the reason why my romantic impulse towards death remain unfulfilled in reality was the immensely simple fact that I lacked the necessary physical qualifications" (p. 75). To metamorphose into a truly existent being, he had to overcome his frail constitution and gain both strength and flesh, which he'd accomplished by the time *Sun and Steel* was written.

In the essay, Mishima likens his situation to that of an apple. Though singular, the apple possesses two layers of existence. The first is superficial, visible to the human eye and reflects color when its opaque surface is struck by light. The second is deeper, impenetrable by human sight, consisting of a core that houses the very seeds of life. To the readers of *Sun and Steel*, Mishima posits this question: How does one reconcile the apple's contradictory existences? His response: "It is for a knife to be plunged deep into the apple so that it is split open and the core is exposed to the light—to the same light, that is, as the surface skin" (p. 63). But this creates a dilemma, because in order to expose the life-bearing core the surface must be sacrificed, the skin irrevocably destroyed.

The phenomenon Mishima describes is analogous to death, a time when the body's end gives birth to another form of existence unreachable during life:

> That, precisely, is when the knife of the foe must come cutting into the flesh of the apple—or rather, the body. Blood flows, existence is destroyed, and the shattered senses give existence as a whole its first endorsement, closing the logical gap between seeing and existing. . . . And this is death. (p. 65)

Mishima closed the gap between seeing and existing by plunging a knife into his own substantiated flesh.

SUMMARY AND CONCLUSIONS

Yukio Mishima's life had been one of struggle in achieving an authentic existence. From birth until the age of 12, he was raised by a sick and domineering grandmother who instilled in him the crude ways of her samurai lineage. Without a mother and father to provide him comfort and affirmation, Mishima felt increasingly incorporeal, which was exacerbated by his grandmother's proximity to death. Confined behind the gates of the Hiraoka household, he felt painfully excluded from the comings and goings of life, and so he began to live vicariously through the (imagined) sorrows of others, filling the void that resided within him. But the act proved insatiable. He developed a thirst for blood that was quenched only by fantasies of men fated to die.

To young Mishima, the first step to feeling alive was to experience the finality of others' lives. After all, to die is to have been alive—an endorsement of existence. He was enamored with young men who possessed the flesh that he coveted, and this realization dawned on him during a chance encounter with a herculean boy named Omi. In his fantasies, Mishima basked in the role of executioner, slaying (in theatrical fashion) princes from distant shores as well as his own unwitting classmates. Deep inside, it was the ecstasy of his own death that he longed to experience.

The subjective experience of incorporeality, the pervasiveness of death, and the longing for death to authenticate one's being were themes that crystallized during Mishima's formative years and were concretized throughout adulthood in his novels and plays. One can say that the characters in Mishima's writings were projections of himself and his fierce struggle to become existent through death. However, it is not the author that dies, but fictional stand-ins who approach finitude with every page turned. His writings were building up the crescendo to authentication, with one final note missing: the author's own death.

Unable to achieve what he was seeking through writing, Mishima continued his project of solidifying the flesh and substantiating the self by practicing various forms of martial arts. Once material, he rehearsed his death in theatrical and cinematic productions by playing the same characters he'd consigned to die in his writings. Eventually, the rehearsal ended, and the day of denouement arrived. At the top floor of the Imperial Palace, Mishima embodied the samurai, the epitome of Japan's martial tradition from a bygone era. Writes Miller (1972):

> Fortunately for Mishima, he was able to blend all his notion about taking his own life with the higher one of thereby serving his country. It was the artist in him, no doubt, that decided to make the best use of death. (p. 11)

Mishima committed the ritual suicide of *seppuku* to convince the people of Japan to wrest themselves free of the Green Snake. In doing so, he resurrected a phantom tradition and finally rendered himself whole.

Chapter 9

"Beauty Is a Dissident Force"

The Case of Reinaldo Arenas

Reinaldo Arenas was a gay Cuban author who wrote defiantly against Fidel Castro's totalitarian regime, earning him a special place in Latin American literature. He wrote 11 novels during his lifetime and was also prolific in other genres, including poetry, short stories, essays, and plays, many neither published nor translated into English until after his death. He is perhaps best known for his memoir, *Before Night Falls* (1993), named one of the 10 best books of the year by *The New York Times* (Echevarria, 1993). It was later adapted into a critically acclaimed film of the same title (2001) by director Julian Schnabel, with Oscar-nominated and Academy Award–winning actor Javier Bardem starring as Reinaldo. He also wrote *Hallucinations* (2001), elsewhere known as *The Ill-Fated Peregrinations of Fray Servando*, whose French translation shared first prize with *100 Years of Solitude* by Garcia Marquez.

Unafraid to challenge the status quo, Reinaldo Arenas celebrated his taboo sexuality and exposed via his writings the extent to which tyranny corrupts people, places, and the very notion of beauty itself. In this chapter, I illustrate the lengths individuals will go to reclaim the freedom denied them—by addressing the far-reaching effects of social and political trauma on Reinaldo's creativity and his creative attempts to subvert that very trauma. I explore the notion of the artist as an agent of social change and the body as a vehicle for enacting that change. Toward that end, I reference his (semi) autobiographical projects to unveil the "secret history" of Cuba and their role in helping him to endure enslavement, captivity, and exile. I conclude with the human meaning of his suicide in the context of his declining health due to AIDS and the larger drama of Cuba's liberation.

COMING OF AGE IN A REVOLUTION

Reinaldo Arenas was born on July 16, 1943. He grew up under conditions of abject poverty during the reign of Fulgencio Batista, whose economic policies widened the gap between the rich and the poor. Reinaldo lived in a *bohio*, a small hut with a thatched roof and dirt floor, with his depressed mother, domineering grandparents, 10 unmarried aunts, three married uncles, and their children. His father, whom he met only once in his lifetime, left his mother before he was born, and she never truly recovered from this betrayed love. The family was so poor that sometimes, dirt was the only thing there was to eat.

As a child, Reinaldo had no books, no literary influences, and no access to formal schooling. Despite his family's poverty, Reinaldo described his childhood in the countryside as "the most creative time of my life . . . a world of pure creativity" (Arenas, 1993, p. 6), his proximity to nature fueling his imagination. The countryside was an enchanted land full of magic and mystery, and to the young Reinaldo, every member of his family assumed a fairy tale–like role. For instance, his grandmother, the family matriarch, was high priestess, a fiercely religious yet superstitious woman who could divine the medicinal properties of herbs through smell and forecast the weather by looking at the movement of stars.

Due to the terrible economy, Reinaldo's extended family was eventually forced to sell their countryside home, marking the end of the best years of their lives. They moved to the desolate town of Holguin, which he likened to a gigantic tomb. Divorced from nature, the young Reinaldo filled time by writing diatribes in which he complained bitterly about his living situation. The family's plight was symptomatic of the larger Cuban predicament, with the poor, dislocated, and disenfranchised becoming increasingly dissatisfied with the regime. Dissatisfaction soon turned into unrest, and finally, into a revolution that sought to overthrow Fulgencio Batista. Reinaldo, by then an adolescent, ran away from home to join a local group of insurgents—not because he believed in their cause, but because he was bored with his monotonous life. However, he was deemed too young and inexperienced by the group, which had long stopped accepting new recruits.

The Batista regime was abolished in 1959 when Reinaldo was 16, and Fidel Castro was installed as the new leader. The dawn of the Castro regime was initially met with celebration. The documentary novel—testimonies against the Batista regime, told from the point of view of the marginalized—came into vogue (Soto, 1994). The new regime promised a Cuba of abundance and introduced reforms in healthcare, economic planning, and education.

The international opinion on Castro was rather divisive, however. In the eyes of his advocates, he was a champion of Western anti-imperialism and humanitarianism; in the eyes of his detractors, he was a tyrant and perpetrator of human rights abuse. The view offered by Reinaldo in his writings leans heavily toward the latter. Public executions of Batista's defeated soldiers were a daily occurrence in the early years of Castro's reign, and there was much lust for blood. In his memoir, Reinaldo recounts the pleas of a grief-stricken mother to spare the life of the man who'd *killed* her own son, to no avail. People accused coworkers, neighbors, relatives, and immediate family members of supporting the fallen regime, even if it wasn't true—in order to curry favor with the new regime, and as payback for the most trivial of slights. "Under a sinister political system," laments Reinaldo, "people turn sinister as well" (Arenas, 1993, p. 82).

Offenders were humiliated publicly and punished unjustly. Women found guilty of adultery were brought to public assemblies, their indiscretions made known to their husbands and kin, while married men with multiple mistresses were spared such proceedings. Laborers in sugar plantations who took a weekend off to visit their families were court-martialed for desertion and sentenced up to 30 years in jail. Free-thinkers, artists, homosexuals, and women who led free sex lives were "rehabilitated" or "parameterized." Rehabilitation involved publicly denouncing one's counterrevolutionary leanings and embracing the regime, while parameterization forced subjects who failed to conform to socially acceptable standards into seclusion. Parameterized men were terminated from employment and brought to forced labor camps, which Reinaldo described as far worse than Dante's last circle of Hell. To escape duty, many resorted to extreme measures, from amputating their fingers to hacking at their legs with a machete.

The Cuban economic infrastructure also crumbled, especially after Castro funneled so much of the labor force toward harvesting 10 million tons of sugar. The plan failed, of course, as his chief sugar adviser predicted, for it had been impossible from the start, making Castro the laughing stock in the international arena. Consequently, Cuba was forced to rely on the former Soviet Union for economic assistance, but with the adoption of Soviet-style Communism, the land ceased to belong to the people. Farmers were stripped ownership of lands that had belonged to their families for generations. Many areas suffered gross neglect, with garbage accumulating for up to three years before it was collected. Use of the beach, which was once open to the general public, now required monthly dues that only the rich could afford.

Castro's regime saw the decline of literature as well, figuratively and literally. Books with seditious content disappeared from libraries, gathered and set ablaze in *Fahrenheit 451* fashion. Castro's definition of counter-revolutionary was quite broad, encompassing books that were nonutilitarian, politically apathetic, and did not advance his regime's cause. Experimental writing was deemed especially bourgeois. Besides the documentary novel, which aired complaints about the previous regime, only the detective novel was considered publishable, for it hewed closely to the ideological formula of citizens and police working together to bring counterrevolutionary villains to justice. The number of published novels dropped precipitously, leading to a chasm within the literary community between those who pledged allegiance to the revolution and those who refused to compromise their artistic integrity and personal vision; the latter were branded "CIA agents" and "agents of cultural colonialism." Reinaldo succinctly but powerfully described Castro's regime as "the drums of militarism stifling the rhythm of poetry and life" (Arenas, 1993, p. 93).

In sum, the Castro revolution replaced one repressive regime with another. As the weeks and months rolled into years, desperate people sought escape, even if it meant risking death. Some swam miles for American shores but drowned. Others tried to cross the electric fence surrounding the American Naval Base in Guantanamo Bay, only to be machine-gunned by Cuban troops. In one striking instance of desperation, two men attempted to hijack a plane and fly it out of Cuba. None of the passengers assisted Castro's police, since they too wanted the plane hijacked; they were later arrested on suspicion of aiding and abetting. Reinaldo knew the culprits personally and dedicated a short story in their honor.

Against this backdrop of political repression, Cubans were committing suicide en masse. Some jumped from balconies and splattered against pavements; others slit their wrists and throats or swallowed poisonous concoctions. The suicides were disproportionately women, homosexuals, writers, and other creative types, who chose to end their lives to reject a life of continuing compliance. In a place where expressive freedom was stifled, suicide was the only authentic action possible, but one could argue that it was also a form of surrender, a tragic sequel to compliance. For the years and decades to come, Reinaldo would choose resistance through literary channels.

LITERATURE AS POLITICAL SUBVERSION

Reinaldo himself realized that the free education he was receiving was indoctrination and militarization, thinly disguised. For instance, in order to pass as an agricultural accountant, a student must be deemed physically fit to climb mountains. The man of numbers (or letters) was also trained to be a man of arms. After graduating from the Universidad de la Habana, Reinaldo worked in the National Library. It was during this time that his desire to be a writer crystallized. He was not only surrounded by books, but he discovered two mentors in Lezama Lima and Virgilio Piñera—both homosexuals and both writers of international acclaim who wrote critically of the Castro regime.

Piñera, for example, wrote a damning story in which a prized diamond called Delfi (anagram for "Fidel") is discovered to be a fake and is flushed down a toilet.

Lima and Piñera held clandestine meetings where writers could share works-in-progress. Reinaldo himself was not openly counterrevolutionary, at least not in the beginning; he initially hid his rejection and disdain of Communism. But over time, due in part to the writing community he now belonged to, his writings became more and more transgressive, until he himself fell out of favor with the regime. Reinaldo saw totalitarianism as anathema to creativity: "Under a dictatorship, beauty is always a dissident force, because a dictatorship is itself unaesthetic, grotesque" (Arenas, 1993, p. 87). He described creativity as a "mysterious visitation," demanding the writer to be vulnerable and have faith in his words. For Reinaldo, the task of the writer is to describe the world, in all its horrors, through the eyes of the very people the regime sought to eliminate. He would rather be branded a traitor than be called a law-abiding citizen.

As mentioned, the documentary novel was one of few literary forms approved by the government. The regime praised the genre for its documentary realism, its linear chronology, and its use of official, historical documents, like news clippings and photographs, to authenticate the testimony contained therein. When studying Reinaldo's works, one cannot take for granted the formal and technical aspects of his writings. Form can be just as transgressive as content, especially in a country where freedom of expression is sought rather than given, and where the definition of art is tightly regimented by the state. Thus, deviations from literary conventions can themselves be forms of protest, and the novel the site of fierce ideological battles, which Reinaldo was prone to wage.

Like the documentary novel, many of Reinaldo's novels also take the form of testimonies. However, their protagonists are individuals marginalized by the *Castro* regime (mostly homosexuals), *not* the Batista regime. Sometimes the narrator is not one character but many, calling the reliability of the testimony into question. Occasionally, Reinaldo would paste real but frivolous documents (like receipts) onto his manuscripts to satirize the abundance of bureaucratic documentation so prevalent in revolutionary Cuba. Rather than past tense, his stories are often narrated in *present* tense, heightening immediacy and the sense that oppression is ongoing, with no foreseeable end in sight.

In his writings, *subjective* truth takes precedence over realism and objective truth. For Reinaldo, no truth is neutral, and sometimes, there is more truth in fiction than what poses as verifiable history. His novels alternate between dreams and reality, waking moments and fantasy, with real and imagined characters walking alongside one another, suggesting that the real and the imagined are both legitimate experiences. Death is not always the end for his characters; a character who dies in one page might return in the pages that follow, behaving as if nothing tragic had happened. As absurd as this may seem on the surface, the underlying message is that for subjects of totalitarian regimes, what is most frightening isn't death, but the notion that suffering is never-ending. Totalitarianism is the abyss of madness itself, institutionalized.

Consistent with his antidocumentary stance, Reinaldo eschewed linearity and causality. His novels are seldom told chronologically and instead adopt a fragmentary dramaturgy that reiterates events from different perspectives and from alternating timelines, in the style of Akira Kurosawa's film *Rashomon*. For instance, *Hallucinations* (*El mundo alucinante*) (2001) has three versions of the first chapter, while the Prologue to *The Color of Summer* (*El color del verano*) (2000) can be found midway through the 400-page novel. Just as importantly, the structure of his works is inextricable from their emotional tone, and the novella *Old Rosa* (1989) is most exemplary.

This 100-page work is divided evenly between two connected stories, "Old Rosa" (*La vieja Rosa*) and "The Brightest Star" (*Arturo, la estrella mas brilliante*). The first follows the titular character as she loses the land (and with it, her sanity) that had been in her family for generations after Castro's rise to power. The second follows Old Rosa's son, Arturo, who is locked up in a concentration camp for homosexuals, where he, too, loses his sanity. "Old Rosa" is told in a single unbroken paragraph, while "The Brightest Star" is told in a single unbroken *sentence*. Readers are not afforded the solace of a paragraph break in the former or a period in the latter. The effect is one of dangerous immersion, and possibly, submersion and suffocation so that readers acutely feel the sense of entrapment felt by the characters.

Every now and then, Reinaldo would blend the tragic with the comedic. He described humor as one of humanity's fundamental gifts: "If we lose our smile, we don't have anything" (quoted in Soto, 1994, p. 152). For Reinaldo, the serious tone of the documentary novel has a distancing effect, whereas humor comes closer to evoking reality. He used his writings to launch scathing attacks on Fidel Castro, on "friends" and neighbors who had informed on him, and on writers who won literary prizes for supporting the regime. For example, the heterosexual protagonist of a documentary novel, or the presumably heterosexual author of said novel, might make a cameo appearance in an Arenas novel dressed in drag. A number of his attacks take the form of obscene tongue twisters that became popular throughout Havana despite (or perhaps because of) their assault on conservative tastes. *The Color of Summer* is especially rife with them; of the 115 vignettes constituting the novel, 30 are tongue twisters. One in particular calls into question the sexual orientation of the author Miguel Barnet, thinly disguised here as "Barniz":

> Bibulous Barniz, like some burlesque burgher, stood imbibing beer in a bar in Borneo . . . when a bearded Bedouin . . . putting back bourbon after bourbon, tipped his biretta and proffered him his prominent protruberance. Barniz, bedazzled by the Bedouin . . . put by his beer and imbibed the bubbly brew produced by the barbarian's protruberance. Oh, what a bubbly brew the bibulous Barniz imbibed! (Arenas, 2000, p. 115)

The vignette describes a bar encounter between "Barniz" and a Bedouin that ends with fellatio, which excites the former greatly—an implication that would have given the real-life Barnet great displeasure.

This level of obscenity is not unusual in Reinaldo's writings. In another novel, *The Assault* (*El asalto*) (1994), the narrator-protagonist of a dystopian society slays the "Represident" with his own member, causing the tyrannical dictator to explode. It is unsurprising that none of Reinaldo's novels ever saw the light of day in Cuba. No reputable press would have dared to publish a novel that skewers Castro and provides hyperbolic depictions of gay sex. But Reinaldo's novels did see the light abroad, with the help of foreign friends who smuggled them out of Cuba. For example, *The Palace of the White Skunks* (*El palacio de las blanquisimas mofetas*) (1990) was smuggled out as a botany book by a group of French surrealists. Although they were well-received overseas, Reinaldo did not receive a single *peso* for his efforts.

THE LITERARY AND THE EROTIC

The suppression of creativity in Cuba was accompanied by widespread sexual repression. Hotels rented rooms to heterosexual couples only, and as mentioned, homosexuals were sent to concentration camps disguised as rehabilitation camps. But this sexual repression provoked an equal but opposite response: a sexual counterculture and revolution. There was a huge surge in sexual activity between young men; while most practiced discretion because informants were everywhere, even in the home, some took their romps to the public—on treetops, in public transit, in the back of pickup trucks, and in plain sight of astonished onlookers. Reinaldo participated heavily in these escapades. "I came to the conclusion, after complicated mathematical calculations, that I had sex with about five thousand men," he writes in his memoir (Arenas, 1993, p. 93). "We would perform erotic maneuvers worthy of professional tightrope walkers . . . The erotic and the literary went hand in hand" (p. 101).

It is too easy to dismiss these romps as needless risk-taking or promiscuity, to suggest that Reinaldo had a death wish because his sexual acts were putting his life and reputation on the line. But if we were to honor Reinaldo's own embodied experiences, we would instead find that erotic contact, like writing, was both a celebration of existence and resistance to forces of domination. By participating in the sexual revolution, Reinaldo was engaging in a queer world-making practice through which a repressive, heteronormative society is creatively navigated, and in which the formation of queer social relations becomes a strategy for survival. As Rivera-Servera (2012) writes about queer Latino/a sexualities: "Latino/a queer spaces are not always physical structures dedicated to such an identity. They are often times *claimed* through practices of quotidian as well as activist intervention" (pp. 29–30). In other words, embodied practices such as dress, style, speech, gesture, and movement, including sexual movements, can extend the boundaries of oft-circumscribed and oft-hidden queer spaces, however tenuously. Thus, in the context of Fidel Castro's Cuba, sex is not merely sex, but the embodiment of resistance and the possibility of change. But resistance seldom goes unpunished, and unfortunately for Reinaldo, his sexuality would land him in forced labor.

TWICE IN CAPTIVITY

In 1972, Reinaldo was parameterized for his blatant homosexuality. For a year, he endured brutal living conditions and forced labor in a sugar plantation, which he documents in the narrative poem *El central* (1984). Reinaldo was able to write *El central* because a friend named Reinaldo García-Ramos—whom he refers to as "R" in the book's dedication—smuggled 87 "clean white pages" into the camp. *El central* conjures violent imagery like eyes lost to the sharp ends of sugarcanes, backs bloody from lashings, hands lopped off by sugar-mill machinery, and fingers broken from scratching endlessly at the ground, clearing more land for more sugarcanes in order to meet Castro's insane project of raising Cuba's sugar output exponentially. Under such conditions, the "highest aspirations are for a hat or a pair of sun glasses" (p. 57), to defend oneself against the sun's unbearable heat and light, and the only solace to be found lies "in the midday halt for a drink of dirty water" (p. 44).

El central is not solely about sugar mills, however. It is a work in which two epochs meet, in which past and present Cuba interweave. In order to illustrate history's circularity, Reinaldo juxtaposes the brutal conditions in Castro's beloved sugar mills, with the colonization of indigenous Cubans and enslavement of Africans by Spanish conquistadors. Natives were flogged, as were slaves, as were forced laborers. The cargo of Africans was transported by ship; the cargo of Cubans was transported by bus. Natives filled the pockets of rich landowners, who centuries later would sweeten their coffee with sugar cubes made by blistered hands. In both epochs, lives were ended at the whim of the whip holder; in both epochs, the banner of progress was violence, thinly disguised as domestication of the "wild" African, redemption of the indigene's soul, and creation of the Cuban national subject.

For Reinaldo, creativity and imagination were critical to survival. As he writes in *El central*: "We continue working on you, poem,/ above the hysteria of the crowd/ and beyond the slogans from the loudspeakers" (p. 90). To write is to resist enslavement of the spirit, to keep "memories from rusting" (p. 50) and speak the unspeakable, for "a place were nothing can be told is a place where the most must be told" (p. 56).

A yearlong stint in the sugar mills did not deter Reinaldo, and over time, through his writings, he continued to say the unsayable, becoming a real thorn in Castro's backside. Because Castro feared international scrutiny and backlash, execution of Reinaldo was out of the picture, and so the Cuban government falsely charged Reinaldo with the murder of an old woman and the rape of a young girl, landing him in El Morro.

Of all the concentration camps, El Morro was among the worst. The cells were filthy, with feces and urine reaching up to the ankles. Guards employed ruthless interrogation tactics, often locking prisoners inside cells filled with hot steam. The inmates were equally ruthless, resorting to violence and murder at the slightest provocation, including slitting the throats of sleeping inmates. Reinaldo attempted to end his life inside El Morro by overdosing on the hallucinogenic drugs he'd smuggled from outside. Fortunately, he failed. In order to survive, he wrote prodigiously inside his cell using the pens and papers he'd also smuggled. His manuscripts were destroyed upon discovery by guards, but he painstakingly rewrote them. To protect himself from the aggression of the other inmates, he taught them how to speak French and wrote love letters on their behalf, putting himself in their good graces.

Reinaldo led a celibate life in captivity. On the surface, this seems counter to his belief that the literary and the erotic went hand in hand. However, love-making in prison was for him an act of subjugation to the state; "love has to be free, and prison is a monstrosity where love turns into bestiality" (Arenas, 1993, p. 187). In captivity, the symbolic meaning of sex was inverted, and celibacy now occupied the same semiotic space sex had vacated.

The Cuban government was quite fickle in deciding the official grounds for his prosecution. During trial, attempts to indict him for the corruption of minors failed miserably, mainly because the adolescent who was bribed to testify against him, testified on his *behalf* instead. Had Reinaldo been found guilty of this charge, his sentence would have been indefinite, as opposed to two years for "lascivious abuses," a sentence that was lengthy enough for such a vague charge.

ESCAPE AND EXILE

Upon his release from El Morro, Reinaldo discovered that so many manuscripts he'd stashed in secret locations or entrusted with others had been found, confiscated, and destroyed. He also realized that he could no longer delay his escape from Cuba. Flash forward to 1980, the Cuban people were now so dissatisfied with the Castro regime that thousands sought asylum in the Peruvian embassy. In response, Castro opened the port of Mariel. Those who wanted to leave, including homosexuals, could leave. As far as he was concerned, these so-called degenerates were no longer his concern, with the exception of intellectuals. Writers and degree holders were especially dangerous to be let out of the country because they posed the greatest threat to Castro's international reputation. They were blacklisted from leaving, and this list included Reinaldo Arenas.

What was Reinaldo to do? Fortunately, Cuba's identification system was not so sophisticated at the time. He changed his last name on his ID by replacing the "e" with an "i" so that it read "Arinas," a perfectly viable Spanish surname. He went to the port of Mariel, told the guard that he was homosexual, and was subjected to a series of psychological tests designed to ascertain the validity of his sexuality. The psychologist on site asked if he was on the giving or receiving end; he said receiving. The man then asked him to walk a straight line, to which he gave the most flamboyant shuffle. By the time the police suspected anything, he was already in the middle of the sea on a voyage to distant shores.

Miami, Florida was his first stop, but he felt no happiness there. He felt like an exile among exiles because from his point of view, Miami's Cuban literary community had abandoned its obligation to expose the regime's tyranny. Topographically, Miami resembled Cuba, but the similarities ended there; it was a pale imitation of his homeland. His next stop was New York City, and in the beginning he was mesmerized—by the diversity of its people, by its tall skyscrapers, and by the winter snow. But the dirty beaches of New York were nothing like Cuba's warm blue seas, a contrast made even more stark by winter's icy temperature.

To make matters worse, Reinaldo was horrified by the pro-Castro attitude shared by the intellectuals there, who sang praises of Castro's social welfare programs. Meanwhile, publishing houses that made fortunes from his writings, without him seeing a penny in return, were now telling him he never should have left Cuba. No longer a "suffering artist," they were less inclined to publish his works. But Reinaldo did continue to suffer:

> An exile has no place . . . because the place where we started to dream, where we discovered the natural world around us, read our first book, loved for the

first time, is always the world of our dreams. In exile one is nothing but a ghost, the shadow of someone who never achieves full reality. (Arenas, 1993, p. 293)

Exile had a derealizing effect, and he felt trapped between past and present, dream and waking reality. He felt grief and longing for Cuba, to which he could never return. What was he to do but to scream: "I scream, therefore I exist" (p. 301). And so he screamed, with his body and with his pen, to maintain his tenuous existence.

THE PENTAGONIA

Reinaldo cruised for sex in New York as he did in Cuba. Unfortunately, the United States was in the grip of the AIDS epidemic, which he contracted. AIDS made writing and living increasingly burdensome. He fell ill with pneumonia, Kaposi's sarcoma, phlebitis, and toxoplasmosis (blood poisoning), requiring multiple hospitalizations. Speaking through one of his characters in *The Doorman*, he writes: "What is freedom when your body is weak and racked by all sorts of diseases? Freedom would become as meaningless and loathsome as life itself under those conditions" (Arenas, 1994b, p. 157). Given its systematic and cruel way of killing, he suspected that AIDS might have been man-made, and he interpreted the silence surrounding it as a concerted effort by those in power to eliminate the marginalized, in this case, homosexuals.

He was in a race against time, his sense of urgency captured by the title of his memoir, *Before Night Falls*. He refused to die until his two "autobiographies"—one of his own life, and one of Cuba—were complete. And if he were to die, it would be on his own terms. He once received rat poison in the mail, with a note urging him to end his life. It had presumably been written by someone unhappy with his writings and his dissident spirit. The incident only sparked his determination to continue writing until his body no longer allowed it.

Reinaldo was dead set on finishing his magnum opus, the Pentagonia. Also known as the "Five Agonies," the Pentagonia is a quintet of novels that is both autobiography and "secret history" of Cuba. Though works of fiction, they are, in Soto's (1994) words, "valid testimonies of human dignity in the face of oppression" (p. 40). At over 1,500 pages, the content of these works is beyond the scope of this chapter, but their overarching themes and characteristics warrant a passing remark.

With the exception of *The Assault* (1994a), the final installment (more on this ahead), the protagonists find themselves at the receiving end of an abusive totalitarian system, and they must invent new selves and new worlds to survive their hostile surround. For instance, *Singing from the Well* (1987), the first installment, is told from the perspective of an imaginative child who seeks refuge from his tyrannical grandfather (a stand-in for Castro) in a fantastical world of his own making. *The Palace of the White Skunks* (1990), the second installment, puts readers in the shoes of a dissatisfied young man who joins the revolutionary usurpers of Batista's fallen regime. *Farewell to the Sea* (1985), the third installment, follows a homosexual who is forced to lead a double life as a happily married man; the novel, his confession, is told in verse, illustrating at the meta-level the power of creativity to unveil falsehood. The protagonist perishes in each work but is symbolically reborn in the next installment with the same purpose: "to sing the horror and life of the people" (Soto, 1994, p. 40), to affirm creativity's enduring power over repression.

The novels also affirm the power of creativity through its style and form. *Singing from the Well* blurs the line between dreams and reality, illusion and fantasy, with recently deceased characters returning to life several pages later—an affront to the documentary novel's commitment to verisimilitude and factuality. *The Color of Summer* (2000), the fourth installment, a tongue-in-cheek "celebration" of Castro's 50th year in power, throws the documentary form's linearity out the window by putting the novel's chronological beginning in the middle. And again, *Farewell to the Sea* is a novel told *as* poetry. Thematically, the sea is a recurring motif, representing freedom through imagination and the expanse of the human spirit.

The Assault is remarkable in that its protagonist is not one of the marginalized, but a high-ranking official of the fictitious Bureau of Counterwhispering. This protagonist takes delight in prosecuting "whisperers," individuals who allegedly speak ill of the regime, an offense that is punishable by death. He is in search of his mother, whom he believes to be a mastermind whisperer, so that he could "liquidate" her and earn the praise of the Represident himself (that the head of state is called Represident speaks volumes). By casting such a detestable person in the role of narrator, the author is able show the extent to which a corrupt regime can warp personality.

The satirical novel imagines a fictionalized Cuba in the not so distant future. In this dystopian society, there are only two social roles: accuser and accused. People are but animals whose "eyelids are always half closed" out of fear that "if they open their eyes completely they could offend some agent" (p. 19). Sex is devoid of passion and meaning, enacted only for the utilitarian purpose of procreation; a Breeding Permit is required and the coupling is timed and watched by agents. Only once a year are people allowed "to forget . . . that they themselves are vermin" (p. 76), and that is during the Represidential anniversary (or Represiversary). On this day, it is permissible to hunt down and exterminate cockroaches, to transfer one's oppression onto lesser creatures.

The Assault brings the quintet to a finish by having the regime collapse under its own weight. The nameless protagonist finally secures an audience with the Represident, only to discover that the Represident is none other than his mother. In what can only be described as a preposterous turn of events, he attacks and slays her with his member, whereupon "she explodes in a blast of bolts, washers, screws, pieces of shrapnel-like tin, gasoline, smoke, semen, shit, and streams of motor oil" (145). Witnessing this, the crowd below returns to their senses, killing every agent in sight. Such is Reinaldo's wish for Cuba—for the tyranny to engulf and ultimately destroy itself.

It took Reinaldo 30 years to complete the Pentagonia, with the first installment written when he was only 22. Subsequent installments had to be rewritten multiple times because they were confiscated and destroyed by Castro's police, with *The Color of Summer* alone undergoing five iterations. For this reason, the quintet was never published in the intended order. His persistence in ensuring that his works survived, when others would have surely given up, is a testament indeed to the moral and creative courage (May, 1975) he possessed.

DEATH AND LEGACY

Before his death, Reinaldo sent copies of a handwritten letter to his friends and various news outlets. The letter, appended to his memoir, reads:

> Due to my delicate state of health and to the terrible emotional depression it causes me to not be able to continue writing and struggling for the freedom of Cuba, I am ending my life. During the past few years, even though I felt very ill, I have been able to finish my literary work, to which I have devoted almost thirty years. You are the heirs of all my terrors, but also of my hope that Cuba will soon be free. I am satisfied to have contributed, though in a very small way, to the triumph of this freedom. I end my life voluntarily because I cannot continue working. Persons near me are in no way responsible for my decision. There is only one person I hold accountable: Fidel Castro. The sufferings of exile, the pain of being banished from my country, the loneliness, and the diseases contracted in exile would probably never have happened if I had been able to enjoy freedom in my country
>
> I want to encourage the Cuban people out of the country as well as on the Island to continue fighting for freedom. I do not want to convey to you a message of defeat but of continued struggle and of hope.
>
> Cuba will be free. I already am. (Arenas, 1993, p. 317)

One need not look beyond this letter to apprehend Reinaldo's reasons for ending his life. He had completed his lifelong projects, and his ailing body had no more words to offer. His suicide is neither defeat nor surrender but emancipation, and his letter, an indictment of Castro and a call to arms, mobilizing Cubans at home and overseas to continue the struggle for liberation.

Reinaldo Arenas died in his Manhattan apartment on December 7, 1990.

Chapter 10

The Drama of the Disintegrating Self

The Case of Robin Williams

On August 11, 2014, a dark cloud descended: Robin Williams, the man who had brought joy into millions of homes throughout the world, was pronounced dead. He had taken his own life. Countless people took to social media to express their profound sadness and loss; in his tribute to the fallen actor and stand-up comedian, former U.S. president Barack Obama encapsulated America's collective grief as follows:

> He was an airman, a doctor, a genie, a nanny, a president, a professor, a bangarang Peter Pan, and everything in between. But he was one of a kind. He arrived in our lives as an alien—but he ended up touching every element of the human spirit. He made us laugh. He made us cry. He gave his immeasurable talent freely and generously to those who needed it most—from our troops stationed abroad to the marginalized on our own streets. (quoted in Kaplan, 2014, p. 4)

Making his debut on the hit TV sitcom *Mork & Mindy* (1978–1982) as an alien from planet Ork, Williams would go on to perform in the big screen in a number of starring roles—from radio disc jockey Adrian Cronauer in *Good Morning Vietnam* (1987), to the gender-bending Daniel Hillard/Euphegenia Doubtfire of *Mrs. Doubtfire* (1993) fame, to widower and psychotherapist Sean Maguire in *Good Will Hunting* (1997), for which he won an Oscar for Best Supporting Actor.

As his decades-long career illustrates, Williams's acting possessed both breadth and depth. He was capable of inhabiting a multitude of roles, and through his embodiment of those roles eliciting a range of emotions from viewers. One moment, as the Genie of *Aladdin* (1992), he provokes uncontrollable laughter with his wild voice impersonation of 52 distinct characters. The next moment, he elicits both fear and pity as a lonely photo technician whose obsession with a particular family takes a decidedly dangerous turn (*One Hour Photo*, 2002). Williams had "the ability to go from manic to mad to tender and vulnerable" (Dougan, 1998, p. 176), and so immersed was he in his roles that during the filming of *Mrs. Doubtfire*, members of the cast and crew, and the general public, treated him as if he really were an old lady.

But as Obama's tribute makes clear, the world did not only lose a talent; it lost a kindred spirit. Robin Williams was not only a good actor but a good human being. When Christopher Reeves of *Superman* fame was in the hospital following the tragic horseback-riding accident that rendered him quadriplegic, Williams, in full regalia, arrived as a Russian proctologist, bringing laughter back into his best friend's life. Similarly, when Steven Spielberg fell into a deep depression during the filming of *Schindler's List*, Williams spent countless nights on the phone lightening the director's dark moods with his irreverent humor. His uncanny ability to make others feel better, including those with the most sour disposition, would earn him the nickname "Doctor of Soul" (Associated Press, 2015, p. 123).

His spirit of generosity extended to strangers as well, evident in his involvement in charitable causes like the Challenged Athlete Foundation, which provides prosthetics to athletes with disabilities, and the Starbright Foundation, which endeavors to make the wishes of terminally ill children come true. Throughout his career, Williams also took part in six United Service Organizations tours, entertaining more than 89,000 servicemen and women stationed across 13 countries (p. 111). And with his good friends Billy Crystal and Whoopi Goldberg he founded Comedy Relief, which raised funds for the homeless. Unlike many celebrities, however, Williams was unconcerned with cultivating a star persona; he did not take on too many causes to avoid diluting his involvement's significance. The men, women, and children who had the pleasure of meeting him also described him as genuine and personable. He was not one to refuse an autograph, and according to one of his biographers, "even his worst detractors had to concede that he was an exceptionally generous man" (Herbert, 2014, p. 148). He genuinely wanted to make people laugh and smile.

THE VERDICT

The suicide of Robin Williams was unfathomable to those who conflated the life with the work, for he was the quintessential happy man in their eyes. Those more familiar with his biographical life made sense of the suicide by recourse to the actor's substance abuse history; he'd been spotted in a rehab facility just months prior to his death, after all. But as Susan Schneider, Williams's third and latest wife, pointed out, Williams entered the facility not because he had relapsed, but to reinforce his commitment to sobriety (Yahr, 2014). And there's no reason to doubt her testimony to the press; toxicology reports revealed zero traces of drugs and alcohol in his system. Aside from substance abuse, the news offered two other explanations for the suicide: Williams's diagnosis with Parkinson's disease and Lewy body dementia (LBD) (which I will return to shortly), and his "mental illness."

"This is an important story about a horrific disease: depression," wrote one commentator (Vislocky, 2014, p. 24). "America has to wake up and realize this is as serious as cancer, and more funding and awareness has to be raised." According to a staff writer at *The Christian Science Monitor* (Goodale, 2014), depression, alongside drug addiction, make up the "twin demons" of Williams's career. Psychiatrists, both armchair and accredited, took to the soapbox as well. "We have to be ever mindful that depression is a real disease, it is common, it is serious, but it is treatable, and we have to keep talking about it," says Dr. Harry Croft (quoted in Monde & Pesce, 2014, p. 6). "It's a brain disorder, and it can affect anybody—the rich, the famous and the rest of us." This disorder can make people "forget all the wonderful things in their lives," according to Dr. Julie Cerel (quoted in Weintraub & Kelly, 2014, p. 3D). "Having depression and being in a suicidal state twists reality. It doesn't matter if someone has a wife or is well loved."

The verdict, it would appear, is that depression "killed" Robin Williams. But others qualified the diagnosis by claiming that Williams was not only depressed but manic as well. More specifically, he was hypomanic. "Hypomania is exhibited in creative people, and successful entrepreneurs," says Dr. Susan Biali (quoted in Stewart, 2014, p. 38). "They're fast talkers, full of energy, funny, don't need a lot of sleep—and their lives are often functioning very well. But it may alternate with bouts of depression." In his letter to the editor of *The New York Times*, Dr. Henry J. Friedman (2014) says the death of Robin Williams highlights "the importance of differentiating types of depression, particularly bipolar from other types of depressive disorders" (p. 18).

The greatest irony in all of these efforts to pinpoint Williams's brand of mental illness is that the actor himself never admitted to being mentally ill. He once told Terry Gross on NPR's "Fresh Air" (quoted in Stewart, 2014):

> No clinical depression, no. No, I get bummed, like I think a lot of us do at certain times. You look at the world and go, "Whoa." Other moments you look and go, "Oh, things are OK." Do I perform sometimes in a manic style? Yes. Am I manic all the time? No. Do I get sad? Oh yeah. Does it hit me hard? Oh yeah. (p. 38)

The above testimonials, which are representative of the wider coverage of Williams's death in high-circulation papers, operate from the assumption that mania, depression, and mental illness in general are endogenous in origin, arising from *within* the individual—specifically, the human brain. The illness takes a life of its own as if the sufferer were possessed by a demon. What's significant is that the experts make no reference to the concrete details of Williams's life, *except* when looking for confirmation of the illness. They also have no qualms about diagnosing someone who had never set foot in their clinic or office. Williams's exuberance on stage or in front of the camera is but a symptom of (hypo)mania, for example. His creativity is all but pathologized, and his suicide is framed as a depression-induced failure in reality testing; he was well-loved but could not *see* that he was well-loved, nor could he see that he was mentally ill. His death is mobilized in a call to arms to destigmatize mental illness, but in doing so the actor is depersonalized, reduced to abstractions and generalities bearing little semblance to the complexities of his life. Furthermore, his own perspective into his condition—his attribution of depression to very *human* causes—is rendered invalid.

When it became known that Williams had been diagnosed with Parkinson's in November 2013, and may have been exhibiting symptoms as early as 2011 (Bender, 2014), and when the coroner's report later revealed a severe case of LBD (Schneider, 2016), few commentators pointed their fingers at these culprits. But rather than ask what Parkinson's or LBD must have *felt* like from the perspective of Robin Williams, they were more concerned with how the conditions, and the medications used to treat them, might have exacerbated his clinical depression and anxiety (Brown, 2014)—again, without reference to the concrete details of his life. In order to apprehend the role of neural degeneration in Williams's decision to die, it's important to consider the life-worlds of persons with these conditions, in their own subjective terms—for how they interpret the bodily experience of losing their mobility and communicative ability, and the meanings they assign to such an experience.

THE PHENOMENOLOGY OF NEURAL DEGENERATION

Parkinson's is a movement disorder resulting from abnormalities in the extrapyramidal motor system and associated pathways (Marr, 1991), and its main symptoms—collectively referred to as the "symptom triad" (Whitehead, 2010, p. 30)—are tremors, muscle rigidity, and slowness of movement (bradykinesia/hypokinesia). The course of this neurodegenerative disease is 10–25 years, and it is comprised of five stages—Stage 5 being the most severe, with the afflicted rendered so immobile s/he is bound to a bed or wheelchair.

The condition assaults values we hold dear in contemporary American society, "such as independence, competence and decency" (Nijhof, 1995, p.

199). Due to loss of strength and manual dexterity, and the gradual yet painful transition from normal mobility to complete immobility, daily activities such as writing, buttoning one's shirt, tying one's shoelaces, maintaining one's hygiene, preparing meals, and driving automobiles, progressively become more difficult if not dangerous and require tremendous effort. Many individuals with Parkinson's speak of shame when discussing their condition and their growing reliance upon others, and those who depend upon their bodies for their livelihood are especially devastated. Their sense of physical competence is assailed, and unable to partake in roles and activities that once held meaning, their notion of self is radically altered, supplanted by a sick role. Being labeled as "disabled" creates a fissure between past and present selves and can greatly diminish one's sense of self-worth (Martin, 2016).

Parkinson's calls into question the unity between mind and body, for the intact mind is suddenly trapped within an uncooperative body, a body that refuses to look and behave in socially valued ways and capitulate to the person's will (Bramley & Eatough, 2005). When one is unable to speak normally or hold back one's saliva when speaking, or project the emotion one genuinely feels due to rigid facial muscles, one cannot help but feel subjugated by one's own body. While drug therapy can control the symptoms of Parkinson's and lengthen the period of physical independence (though not indefinitely), long-term use can produce untoward side effects like hallucinations and further motor problems like dyskinesia, a state of extreme involuntary movement which causes the limbs to jerk and the face and torso to twist. In other words, even when the symptoms of Parkinson's are attenuated via medication, the body continues to feel alien and unnatural, as if it does not belong to oneself. Moreover, the medicated body is felt by individuals to be in a state of constant flux and unrest—between movement and movement loss, between mental agility and cognitive lethargy.

The disease also thwarts one's ability to communicate verbally and nonverbally. As I mentioned, there is a decrease in the mobility of facial muscles, resulting in what is commonly known as the "mask" or "stare" of Parkinson's (Martin, 2016, p. 313). Reduced facial expressiveness, in concert with stuttering, slurred speech, lowered volume and clarity, and difficulties with sustaining attention, can produce much anger and frustration. It is deeply saddening when one's words and thoughts, once forthcoming, are suddenly choked, held captive within the solitary prison of one's body.

The afflicted can feel especially stigmatized by others. Some express concern about the misattribution of symptoms to deviant behavior—for instance, being perceived as nervous or dishonest when one is trembling or sweating profusely during a stressful encounter, or being perceived as drunk when one misses a step and falls (Martin, 2016). Many resent feeling infantilized, treated as helpless, feeble, or senile, and addressed in a condescending or patronizing manner. Because their partners and loved ones must now shoulder increased responsibility for their welfare, persons with Parkinson's may feel themselves to be a burden. To counteract negative evaluations by others, some engage in activities that test the new limits on their bodies in perilous ways.

To avoid being treated differently, individuals may attempt to "pass" as persons without the disease (Martin, 2016; Nijhof, 1995). One might hide one's trembling hands in one's pockets or behind one's back, for example, or restrict one hand with the other. Attempts to conceal or disguise symptoms can backfire, however. As one person explains, "I look worse when I disguise it because I'm doing contortions" (Bramley & Eatough, 2005, p. 230). When unable to hide symptoms, and when unable to publicly present themselves in ways that align with their desired image of self, the individual might avoid social interaction and withdraw from public view altogether, so as not to risk further embarrassment or shame. Combined with a more tightly regimented life in which periods of rest and activity are planned, the feeling of being under constant surveillance, and the subsequent retreat from participation in social life, can lead to a deep sense of isolation and shrinkage of one's world.

In sum, Parkinson's calls into question one's relationship to self, world, and other. The loss of automation exposes the fragility of the human body, undermining one's agency and sense of security. Avenues for the creative expression of self are stifled by the disjuncture between mind and body. The self is devalued by the stigma of disability, and the world in which one dwells, once expansive in size, is suddenly diminutive. Thoughts of the distant future are truncated and life is lived on a moment-to-moment basis.

I do not paint such a grim picture to suggest that disability is a death sentence or to imply that persons with Parkinson's cannot live a rich and meaningful life in the company of loved ones. Far from it. Rather, I paint such a picture to illustrate how Robin Williams might have experienced Parkinson's, whose symptoms he concealed for three full years prior to his suicide, and whose impact he must have felt long before an official diagnosis, as is the case for most persons with Parkinson's (Marr, 1991). We must bear in mind that for actors and stand-up comedians like Williams, the body itself is the medium, the vehicle for the expression of a creative vision—in his words, "another colour you get to paint with" (Herbert, 2014, p. 172). Because his profession requires the use of the body in its *entirety*, someone as gifted in the expressive arts of performance and rhetoric is sure to suffer greatly when that body is suddenly faced with imminent deterioration. Williams was a fast talker, adept in the arts of mimicry and gesticulation, with a face that could capture pathos, bliss, and every shade of feeling in between. Parkinson's would have undone the very foundation of his craft.

Three months after Williams's suicide, the coroner's report revealed that the actor was suffering from LBD—a diagnosis he was not privy to in life. As his wife Susan Schneider (2016) explains, "Clinically he had PD, but pathologically he had diffuse LBD" (p. 1310). The two conditions fall within the same spectrum of diseases, but on opposite ends; both involve the presence of Lewy bodies, which are responsible for neural degeneration, but unlike Parkinson's, persecution by LBD is swift and merciless. It would appear that Williams was not only losing control of his body; he was losing his mind, and he was painfully aware of it. Billy Crystal (quoted in Herbert, 2014) had said that Williams's "brain is the one thing that's kept him buoyant" (p. 208). But now, the man who once memorized hundreds of lines for the 2011 Broadway production, *Bengal Tiger at the Baghdad Zoo*, could not remember a single line when filming *Night at the Museum 3* four months prior to his suicide. "I just want to reboot my brain," he would say to his wife (Schneider, 2016, p. 1309).

Williams's mind and body were under attack, and in the following excerpt, Schneider provides a more concrete picture of his deterioration:

> Robin was growing weary. The parkinsonian mask was ever present and his voice weakened. His left hand tremor was continuous now and he had a slow, shuffling gait. He hated that he could not find the words he wanted in conversations. He would thrash at night and still had terrible insomnia. At times, he would find himself stuck in a frozen stance, unable to move, and frustrated when he came out of it. He was beginning to have trouble with visual and spatial abilities in the way of judging distance and depth. His loss of basic reasoning just added to his confusion. (p. 1309)

Williams was reportedly sleeping up to 18 hours per day, barely able to climb out of bed (Dillon, 2014). He'd become so reclusive that he installed blackout curtains in his bedroom, the darkening of his world mirroring the darkening of his soul. "Can you imagine the pain he felt as he experienced himself disintegrating?" asks Schneider of her readers (p. 1309).

It should be apparent by now that the imminent deterioration of body and mind contributed to Williams's suicide. However, this tells us nothing about what acting and comedy *meant* for him, besides the obvious fact that they were the source of his livelihood. In order to arrive at their meanings, and to apprehend what was truly at stake for him, we must go even deeper, to the formative years of his life.

THE POWER OF PERFORMANCE

Robin Williams was born on July 21, 1951, to Robert, a senior executive at Ford, and Laurie, an aspiring model and philanthropist. He described his parents as emotionally and geographically distant. They were often away on business or at charitable causes, leaving him under the constant care of nannies. Though he had a privileged upbringing, his childhood was one of unremitting loneliness: "I lived in that big house and I was pretty much alone . . . I was kind of out in a big farm in the country way away from everybody" (Herbert, 2014, p. 154). To complicate matters, he was bullied in school for being short, shy, and stout. Though he had two half-brothers from his parents' previous marriages, they were much older and not very close, and so he made imaginary friends. He reportedly had a massive toy collection, consisting of two- to ten-thousand toy soldiers who kept him company. Though the numbers may have been exaggerated, they nevertheless reveal a need to satisfy an intense longing for human connection, a need that would persist in adulthood.

Williams spent much of his childhood seeking his parents' attention and approval, and in this pursuit, he discovered the power of comedy. His first ever impersonation was of his grandmother, whom he mimicked so accurately, and so irreverently, that his mother was reduced to tears. Comedy thus became his means of sustaining ties with his mother: "I think maybe comedy was part of my way of connecting with my mother—'I'll make Mommy laugh and that will be okay'—and that's where it started" (p. 31). If he could make her laugh, he could win her love. It was also a means of breaking through his father's tense exterior, a distant and pragmatic man who recognized his talents and would later finance his pursuit of acting. Above all, comedy would become Williams's primary means of relating to others:

> And since I was suffering from a case of the terminal shy I couldn't make friends that easily, and I always spent a lot of time in my room and I created my own little world full of all these little characters that had strange and unusual qualities. After a while, I realized that people found these characters funny and outrageous, and then it got to the point where I realized the characters could say and do things that I was afraid to do. (Dougan, 1998, p. 71)

Later in life, Williams confessed to a severe case of "Love Me Syndrome" and an acute fear of abandonment—both rooted in childhood, and both quelled by acting and comedy. In making others laugh, he felt loved, and in feeling loved, he felt less alone. Williams felt most alive when seen by others.

It is not surprising that Williams starred in the role of "man-child" in a handful of movies—a role that fuses together the adult body with the innocence and naïveté of a child. To name but a few examples: In *Hook* (1991), Williams starred as Peter Banning, a father and corporate lawyer who had forgotten he was Peter Pan, and in remembering, rediscovers the magic of his childhood and the magic that continues to surround him. He then starred as Alan Parish in *Jumanji* (1995), a child who becomes trapped in the fantastic world of the titular board game, reemerging decades later as an adult unschooled in the ways of civil society. And in *Jack* (1996), Williams played the role of a 10-year-old boy with Werner syndrome, which causes his character to age four times faster than the average person. The significance of these roles stems not from his authorial control over the script, which varied from movie to movie, but in the resonances between them and his childhood's subjective reality. By Williams's own admission, Jack's lonely childhood, and difficulty making friends, mirrored his; and like young Alan Parish, he was often by himself in a big old house. Meanwhile, playing Peter Banning made Williams realize how little time he had with his parents growing up—a mistake he vowed not to repeat with his own children.

Some have interpreted Williams's embodiment of the man-child as proof of his arrested development. According to one of his biographers, "He never stopped portraying the man-child because he never stopped *being* the man-child" (Herbert, 2014, p. 237). However, such a statement ignores the restitutive power of creativity in the actor's life. Williams himself espoused the view that creativity can be cathartic, a means of addressing personal trauma in a genuine way. It was also his breakwater against deep depression and anxiety: "You look at the world and see how scary it can be sometimes and still try to deal with the fear. Comedy can deal with the fear and still not paralyze you or tell you that it's going away" (Associated Press, 2015, p. 51). By starring as a man-child, Williams not only laid bare the injuries of his past to be empathically received by others; he was also reconciling past with present, acknowledging the enduring impact of his childhood experiences on adulthood.

Obviously, Williams played other roles besides the man-child, which are beyond the scope of this brief study. But the point stands that for Williams, acting and comedy fulfilled the ontological needs of emotional validation and human connection. It is therefore unsurprising that he mined his personal life for material for his stand-up comedy. It is also unsurprising that whenever he performed at college campuses, he would ask the event organizers to place toys of their choosing on the stage, which he incorporated into his act. In doing so, he recapitulated the loneliness of his childhood and the comfort he'd derived from his company of toy soldiers. But in doing so, he was simultaneously *undoing* the loneliness, for he was now partaking in communal laughter.

It is even less surprising that Williams fell into a deep depression after the cancellation of the NBC sitcom *The Crazy Ones* in May 2014, three months prior to his suicide. His career started in television 31 years prior with *Mork & Mindy*, and it seemed that it would end in television. Williams begged for clemency, to no avail. Though the show's cancellation after one season was due to a mediocre script and fledgling ratings rather than the quality of Williams's acting, it was nevertheless felt as radical invalidation of his being. And with his mind and body literally disintegrating, Robin Williams took his life—to thwart the complete eradication of self, and to reclaim agency where it had been lost, so that death, if not life, became his own.

Interlude IV

The Medicalization of Life and Death

As human beings, there is perhaps nothing more terrifying than the thought of our own mortality. From birth onward, every second that elapses brings us closer to life's endpoint. The most nihilistic among us may even see living as nothing more than being in transit. But most of us aren't nihilists. We are taught early in life that existence is to be celebrated. We bemoan the minutes and seconds lost to the drudgery of work, and when the opportunity arises, we throw ourselves onto the path of adventure with reckless abandon. Try as we might to deny it, we are the protagonists of our own narratives.

Our fear of death recedes into the vista, visible but in the periphery, like the moon at daytime. But this fear lies waiting at the threshold of consciousness, for the moment in which background suddenly becomes foreground. All it takes is a little perturbation: the evening news sensationalizing a gruesome traffic accident, or tomorrow's paper with its listing of the recently deceased. And yet, despite periodic reminders of death's arbitrariness and inevitability, and despite our own admission that we *know* we will die someday, the mere resumption of our daily lives makes us forget the reality of our end. The death of the other, often rendered spectacular in fictional and mass media, remains in its own province, far removed from the perimeters of our comparably mundane lives.

But there are some experiences that cannot easily be shaken off, firsthand encounters that make death linger on the rim of consciousness, longer than we are comfortable with. Chronic and excruciating pain. Physical victimization. Diagnosis of a life-threatening illness. The death of a loved one. Suicide.

Suicide is an affront to our most deeply held assumptions about life, an assault on our ontological security. We tell ourselves that our instinct is directed toward the *preservation* of life, not its cessation. The mere thought that the decision to live is reversible, that suicide is free will in its purest and darkest form, is unsettling to us. So what are we to do, but to frame suicide as an anomaly, a perversion, a sickness?

FROM MORAL TO MEDICAL

In the Western world, centuries prior to its association with so-called mental illness, suicide was framed as a failure in morality, an act of deviance or crime (and in many parts of the world today, such as the Islamic Middle East, it is *still* considered a crime). For instance, in Dark Age Europe, suicide attempts were punishable by death, and the material possessions of actual suicides were confiscated by the state rather than bequeathed upon surviving family members (Alvarez, 1973). The depravity of suicide was so severe that the living refused to bury the dead, fearing that physical contact with the decedent's impure body would invite further misfortune, or worse, Death himself. To keep the soul of the deceased from finding its way back to the realm of the living, the body was sometimes buried at a crossroads with a stake through the heart, or in an isolated part of the cemetery under an unmarked grave.

With advances in science and technology, particularly in the arena of medicine, the moral model of suicide slowly gave way to a medical one, though traces of the former continue to linger today. For instance, the words "attempt" or "commit" have retained their criminal overtones when invoked with "suicide," although recent ethnographic work (e.g., Flanigan & Alvarez, 2019) suggests that "commit" remains deeply meaningful to suicidal persons, for it connotes agency and choice as opposed to criminality. But by and large, the rhetoric of crime has been replaced with a rhetoric of illness; rather than criminalized, suicide has become *medicalized* in civil society. The root metaphor (Hillman, 1997), or archetypical role, governing medicine is the promotion of life, under which threats to biological continuity must be averted at all costs. For such threats to be neutralized, they must first be made tangible and concrete. Modern medicine and its specialists have made suicide tangible by locating it within the cells of the body, the human brain, and the double helix of the DNA.

The extent to which mental illness and suicide are driven by endogenous and exogenous factors is subject to continuing debate, and there is ample support for and against the scientific basis of the biopsychiatric (i.e., medical) model. But rather than engage in that debate here, I have decided instead to call readers' attention to why the medical model is embraced so widely in the United States, and to a lesser extent, Western Europe; why Americans treat mental health conditions and suicide as if they are the outcome of heredity and biology; and why attempts to reconcile the nature and nurture positions (e.g., two-hit hypothesis, stress-diathesis model) still assign primary importance to genetic vulnerability and only secondary importance to tragic life circumstances. I then draw attention to the personal and social consequences of our unquestioning compliance to the medical model, and its ramifications for suicidal persons and the so-called mentally ill, whose lifeworlds and creative contributions we jettison. I conclude with a plea to recognize our death denial and remediate our *technocratic mindset* so that we may be able to listen more deeply and truly.

THE MEDICAL MODEL'S ALLURE

The biopsychiatric model continues to hold appeal for several reasons, both psychological and structural. At the individual level, it exonerates clinicians and family members who have lost a patient or loved one to suicide from responsibility. The pain of being a suicide survivor lasts a lifetime. Unlike deaths due to natural and accidental causes, which are the outcome of forces beyond human agency, suicide leaves in its wake questions of culpability and preventability. By ascribing suicide to so-called mental illness, to endogenous forces arising from within, the burden of responsibility is lessened for survivors, even if only slightly. However, guilt is never fully assuaged; it is only masked or disavowed.

Curiously, people who suffer from profound psychological distress are among the biggest advocates of the medical model. As Szasz (2007) suggests, being medicated validates their status as sick patients in need of compassion, care, and support, and it assures friends and family members that they are being rendered harmless to others and to themselves. I will also add that diagnosis with a mental health condition can give unity and coherence to the chaos of madness, giving some sense to experiences that had previously been senseless. For people whose mania, depressed mood, delusions, hallucinations, and addictions—"the psychiatric conditions most intimately linked to suicide" (Jamison, 1999, p. 168)—appear to arise from nowhere, the medical model supplies a coherent narrative that locates the cause of the illness and offers prescriptions for change. After all, a concrete problem can be more readily dealt with than a nebulous one, a matter of turning on (or off) the proper switches in the brain or DNA.

Unfortunately, the adoption of a sick role may inadvertently result in the abrogation of personal responsibility. In a *New Yorker* article, staff writer Louis Menand (2010) relates the story of a woman who, upon recovering from depression, accused her therapist of taking what she had said too seriously. "It was the depression talking," the woman protested. By internalizing such labels as depression, bipolar, or borderline (now a defunct diagnosis), one essentially *becomes* the disease. Agency and self-determination are surrendered to the disease, which is understood as exerting control over every aspect of the individual's life.

As mentioned, the medical model promises actionable solutions. If suicide is due to mental illness, and mental illness is a biological aberration, a bona fide disease rooted in neurotransmitter activity gone awry, then it can be abolished from the face of the earth. In contemporary American society, psychopharmacology is the magic bullet, a powerful talisman in our arsenal against the many incarnations of death, which can be dispensed with swiftness and en masse. Many patients are expected to be on medications for the rest of their lives, despite the fact that the drugs they are taking—drugs that alter cortical activity in ways yet unknown—have been tested in clinical trials lasting no longer than six to eight weeks (Breggin, 2008; Reznek, 2016; Whitaker, 2003, 2010).

At the structural level, the medical model supplies a universal language for mental health professionals. Depression is depression and bipolar is bipolar for the clinical psychologist, the biopsychiatrist, and the social worker alike. In theory, the existence of a central, unifying discourse means that miscommunication is minimized and the success of concerted efforts to treat patients maximized.

Financial considerations play a significant role in keeping the gears of the medical model spinning. Although many in the field of psychiatry are empathetic listeners willing to acknowledge the limitations of science, there is no denying the allure of glowing sums of money, not when biopsychiatrists derive much revenue from pharmacologic counseling alone, with individual consultations lasting as little as 15 minutes (Breggin, 1994, 2008). The mother of David Foster Wallace, the infamous author of *Infinite* Jest who hanged himself in 2008, lamented that her son's first visit to a psychopharmacologist lasted a mere three minutes (Max, 2009). Pharmaceutical companies provide the bulk of financial support to organized psychiatry, and medical schools accept money from Big Pharma, which trickles down to professional publications being pressured into exaggerating the effectiveness of drugs and downplaying their adverse side effects. Big Pharma supports much research into the efficacy of modern treatment (largely chemical based), often with the predictable results that such investments would yield. Even the activities of grassroots advocacy groups, including the National Alliance on Mental Illness, are underwritten by drug companies. As it stands, it can be very difficult to disentangle profit motives from a genuine desire to ameliorate suffering and promote well-being.

The alliance between medicine and state, or what the late Thomas Szasz (2007) called *pharmacracy*, ensures that the machine is well oiled. The medicalization of madness and suicide legitimizes them as subjects of rigorous scientific inquiry. This attracts state and federal funding to support the activities of scientists and academics in university and laboratory settings. In turn, empirically validated treatment forms—psychopharmacology, electroconvulsive therapy (ECT), psychiatric hospitalization—which privilege efficiency and expediency, are generously reimbursed by health insurers, while social rehabilitation and psychotherapy get little to no coverage unless paired with a regimen of drug treatment. Professionals who refrain from prescribing the routine course of treatment run the risk of being sued for malpractice and nonadherence to standards of care, a risk that rises dramatically if a patient were to attempt or commit suicide.

ON STIGMA AND FATALISM

Presumably, the biopsychiatric model reduces the societal stigma of suicide by lessening the social distance between those who are mentally ill and those who are not. Paired with the rhetoric of epidemic, which inflates prevalence estimates by administering diagnostic surveys to community members who aren't even in treatment, and includes millions of people who are reacting *appropriately* to stressful life circumstances (Horwitz & Wakefield, 2007), a sense of shared humanity is created. We are brothers and sisters united by a common public health problem, one that could affect *anyone*—directly if one has been diagnosed, and indirectly if one has an afflicted family member.

However, there is growing evidence to suggest that the model might actually achieve the opposite outcomes. For instance, Mehta's study (cited in Watters, 2010) finds that people who espouse endogenous explanations for their condition elicit *less* sympathy and greater hostility from others, and they may be faced with the additional challenge of finding companionship, love, and acceptance. As she explains, viewing people as inherently flawed "sets them apart and may lead to our perceiving them as physically distinct. Biochemical aberrations make them almost a different species." People who espouse psychosocial explanations, on the other hand, are treated with empathy and protected against the charge of being weak so often directed at the mentally ill. In other words, it is not disease that unites, but relatable human experiences. Disease may actually alienate.

If the so-called mentally ill is seen as subhuman, it stands to reason that the suicide or suicide attempter is also seen as subhuman—by the general public, and at times, mental health professionals themselves. About Virginia Woolf, one psychologist disparagingly remarked, "There was enough mental illness in this family, past and present, to keep a psychiatric hospital in business" (Kottler, 2006, p. 107). This same author described Sylvia Plath as a "hopeless case" (p. 30), and Judy Garland (an equivocal suicide) as "one of the most notorious therapy failures in history" (p. 44). One hopes that his condescending attitude does not extend to suicidal persons entrusted with his care.

"Geneticizing" mental illness suggests that there is something about the person that is immutable. The attribution of conditions like depression and schizophrenia to biogenetic causes can result in what Phelan and colleagues (2006) call *prognostic pessimism*, the belief that the afflicted will never get better. Following this line of thought, the attribution of suicide to endogenous causes can likewise engender *fatalism*, and we find this in so many biographical accounts. For example, in her biography of Iris Chang, Paula Kamen (2007) writes that Iris's bipolar disorder "was so extreme in the end that it was comparable to an advanced cancer, a far-gone tumor" (p. 271), calling it the "main villain" and downplaying the role of "her grisly subject matter" (ibid.). She wonders if Iris had been aware of her genetic susceptibility, or if her family had even "shared" this information with her, as if they had privileged access to her genetic blueprint. Curiously, Ying-Ying Chang (2011), Iris Chang's mother, disagrees with the diagnosis of bipolar disorder and suspects that the symptoms Iris exhibited might have been produced by the medications she was taking, which is consistent with Whitaker's (2010) observation that conventional psychiatric treatments often produce the symptoms they were meant to alleviate.

We see such pessimism again in Shneidman's (2004) writings on "Arthur," a book-length primer on the psychological autopsy method and a reconstruction of the decedent's plunge into suicide. According to Arthur's best friend, "the chemistry in the brain is off" (p. 94), which is corroborated by Shneidman's own remark that "Genes and fortune bent Arthur to his end" (p. 163). Arthur's former psychiatrist is equally fatalistic: "I vividly remember his first visit because my impression was, clearly, that someday he was going to commit suicide" (p. 143). There is a sense that the suicide could not have been averted, and we can trace the allure of biological predestination to the need for closure, a need to mitigate the impotence and guilt brought forth by devastating tragedy.

It is not unreasonable to think that altercasting the so-called mentally ill and suicidal person as subhuman justifies their cruel and inhumane treatment under the guise of care. The history of psychiatry is itself a catalog of such treatment, which included bloodletting, ice baths, insulin therapy (which induces hypoglycemic comas), and transorbital lobotomy, which severs the connection between the frontal lobe and the rest of the brain by shoving an ice pick through the eye sockets (Whitaker, 2003). Less severe but similarly degrading, one can add to the annals of psychiatry the embarrassing removal of front teeth. Virginia Woolf had several teeth extracted by a specialist who subscribed to the "focal infection theory," a belief that maladies both physical and psychological were caused by a nest of bacteria in the teeth's roots (Brooks, 2012).

Today, we have the likes of ECT, which unleashes upon the brain enough electricity to power industrial machinery, well beyond the range of human physiology, and which has a scathing effect on human creativity and autobiographical memory (Breggin, 1994). It destroyed the actress Frances Farmer's (another suicide) ability to act, and Ernest Hemingway could not write a single sentence after being subjected to multiple rounds. David Foster Wallace himself received a dozen rounds, all of which proved inefficacious (Max, 2009). ECT can be so terrifying to those who have experienced it firsthand that many would opt to die rather than suffer another round.

IMPLICATIONS FOR SYMBOLIC EXPRESSION

Biogenetic explanations for mental illness and suicide may reduce blame by placing the locus outside the person's control. However, they may also increase perception of the individual's dangerousness (Kvaale, Haslam, & Gottdiener, 2013) and result in withdrawal of social support, harsher treatment, and interpersonal isolation. Even though suicidal ideation is a normal response to overwhelming situations, deeply depressed people have a difficult time opening up about their thoughts and feelings when these are taken as signs of genetic inferiority and moral failure. When words are choked, the person is robbed the opportunity to partake in the communality of living, to have one's story heard and acknowledged by empathetic others. Rather than dissipate, the suicidal impulse festers and grows as a result.

I agree with Reznek (2016) when she writes: "We have evolved into the quick fix culture. We want results now and we don't care how they are achieved. If something can be achieved easily, rather than with effort, dedication, and hardship, we take the easy route" (p. 120). The emphasis on expedient treatment forms that privilege rapid symptom elimination, at the expense of longer-term engagement and care, precludes important stories from being told and *owned*. Even when the words are forthcoming, we render ourselves so numb to the feelings elicited by loss that the words fail to move us. Or we plumb stories for symptoms so that the other remains an "other," even though "the vicissitudes of life naturally produce much depression, anxiety, and grief" (Horwitz, 2002, p. 159). We are no different from the people who marveled at the naked emperor's new clothes. When we think someone is mentally ill, we look for the symptoms that corroborate the illness—even when the symptoms aren't there, and even when doing so devalues the person's life. The discourse on suicide in particular is abundant with "disease sniffing" of the highest order, and creative people are among its favorite targets.

For example, Vincent van Gogh has been diagnosed with no less than 150 (and still counting) physical and psychiatric disorders by scholars of all stripes (Maire, 1971). Just as astounding, the authors of these pathographies ruthlessly dissected his paintings in their search for symptoms of the presumed disorder. Similarly, when Iris Chang's suicide became news, her relentless quest to rescue historical truth from oblivion was reframed by mass media as mania, and Robin Williams's exuberance on stage and on the screen was likewise treated as such. I am not suggesting that mania doesn't exist, for mania is a very real and harrowing phenomenon. Rather, I'm suggesting that instead of looking *for* symptoms, that we look *at* symptoms as metaphors, as veiled references to the tragic circumstances that gave birth to them in the first place. The symptom is not the end of the story. It is the beginning. But we live in a time and place "where talking to people and getting their life story is considered passé" (Reznek, 2016, p. 114).

Sadly, human creativity, that timeless expression of our collective and innermost being, has also become medicalized. Many scholars speak of the link between creativity and so-called mental illness. They speak of the creative edge bipolar disorder and psychotic states confer, such as increased productivity, defiance of societal conventions, indifference to audience expectations, elevated mood, which may sharpen creative thinking, and combinatory thought, in which incongruous images and ideas are merged (Jamison, 2003; Nettle, 2001). While suffering and creativity are in many cases joined at the hip, medicalizing creativity has the tragic outcome of reducing symbolic expression to illness manifestation. Instead of attempting to see the world as it is seen by the suffering artist, the misunderstood misfit, the deviant extraordinaire, many contemporary studies are nothing more than glorified fishing expeditions, the catch being an official diagnosis.

When creativity is pathologized, suffering is also romanticized, stripped of its horrific brutality and reality. In an interview with Tim Jonze (2014) of *The Guardian*, the American singer-songwriter Lana Del Ray, when discussing Amy Winehouse and Kurt Cobain, remarked: "I wish I was dead already." The implication was that stardom is synonymous with suffering, tragic death with iconicity and immortality. Frances Bean, daughter of Kurt Cobain, took to Twitter with this impassioned message to Del Ray: "The death of young musicians isn't something to romanticize. I'll never know my father because he died young and it becomes a desirable feat because people like you think it's cool. Well, it's fucking not." Indeed, there is nothing alluring about Cobain putting the barrel of a shotgun in his mouth and squeezing the trigger.

Above all, the articulation of creativity (and suicide) with so-called mental illness conceals the fact that we are all inherently creative, and that we all suffer at some point in our lives. If we are to believe Hillman (1997) that the seeds of life and death reside within each other, then to medicalize creativity and suicide is to devalue life and death. Symptoms that appear nonsensical, or as mere by-products of disease, become intelligible when situated within the context of an individual's story and lifeworld. Many people who suffer from psychosis speak in "gibberish" that, once decoded, reveal hidden landscapes of pain, suffering, neglect, betrayal, loss, but also, love, beauty, creativity, humanity, and life. The same can be said of the most abstract of paintings. What does one make of Mark Rothko's use of bleak colors in the months leading to his suicide? Much, if one listens to the language of his canvas, for his paintings contain "all my feelings about life" (quoted in Ravin, Hartman, & Fried, 1978, p. 78).

TECHNOCRATIC DEATH DENIAL

We have stopped listening to stories, and instead, convinced ourselves that death and misery can be banished from the body, that true happiness is available in pill form. We are forever adding new talismans to our growing arsenal against death. Our situation is comparable to that of vampire slayers, but instead of crucifixes and vials of holy water, we have machines that unleash electricity upon presumably defective brains. But we are not slaying vampires, nor can we slay death, for it is built into the fabric of human existence.

Make no mistake, we should do everything in our power to prevent a suicide. I do not deny the testimonies of people who can attest to having been helped by existing treatment regimens and the medical model writ large (e.g., Casey, 2002; Wurtzel, 1994). The problem is not the application of science and technology to many arenas of life and death, but what Moller (2000) calls the *technocratic* mindset, which privileges efficiency and rationality without consideration of "the moral and cultural consequences of technological dependence" (p. 54). As I argue elsewhere (Alvarez, 2017), this technocratic mindset has given way to a technocratic *death denial* that is visible in visual culture, behavioral medicine, and end-of-life care. Death is rendered spectacular in fictional and mass media, people are anesthetized to the affective dimensions of loss, and those marked by death, including suicidal persons, are hidden behind institutional walls. Sequestration of the so-called mentally ill is indeed a new spin on timeless fears of death contagion.

As Becker (1997) points out, the fear of death undergoes rather complex "elaborations" and "transmutations": in our conformity to and secure dependence on societal norms; in our relentless search for answers to the most puzzling questions life generates; and in the American urge to *heroism*, to stand out and be of greater value than anything or anyone else. I would not go as far as Becker to suggest that fear of death underlies every waking human activity, or that it demands the daily expenditure of much psychological energy (Zilboorg, 1943). But I do agree with Becker that what he calls "utopian science" bears some responsibility in camouflaging, through denial, humankind's terror of mortality.

Technocratic death denial reduces humans to mere assemblages of raw materials, to component parts of a larger social machinery, which continues to justify subhuman treatment of the so-called mentally ill. We need to remediate this mindset so that technology is used in the service of humankind, in order to facilitate creativity, symbolic expression, and deep listening. Toward that end, we *should* stare at the black sun of death. We should stare at the shadows it casts, but most importantly, at the person upon whom its harsh lights fall.

Conclusion

And so, we have reached the end of our journey together. Throughout, we have seen that creativity can fold unto itself the horizons of past, present, and future. We have also seen that creative work is paradoxical in that it can protect one from the brunt of trauma, yet act as a vector of trauma and retraumatization. Of course, creative work can be enlisted in the service of healing, especially when used teleologically and in the context of a facilitative intersubjective surround. Otherwise, Death takes the hand of the creator, leading them to the maw of the abyss.

We have seen, too, that suicide can be a means of authenticating the self (in the broadest possible sense), despite the simultaneous negation of self it entails. As I have illustrated, the symptoms of suicidal depression are themselves concretizations of threats to selfhood that the act of suicide seeks to overcome. Paradoxically, creativity can serve similar psychological purposes, by concretizing threats to self and efforts at self-restoration. Taken together, creativity and suicide can both authenticate the self, and I argue that this synonymity may underlie their coexistence.

I also argue that the medicalization of suicide and creativity is itself paradoxical. In our highly technocratic and elaborate attempts to thwart suicide and forestall Death's knock on our doors, we inadvertently (or perhaps willfully) disavow life. Although organized psychiatry, pharmacracy, and the like are partially responsible for the dismissal of suicide narratives and reduction of creativity to illness symptoms, the blame also falls heavily on our shoulders. We stigmatize and trivialize because it is much easier, and more preferable, than staring into the abyss.

But what do we see when we decide to take a long, hard look? To answer that, let us revisit the lives—and deaths—of the 11 phenomenal individuals to whom I have dedicated the last 13 years of my life.

TRAUMA AS PRELUDE TO CREATIVITY

It goes without saying that all 11 people featured in this book were intensely creative during their lifetime, although their commitment to their craft manifested at different points in the life cycle. All experienced trauma and loss, though the nature of such experiences, and the ways in which these informed and were addressed by their work, exhibit many variations.

Eight of the 11 used creativity to work through personal crises that have origins in their formative years. For Phyllis Hyman, Kurt Cobain, and Theresa Duncan, creativity validated the emotional truth of a shattered childhood. It was also their ticket out of an intersubjective surround that was hostile to their needs. Theresa swam her way through written words to faraway lands, her narrative video games encapsulating her quest for emancipation. She was silenced as a child, and in creating, she sought to overcome that silencing. The songs of Phyllis evoke the family dysfunction of her Pittsburgh home and her deep desire for its undoing. The same can be said of Kurt's music and the enduring impact of his parents' divorce, which produced in him a state of *homelessness* in both physical and existential senses of the word.

For Robin Williams and Yukio Mishima, creativity fulfilled the ontological need for human connection that was felt to be largely absent in childhood. Robin grew up feeling alone in a big empty house, his care relegated to nannies by his geographically and emotionally distant parents. Through comedy and acting, he found a way to connect with his mother, and eventually, the larger human and social surround. Yukio's case is more extreme. Sheltered by a strict and overbearing grandmother who descended from a samurai lineage, Yukio felt no connection to others whatsoever, and therefore, unalive. Through writing, he could experience others' suffering, and in the process, flicker into being.

Others enlisted creativity in the project of mourning, memorializing, and in some cases, resurrecting the dead. Jeremy Blake memorialized his father in several of his artworks, which serve as elegies, or lamentations for the dead. Alan Turing became a serious mathematician and scientist to keep the love of his childhood alive and later create an artificially intelligent body to house the boy's spirit, in essence resurrecting him. Sylvia Plath's poems, which she crafted to please her father when he was still living, became a conduit to his resurrection. It also assumed the purpose of grief work; prohibited from attending his funeral and his grave, she wrote poetry (and memoir disguised as fiction) to communicate the depths of her loss.

For the remaining three—Iris Chang, Kevin Carter, and Reinaldo Arenas—creativity authenticated not only the truth of individual experience but that of collective human suffering and memory. This is not to deny the resonant power of individuals like Sylvia Plath, whose confessional poems spoke to female subjectivity, or Kurt Cobain, whose grunge music echoed the angst and alienation felt by an entire generation. But the aforementioned three *directly* addressed nefarious agents of historical revisionism in order to expose ruthless regimes, validate the experiences of the downtrodden, and rescue truth from oblivion. In short, they used historical trauma as material for their works for subversive purposes.

Iris set the record straight by exhuming the bodies of the Rape of Nanking, to everyone's horror, including her own. In doing so, she restored a crucial portion of Chinese history to its rightful place. Through photography, Kevin exposed the horrors of apartheid South Africa, authenticating the lived reality of Blacks, whom he treated as his reference points. Eschewing documentary forms, Reinaldo used satirical fiction to launch scathing attacks on Fidel Castro's regime and its marginalization of peripheral others. In a parallel act of creativity, he also used his virile body to contest the wholesale political and sexual repression of his time.

CREATIVITY AS PREQUEL TO TRAUMA

The salvific powers of creativity are undeniable. It can validate the emotional truth of profound experiences, including and especially traumatic ones. It can be a vehicle for mourning and making sense of losses, individual as well as collective, and through it, feel the continuing presence of lost others. And it can fulfill various ontological needs, including human connection, a sense of purpose and agency, and a feeling of continuing aliveness. But as the 11 case studies illustrate, there are limits to creativity's restorative power, and in several unfortunate cases, it can beget more trauma.

The most obvious examples come from Kevin Carter and Iris Chang. Both worked with extremely dark subject matter. The primary trauma of bearing witness to the "hostel wars" between opposing factions of Black South Africans made Kevin question his moral adequacy, which was compounded by his prize-winning photo of the "little girl" and the vulture. How ironic that photography endowed him with purpose after his first suicide attempt, only to traumatize him so. Iris never witnessed the horrors of Nanking or Bataan, but she was vicariously traumatized by prolonged encounter with archival records of the dead and oral testimonies of the living. Worse, she began to see the world through the lens of massacre victims, making her intensely paranoid. If creativity can bridge past and present, then this bridge flooded Iris with the memories and feelings of the dead.

Both Kevin and Iris were so empathetic they felt the physical and emotional suffering of their subjects. For them, creativity served as a bridge between self and other as well, and with this came attendant dangers. But one need not work with terribly dark subjects to experience the contagious effects of creativity. Jeremy Blake's creative partnership and relationship with Theresa Duncan deepened the bond between them, to the extent that whatever tumultuous feelings she felt, he too felt.

One outcome of creative work that targets systems of inequality and suffering is that one becomes the target of those very systems. It's unclear to what extent Iris was hounded by right-wing extremists and ultranationalists, but at the very least, she was on the radar of two global superpowers (Japan and the United States). Something similar can be said of Theresa's adversarial relationship to the Church of Scientology, though her work was never expressly social justice–oriented. Reinaldo Arenas also painted a target on his back with his transgressive fiction and embodiment of gay identity, but from his point of view, creativity was not a source of trauma. On the contrary, it was sustaining and life-giving, helping him to endure forced labor, imprisonment, and later, exile.

For those who mine or exploit personal traumas in their creative work, it can run the risk of repetition without resolution, if not retraumatization. For Phyllis Hyman, Kurt Cobain, and Sylvia Plath, creativity was authenticating while also *reactivating*. The nuclear crises of their lives were transposed onto their art, which in turn were transposed back onto their lives. Phyllis sang of finding and losing love, and countless times did she find and lose love in life. Kurt repeated the trauma of his fractured childhood in his music (and in his drawings), and he was extremely sensitive to threats to the integrity of his new family. Sylvia sought to resurrect Daddy in her poetry, only to realize that continuing to tread this path will eventuate in deathly reunion.

But even when it reactivates past trauma, creativity allows for the imagination of pathways to alternative (if not better) lives. The form, function, impact, and meaning of creativity in a person's life is fluid rather than static. For Sylvia, the symbolic function of creativity changed from reunion with to exorcism of father, and from supplication to repudiation of mother. In order for her to thwart engulfment and remain agentic, such a change had to occur. For Iris, Phyllis, and Kurt, the promise of undoing trauma's devastation of the self manifested in other generative acts: the miracle of conception and birth and the creation of a new nuclear family. When one creative pathway to emancipation becomes impotent, other pathways take its place. Multiple pathways can also be active simultaneously.

But sometimes, creative work isn't enough, especially in the absence of a facilitative human surround, or when traumas run so deep that the empathic attunement supplied by others cannot be felt. Writing alone could not render Yukio Mishima corporeal or give him the necessary qualifications for the existence he coveted. It brought him to a crescendo, but there was always a missing note. Finally, circumstances beyond the person's control may impinge upon the creative process and its restitutive functions.

THE MANIFOLD HUMAN MEANING OF SUICIDE

No one can deny that the individuals profiled in this book chose the door of self-destruction as an alternative to the intolerable pain, suffering, and helplessness that they perceived to stretch endlessly ahead. One might say that in ending their lives, they seized power in the cavern of powerlessness. Of course, the opposite can also be said: that their suicide was total surrender. But in any given case, the human meaning of suicide is manifold. Some meanings are foregrounded by the act, some quietly recede into the horizon, and some are so contradictory they resist reconciliation. Once again, here are the meanings that arise from a careful study of these individuals' lifeworlds.

Suicide can be a means of preserving agency, of hanging onto the last shreds of one's capacity for self-determination. In many instances, suicide is pushback against forces of negation, real or imagined: "I kill myself, therefore I am." For Theresa Duncan, Iris Chang, and Yukio Mishima, these forces are larger than life: the Church of Scientology, agents of historical revisionism, the Green Snake's promise of modernization. In the case of Yukio, self and society became so entwined that personal threats to authenticity were transposed onto the national stage, namely, traditional Japan's corrosion by Westernization. In some cases, the relationship between self and society is inverted, so that the drama of a nation is enacted in the body. Reinaldo Arenas ended his life not as surrender to, but as a final stand against Castro's regime.

The forces of negation in a suicidal person's life need not be so monumental. For Sylvia Plath, it was the threat of engulfment by mother and father that set off her ritual of suicide. Through death and rebirth, she sought to (re)claim ownership of a life that was her own. Robin Williams (and to some extent, Reinaldo Arenas) forestalled the ravages of illness on mind and body through suicide, taking control of its trajectory and thwarting the total dissolution of self. Indeed, a self on the brink of negation can salvage itself through life's cessation. We also see this in Kevin Carter, who felt as empty as a vacuum; he killed himself before the vacuum could implode.

For three of our subjects, self-destruction has the added meaning of symbolic reunion. Jeremy Blake could not conceive of a world in which Theresa didn't exist. If he could not be with her in life, then he would be with her in death. The sea represented for him the channel he must traverse to reunite with his lost love, and he made that voyage seven days after her suicide. Alan Turing engaged in a lifelong project of resurrecting his beloved Christopher. When scientific avenues to reunion were suddenly closed off, he sought a more magical means: Snow White's poison apple. Although suicide was exorcism for Sylvia Plath, let's not forget that its original meaning and function was reunion with Daddy, which proved to be untenable.

Suicide can also take on the meanings of liberation and expiation. Did Theresa not also end her life to liberate Jeremy from the grips of her madness? As his muse, the font of his inspiration, it was her avowed duty to see to it that his creativity flourished—even if that meant removing herself from his life. And did Iris Chang not fire a gun at herself out of remorse for her son's diagnosis with autism? These two cases raise another paradox of suicide. To kill oneself is one of the most crushing things one can do to loved ones, and yet, many individuals terminate their lives believing that others' lives will be better for it. Perhaps this is why Alan Turing made his suicide look like an *equivocal* suicide—to leave the possibility of it being an accident open to his mother. The suicide's consideration of others is evident as well in Sylvia Plath, who made sure that her children had milk and cookies in their sealed bedroom should they go hungry at night. But Jeremy was not spared the horror of Theresa's suicide. Neither were Sylvia's children; her son Nicholas would go on to commit suicide later in life (O'Connor, 2009).

Lastly, suicide can serve as a *testimony*—to the truth of individual and collective trauma, and to the facticity of one's existence. The following passage has bearing here:

> The act of killing oneself can function as the ultimate symbol of an emotional murder that has taken place long before. . . . If someone's soul has been murdered, that person may elect to carry out the deed in physical, literal terms. The act of killing oneself thereby symbolically expresses the truth of an experience that has been denied and erased. The brutal fact of the person's death then stands before the world, ineradicably testifying to the tragedy that no one wanted to confront. (Atwood, 2012, p. 154)

Kurt Cobain felt himself die when his parents divorced and he lost his original family. The trauma of that loss sought recognition through his music, his artwork, his murderous fantasies, his somatized distress, his substance use and abuse, and his self-destruction. Theresa never openly spoke about the traumas of her childhood; she could only allude to them. When this silencing was repeated in adulthood, she ended her life, an act that could neither be undone nor contained. Reinaldo Arenas represented all the lives the Castro regime had disappeared. In taking his life, he communicated to the entire world the truth of the magnitude of Cuba's loss. And lastly, Yukio Mishima, who never felt himself alive, asserted the truth of his existence in death.

PATHWAYS FROM CREATIVITY TO SELF-DESTRUCTION

We have addressed the manifold human meanings of the impulse to create and the lure of self-destruction's call. We have also unveiled some of the paradoxes immanent to creativity and to suicide, respectively. This brings us to the original paradox that led to the creation of this book in the first place: the coexistence of life and death, creativity and suicide, the celebration and cessation of being. Below, I re-present the parsimonious model (posited in the Introduction) that traces the pathway from creativity to suicide:

> *Creativity fulfills various ontological needs that have been thwarted by nuclear crises in a person's life. If creativity loses its potency, or forces beyond the person's volition impinge upon creativity's restitutive powers, other creative pathways may emerge. If these too are rendered impotent or choked off, suicide may surface—as a final stand against forces of negation, and as the ultimate resolution of the original crises.*

Now, let us see one last time how this general principle unfolds and undergoes transmutation in each of the lives featured in this book.

Iris Chang sought to rescue historical truth from oblivion after witnessing photographed atrocities of Japan's war crimes in her motherland. The years-long endeavor traumatized her and made her question her ontological security. In a project to undo her own dying, she participated in the creative act of conception and birth, but her son's diagnosis with autism shattered all hope. As a final statement against forces she perceived were persecuting her, and as expiation for her "crime," she ended her life.

Kevin Carter photographed the horrors of apartheid to restore the integrity of Black South Africans and imbue his own life with purpose. But no sooner did he feel his moral inadequacy, which was compounded by the attacks of critics. He continued to produce in spite of this, but the end of apartheid, the loss of his "good" double, and one last botched assignment reaffirmed the worthlessness he originally felt, which he resolved through death.

Phyllis Hyman sought a ticket out of her broken home through music, which concretized the dramas of her childhood and her yearning for its undoing. But the pain of her losses in the past and the present could not be undone by music alone, and by resorting to drugs, she further undermined her craft and relation to other people. Broken, exhausted, and convinced she was doomed to spend the rest of her life alone, she put herself to sleep—her lonely death a testament to her pervasive aloneness in life.

Kurt Cobain was devastated by the divorce of his parents and subsequent dissolution of the nuclear family. The emotional truth of his psychic death was kept alive by various pathways to concretization, most notably his music and his obsession with (self) destruction. The birth of his daughter promised renewal of the lost family, but losing custody of Frances (albeit temporarily) due to past drug charges brought the original trauma back in full force, undercutting the resurgence of his creativity. One can sense echoes of the violent death he felt himself undergo as a child, in the violence of his method of suicide.

Sylvia Plath used writing and poetry to wrestle herself free from engulfing paternal and maternal influences, which were rooted in her father's death and the absence of her mother's love. Her suicide attempts, ritualized in a cycle of (near) death and rebirth every 10 years, fulfilled a similar function, but more potently, especially when her creative abilities came under attack (e.g., Harvard's rejection letter). Overcoming death meant that life was rightfully hers, but sadly, she did not overcome it the third and final time.

There is much silence surrounding Theresa Duncan's childhood, and the act of creating via storytelling may have been her way to overcome that silence. Whether or not the Church of Scientology was truly after her, the fact remains that her creative projects were stopped in their tracks, at which point, madness became her mouthpiece. But the madness that gripped her gripped Jeremy as well. Her suicide is manifold in meaning: as liberation of her love, as resistance against silencing by the church, and as ultimate expression of the human "need to tell stories," as she writes on her blog on the day of her death.

Jeremy Blake created artworks that were self-referential social critiques. They communicated the subjective truth of his experiences, and when he and Theresa were in the grips of paranoia, this too found its way into his art. His creativity was forever dashed when his lover and muse of 10 years died. In the immediate aftermath of her death, he resolved to dedicate his future artworks to her. But upon realizing that life without his other half was not worth living, he sought to overcome his loss through reunion in the afterlife.

Alan Turing also sought reunion with his lost love through suicide, but this was only after all creative pathways to reunion in life were choked off. The childhood trauma of losing Christopher jump-started a lifelong scientific endeavor to resurrect him—with Alan himself, and later, an intelligent machinery, serving as potential vessels for the spirit. However, the societal prejudice of Alan's time conspired to bring about an end to this project, and if it could not continue in the physical realm, it would do so in the spiritual realm.

Because of his upbringing, Yukio Mishima never felt existent as a child, and he sought to overcome his feeling of unreality through writing, via identification with protagonists fated to die. But writing, by itself, could never fully endorse his existence; it was only a partial antidote. After materializing his self through a strict regimen of martial arts (another concretizing pathway), he committed the ritual suicide of *seppuku*. Something that dies must have therefore lived, and in death, Yukio felt himself finally come into being.

Reinaldo Arenas used writing and his virile body to protest the wholesale oppression of disenfranchised Cubans under the Castro regime. The generative power of creativity helped him endure the horrors of forced labor in the sugar plantations, imprisonment in El Morro, and exile to the United States. And then he contracted AIDS. In the face of declining health, he managed to complete his memoir and the Pentagonia, and realizing his end was near, he ended his life in one final act of resistance against Fidel Castro.

And finally, Robin Williams, the lonely child in a big empty house who used acting and comedy to feel connected to others. His mind and body were his vehicle for his creative expression, and their assault by neurodegenerative diseases undercut his creativity's connective power. Through suicide, he took control over the trajectory of his illness and forestalled the complete disintegration of his self.

CODA

In *The Denial of Death*, Ernest Becker (1973) wrote that humankind

> accepts the cultural programming that turns his nose where he is supposed to look . . . he learns not to expose himself, not to stand out . . . the result is that he comes to exist in the imagined infallibility of the world around him. (p. 23)

Perhaps it is because highly creative individuals *resist* cultural programming that the world they inhabit seems as if it is in constant danger of coming apart at the seams. Iris Chang stood out and spoke out when she wrote *The Rape of Nanking*, and when Kevin Carter looked where he was not supposed to, he saw a world different from the one white South Africans of privilege inhabited. The world was no longer infallible.

Rollo May (1975) believed that creative individuals express the conscience of the entire human race, and I am inclined to agree. After all, Phyllis Hyman's love ballads, and Kurt Cobain's grunge music, drew thousands of spectators because they sang people's pain, loneliness, and bitter resentment for them, in much the same way Robin Williams's movies bring the nostalgia of our childhood back into our homes. Creativity takes courage, *creative courage* (May, 1975), through which new symbols, forms, structures, and meanings are created, and upon which the foundations of a new and perhaps better society may be built. In light of this, is our technocratic denial of creative people's vision and life not also a denial of humanity's collective conscience?

The pressure to arrive at generalizable results, and to appropriate the procedures of the natural sciences, has made the social and human sciences forget that there is more to lived experience than the transmission of electrochemical signals in the brain. That human beings are more than just assemblies of conditioned responses to pleasant or aversive stimuli. That dimensions of self-world experience always overflow the categories with which we try to capture them. That lives are deeply embedded in numerous intersubjective contexts. That we express the meaning of vitality and suffering in countless ways. And that some express their anguish through the creative act, and others through the cessation of their pulse. Psychology and medicine should open their eyes again, and listen to this forgotten pulse.

References

Aaron, M. (2015). *Death and the moving image: Ideology, iconography and I.* Edinburgh, UK: Edinburgh University Press.

Abraham, K. (1924). Melancholia and obsessional neurosis. In *Selected papers of Karl Abraham.* London, UK: Hogarth Press.

Ackerman, D. (1997). *A slender thread: Rediscovering hope at the heart of crisis.* New York: Vintage.

Akiskal, K., & Akiskal, K. (1996). Abstract expressionism as psychobiography: The life and suicide of Arshile Gorky. In J. Schildkraut & A. Otero (eds.), *Depression and the spiritual in modern art: Homage to Miró.* Chichester, England: John Wiley & Sons.

Alan Turing gets blue plaque. (2012, June 29). *Pink Paper,* p. 19.

Alexander, P. (1991). *Rough magic: A biography of Sylvia Plath.* New York: Viking Press.

Alvarez, A. (1973). *The savage god: A study of suicide.* New York: Bantam.

Alvarez, M. (2017). Technocratic death denial as disavowal of life: Lessons from *Brave New World* and *The Abolition of Man.* In M. J. Boone & K. C. Neece (eds.), *Science fiction and the abolition of man* (pp. 251–263). Eugene, OR: Pickwick.

Alvarez, M. (2018, August 11). The creativity and suicide of Robin Williams: A phenomenological study. *Mad in America: Science, Psychiatry and Social Justice.* Retrieved from https://www.madinamerica.com/2018/08/creativity-suicide-robin-williams-phenomenological-study/

Amsden, D. (2007, August 16). Conspiracy of two. *New Yorker.* Retrieved from http://nymag.com/news/features/36091/

Anderson, P. T. (Director). (2002). *Punch drunk love* [Motion picture]. United States: Sony Pictures Releasing.

Arbus, D. (1972). *An aperture monograph.* Millerton, NJ: Aperture.

Arbus, D. (1995). *Untitled.* Millerton, NJ: Aperture.

Arenas, R. (1984). *El central.* (A. Kerrigan, Trans.). New York: Avon Books.

Arenas, R. (1985). *Farewell to the sea.* (A. Hurley, Trans.). New York: Viking.

Arenas, R. (1987). *Singing from the well.* (A. Hurley, Trans.). New York: Viking.

Arenas, R. (1989). *Old Rosa: A novel in two stories.* (A. Tashi Slater & A. Hurley, Trans.). New York: Grove Press.

Arenas, R. (1990). *The palace of the white skunks.* (A. Hurley, Trans.). New York: Viking.

Arenas, R. (1993). *Before night falls.* (D. M. Koch, Trans.). New York: Penguin.

Arenas, R. (1994a). *The assault.* (A. Hurley, Trans.). New York: Viking.

Arenas, R. (1994b). *The doorman.* (D. M. Koch, Trans.). New York: Grove Press.

Arenas, R. (2000). *The color of summer, or the new garden of earthly delights.* (A. Hurley, Trans.). New York: Viking.

Arenas, R. (2001). *Hallucinations.* (A. Hurley, Trans.). New York: Penguin.

Associated Press (2015). *Robin Williams: Comedic genius.* Miami, FL: Mango Media, Inc.

Atwood, G. E. (1972). Note on a relationship between suicidal intentions and the depressive mood. *Psychotherapy: Theory, Research and Practice, 9*(3), 284–285.

Atwood, G. E. (2012). *The abyss of madness.* New York: Routledge.

Atwood, G. E., Orange, D., & Stolorow, R. (2002). Shattered worlds/psychotic states: a post-Cartesian view of the experience of personal annihilation. *Psychoanalytic Psychology, 19*(2), 281–306.

Atwood, G. E., & Stolorow, R. (1993). *Structures of subjectivity: Explorations in psychoanalytic phenomenology.* Hillsdale, NJ: Analytic Press.

Axelrod, S. G. (1990). *Sylvia Plath: The wound and the cure of words.* Baltimore, MD: Johns Hopkins University Press.

Baird, K., & Kracen, A. C. (2006). Vicarious traumatization and secondary traumatic stress: A research synthesis. *Counseling Psychology Quarterly, 19*, 181–188.

Baranowsky, A. B., Young, M., Johnson-Douglas, S., Williams-Keeler, L., & McCarrey, M. (1998). PTSD transmission: A review of secondary traumatization in Holocaust survivor families. *Canadian Psychology, 39*, 247–256.

Barsotti, N. (2012, December 27). British PM urged to pardon Alan Turing. *XTRA!*, p. 8.

Becker, E. (1997). *The denial of death.* New York: Free Press.

Bender, K. J. (2014, November 8). Robin Williams' autopsy detects no alcohol or illegal drugs. *The Washington Post,* p. A04. Retrieved from www.lexisnexis.com.

Bender, L. (Producer) & Van Sant, G. (Director). (1997). *Good Will Hunting* [Motion picture]. United States: Miramax Films.

Benson, H. (2005, April 17). Historian Iris Chang won many battles/The war she lost raged within. *San Francisco Chronicle.* Retrieved from https://www.sfgate.com/health/article/Historian-Iris-Chang-won-many-battles-The-war-2679354.php

Berger, J. (1991). Uses of photography. In *About looking* (pp. 42–44). New York: Vintage.

Berman, J. (1999). *Surviving literary suicide.* Amherst, MA: University of Massachusetts Press.

Berman, J. (2001). *Risky writing: Self-disclosure and self-transformation in the classroom.* Amherst, MA: University of Massachusetts Press.

Blair, E. (2007, October 27). Exhibit honors young artist whose star was rising. *Weekend Edition Saturday*. Retrieved from https://www.npr.org/templates/story/story.php?storyId=15637707

Blake, J. (2000). *Guccinam* [Time-based painting]. New York: Tillou Fine Art. Retrieved from https://www.tilloufineart.com/artists/jeremy-blake/series/guccinam

Blake, J. (2001). *Station to station* [Time-based painting]. New York: Tillou Fine Art. Retrieved from https://www.tilloufineart.com/artists/jeremy-blake/series/station-to-station

Blake, J. (2002). *Winchester* [Time-based painting]. New York: Tillou Fine Art. Retrieved from https://www.tilloufineart.com/artists/jeremy-blake/series/winchester

Blake, J. (2003a). *1906* [Time-based painting]. New York: Tillou Fine Art. Retrieved from https://www.tilloufineart.com/artists/jeremy-blake/series/1906

Blake, J. (2003b). *Reading Ossie Clark* [Time-based painting]. New York: Tillou Fine Art. Retrieved from tilloufineart.com/artists/jeremy-blake/series/reading-ossie-clark2

Blake, J. (2003c). *Planet waves* [C-print]. New York: Tillou Fine Art. Retrieved from https://www.tilloufineart.com/artists/jeremy-blake/series/c-prints?view=slider#9

Blake, J. (2004). *Century 21* [Time-based painting]. New York: Tillou Fine Art. Retrieved from https://www.tilloufineart.com/artists/jeremy-blake/series/century-21

Blake, J. (2005). *Sodium fox* [Time-based painting]. New York: Tillou Fine Art. Retrieved from https://www.tilloufineart.com/artists/jeremy-blake/series/sodium-fox

Bosworth, P. (1984). *Diane Arbus: A biography*. New York: Norton.

Bowlby, J. (1980). *Attachment and loss* (Vol. 3). New York: Basic.

Bramley, N., & Eatough, V. (2005). The experience of living with Parkinson's disease: An interpretative phenomenological analysis case study. *Psychology and Health, 20*(2), 223–235.

Breggin, P. (1994). *Toxic psychiatry*. New York: St. Martin's Press.

Breggin, P. (2008). *Medication madness: A psychiatrist exposes the dangers of mood-altering medications*. New York: St. Martin's Press.

Brezner, L., & Johnson, M. (Producers), Levinson, B. (Director). (1987). *Good morning, Vietnam* [Motion picture]. United States: Touchstone Pictures.

Brink, A. (1982). *Creativity as repair*. Hamilton, ON: Cromtech.

Brooks, R. B. (2012, May 2). Virginia Woolf's strange treatment to cure her mental illness. *The Virginia Woolf Blog*. Retrieved from http://virginiawoolfblog.com/virginia-woolf-had-teeth-pulled-to-cure-her-mental-illness/

Brown, L., & Graham, M. (2007, December 11). How well did Beck know Theresa Duncan and Jeremy Blake? *New York Magazine*. Retrieved from https://www.vulture.com/2007/12/how_well_did_jeremy_blake.html

Brown, S. R. (2014, August 17). Sad sendoff: Robin's memorial expected to be small, somber. *Daily News*, p. 11. Retrieved from www.lexisnexis.com.

Burke, K. (1963–1964). Definition of man. *Hudson Review, 16*(4), 491–514.

Casey, N. (ed.). (2002). *Unholy ghost: Writers on depression*. New York: Harper Perennial.

Ceglia, L., & Pfeffer, C. (1999). Artists‘ representations of the impact of family suicide during childhood and adolescence. *Journal of the American Academy of Psychoanalysis, 27*(4), 625–657.

Chang, I. (n.d.a). *End of the mirror tunnel* [poem]. Iris Chang Papers (Box 133, Folder 4). Stanford, CA: Herbert Hoover Archives.

Chang, I. (n.d.b). *From the files of the FBI* [short story]. Iris Chang Papers (Box 134, Folder 5, ca. 1970s). Stanford, CA: Herbert Hoover Archives.

Chang, I. (n.d.c). *Racing the hail storm* [short story]. Iris Chang Papers (Box 134, Folder 1, ca. 1970s). Stanford, CA:Herbert Hoover Archives.

Chang, I. (n.d.d). *Secret spys notebook* [diary]. Iris Chang Papers (Box 134, Folder 3, ca. 1970s). Stanford, CA: Herbert Hoover Archives.

Chang, I. (n.d.e). *The case of the meat grinder* [short story]. Iris Chang Papers (Box 134, Folder 5, ca. 1970s). Herbert Hoover Archives, Stanford, CA.

Chang, I. (n.d.f). *The fiasco* [short story]. Iris Chang Papers (Box 134, Folder 5, ca. 1970s). Stanford, CA: Herbert Hoover Archives.

Chang, I. (n.d.g). *The invasion* [poem]. Iris Chang Papers (Box 230, Folder 2, ca. 1970s). Stanford, CA: Herbert Hoover Archives.

Chang, I. (1988a). *The Halloween prince* [short story]. Iris Chang Papers (Box 141). Stanford, CA: Herbert Hoover Archives.

Chang, I. (1988b, November 28). Untitled diary entry. Iris Chang Papers (Box 141). Stanford, CA: Herbert Hoover Archives.

Chang, I. (1995). *Thread of the silkworm.* New York: Basic.

Chang, I. (1997). *The Rape of Nanking: The forgotten holocaust of World War II.* New York: Penguin.

Chang, I. (2000). Untitled entry in notepad, dated August 1-4. Iris Chang Papers (Box 193). Stanford, CA: Herbert Hoover Archives.

Chang, I. (2001, December 24). Betrayed by the White House. *The New York Times.* Retrieved from https://www.nytimes.com/2001/12/24/opinion/betrayed-by-the-white-house.html

Chang, I. (2003). *The Chinese in America: A narrative history.* New York: Penguin.

Chang, Y.-Y. (2012). *The woman who could not forget: Iris Chang before and beyond* The Rape of Nanking. New York: Pegasus.

Charet, F. X. (2007). Writing, healing, and emotional well-being: The theory behind the practice. In C. Mirriam-Goldberg & J. Tallman (eds.), *The power of words: A transformative language arts reader*. Keane, NH: TLA Network.

Chouliara, Z., Hutchison, C., & Karatzias, T. (2009). Vicarious traumatization in practitioners who work with adult survivors of sexual violence and child sexual abuse: Literature review and directions for future research. *Counseling and Psychotherapy Research, 9,* 47–56.

Chu, M. (2004, December 29). Letter of condolence to Brett Douglas and Chang family. Iris Chang Papers (Box 175, Folders 2-4). Stanford, CA: Herbert Hoover Archives.

Cobain, K. (1989). Scoff [Recorded by Nirvana]. On *Bleach* [CD]. Seattle, WA: Sub Pop.

Cobain, K. (1991a). Come as you are [Recorded by Nirvana]. On *Nevermind* [CD]. Santa Monica, CA: Geffen Records.

Cobain, K. (1991b). Lithium [Recorded by Nirvana]. On *Nevermind* [CD]. Santa Monica, CA: Geffen Records.
Cobain, K. (1991c). Polly [Recorded by Nirvana]. On *Nevermind* [CD]. Santa Monica, CA: Geffen Records.
Cobain, K. (1991d). Something in the way [Recorded by Nirvana]. On *Nevermind* [CD]. Santa Monica, CA: Geffen Records.
Cobain, K. (1992). Sliver [Recorded by Nirvana]. On *Incesticide* [CD]. Santa Monica, CA: Geffen Records.
Cobain, K. (1993a). Dumb [Recorded by Nirvana]. On *In utero* [CD]. Santa Monica, CA: Geffen Records.
Cobain, K. (1993b). Heart-shaped box [Recorded by Nirvana]. On *In utero* [CD]. Santa Monica, CA: Geffen Records.
Cobain, K. (1993c). Paper cuts [Recorded by Nirvana]. On *Bleach* [CD]. Seattle, WA: Sub Pop.
Cobain, K. (1993d). Serve the servants [Recorded by Nirvana]. On *In utero* [CD]. Santa Monica, CA: Geffen Records.
Cobain, K. (1993e). Very ape [Recorded by Nirvana]. On *In utero* [CD]. Santa Monica, CA: Geffen Records.
Cobain, K. (1994a). In the pines [Recorded by Nirvana]. On *Unplugged in New York* [CD]. Santa Monica, CA: Geffen Records.
Cobain, K. (1994b). Lake of fire [Recorded by Nirvana]. On *Unplugged in New York* [CD]. Santa Monica, CA: Geffen Records.
Cobain, K. (1994c). The man who sold the world [Recorded by Nirvana]. On *Unplugged in New York* [CD]. Santa Monica, CA: Geffen Records.
Cobain, K. (2002). *Kurt Cobain: Journals*. New York: Riverhead.
Coe, K. (2007, August 2). The Theresa Duncan tragedy. *LA Weekly*. Retrieved from https://www.laweekly.com/the-theresa-duncan-tragedy/
Comas-Diaz, L. (2008). Latino psychospirituality. In K. Schneider (ed.), *Existential-integrative psychotherapy: Guideposts to the core of practice*. New York: Routledge.
Cosens, S. (2012, June 29). Gay codebreaker Alan Turing honoured with Google doodle. *Pink Paper*, p. 2.
Cross, C. R. (2001). *Heavier than heaven: A biography of Kurt Cobain*. New York: Hyperion.
Cross, C. R. (2008). *Cobain unseen*. New York: Little, Brown.
Davis, A. (2013, December 23). Queen pardons gay mathematician Alan Turing. *Windy City Times*. Retrieved from http://www.windycitymediagroup.com/lgbt/Queen-pardons-gay-mathematician-Alan-Turing/45637.html
De Salvo, L. (2000). *Writing as a way of healing: How telling our stories transforms our lives*. Boston: Beacon Press.
Dillon, N. (2014, August 14). Life in darkness: Star a shut-in for days. Trusted pal made grim find. *Daily News*, p. 8. Retrieved from www.lexisnexis.com.
Dokoupil, T. (2007, September 9). Truly, madly, deeply. *Newsweek*. Retrieved from https://www.newsweek.com/truly-madly-deeply-100261
Domino, G. (1988). Attitudes toward suicide among highly creative college students. *Creativity Research Journal, 1*, 92–105.

Dougan, A. (1998). *Robin Williams.* New York: Thunder's Mouth Press.

Duncan, M. (2014, June 21). *Theresa Duncan's, The history of glamour* [Video file]. Retrieved from https://www.youtube.com/watch?v=4Zi_goYyzT8

Duncan, T. (2007a, March 20). Hardy's heart [Blog post]. Retrieved from https://theresalduncan.typepad.com/witostaircase/2007/03/page/4/

Duncan, T. (2007b, March 28). Baby boomer to Wit: Fuck you [Blog post]. Retrieved from https://theresalduncan.typepad.com/witostaircase/2007/03/

Duncan, T. (2007c, April 28). The guessing game [Blog post]. Retrieved from https://theresalduncan.typepad.com/witostaircase/2007/04/index.html

Duncan, T. (2007d, May 6). Politics and the power of the couch [Blog post]. Retrieved from https://theresalduncan.typepad.com/witostaircase/2007/05/page/9/

Duncan, T. (2007e, May 28). The creative process [Blog post]. Retrieved from https://theresalduncan.typepad.com/witostaircase/2007/05/page/2/

Duncan, T. (2007f, June 27). Cloak and dagger on the staircase: Wit spied on, smeared, and physically threatened [Blog post]. Retrieved from https://theresalduncan.typepad.com/witostaircase/2007/06/page/2/

Duncan, T. (2007g, July 2). Baby boomers continue to mystify own measly deaths as apocalyptic [Blog post]. Retrieved from https://theresalduncan.typepad.com/witostaircase/2007/07/page/3/

Duncan, T. (2007h, July 10). Storytelling on the staircase [Blog post]. Retrieved from https://theresalduncan.typepad.com/witostaircase/2007/07/index.html

Dunkley, J., & Whelan, T. A. (2006). Vicarious traumatisation: Current status and future directions. *British Journal of Guidance and Counseling, 34*, 107–116.

Durkheim, E. (1997). *Suicide: A study in sociology.* (J. A. Spaulding & G. Simpton, Trans.). New York: Free Press.

Dyer, E. (n.d.). Eric Dyer's remembrance [Blog post]. *The Wit of the Staircase.* Retrieved from https://theresalduncan.typepad.com/witostaircase/eric-dyer.html

Echevarria, R. G. (1993, October 24). An outcast of the island. *The New York Times.* Retrieved from http://movies2.nytimes.com/books/98/12/06/specials/arenas-night.html

Emery, J. (Producer), & Wise, H. (Director). (1997). *Breaking the code* [Motion picture]. United Kingdom: British Broadcasting Corporation.

Epstein, S. (1995). Elizabeth Layton: Life-long depression, with healing through creativity in later life. In B. Panter, M. Panter, E. Virshup, & B. Virshup (eds.), *Creativity and madness: Psychological studies of art and artists* (Vol. 1, pp. 241–246). Burbank, CA: AIMED Press.

Feirstein, F. (2003). Trauma and poetry: a psychoanalyst's view on the healing power of the arts. *Partisan Review, 70*(2), 255–261.

Fingleton, E. (2008, December 12). Whatever happened to Iris Chang? *CounterPunch.* Retrieved from https://www.counterpunch.org/2008/12/12/whatever-happened-to-iris-chang/

Firestone, L., & Catlett, J. (1998). The treatment of Sylvia Plath. *Death Studies, 22,* 667–692.

Flanigan, J., & Alvarez, M. (2019). Cultural discourse analysis as critical analysis: A view from Twin Oaks and SuicideForum.com. In M. Scollo & T. Milburn (eds.),

Engaging and transforming global communication through cultural discourse analysis: A tribute to Donal Carbaugh (pp. 73–90). Lanham, MD: Fairleigh Dickinson University Press.

Freud, S. (1965). *The interpretation of dreams*. New York: Avon.

Friedman, H. J. (2014, August 16). Treating depression to prevent suicide [Letter to the editor]. *The New York Times*, p. 18. Retrieved from www.lexisnexis.com.

Gardner, H. (1993). *Creating minds*. New York: Basic.

Gay scientist, WWII hero Alan Turing receives posthumous apology from UK. (2009). *Eerie Gay News*, p. 14.

Godard, J. (Director). (1965). *Alphaville* [Motion picture]. Paris: Athos Films.

Goodale, G. (2014). Robin Williams suicide prompts heightened discussion of depression. *Christian Science Monitor*, n. pag. Retrieved from www.lexisnexis .com.

Gosha, H. (Director). (1969). *Hitokiri* [Motion picture]. Japan: Fuji Telecasting.

Heidegger, M. (1996). *Being and time: A translation of Sein und Zeit*. New York: SUNY Press.

Heiman, H. (1976). Psychoanalytic observations on the last painting and suicide of Vincent van Gogh. *International Journal of Psychoanalysis, 57*, 71–79.

Hemingway, E. (1940). *For whom the bell tolls*. New York: Scribner's.

Henderson, P., Rosen, D., & Mascaro, N. (2007). Empirical study on the healing nature of mandalas. *Psychology of Aesthetics, Creativity, and the Arts, 1*(3), 148–154.

Henke, S. (1998). *Shattered subjects: Trauma and testimony in women's life-writing*. New York: St. Martin's Press.

Herbert, E. (2014). *Robin Williams: When the laughter stops 1951-2014*. London, UK: John Blake.

Herman, J. (1997). *Trauma and recovery: The aftermath of violence—from domestic abuse to political terror*. New York: Basic.

Herrera, H. (1983). *Frida: A biography of Frida Kahlo*. New York: Harper & Row.

Herrera, H. (2003). *Arshile Gorky: His life and work*. New York: Farrar, Straus and Giroux.

Hillman, J. (1997). *Suicide and the soul*. Woodstock, CT: Spring Publications.

Hodges, A. (1983/2012). *Alan Turing: The enigma*. Princeton, NJ: Princeton University Press.

Horwitz, A. (2002). *Creating mental illness*. Chicago, IL: University of Chicago Press.

Horwitz, A., & Wakefield, J. (2007). *The loss of sadness: How psychiatry transformed normal sorrow into depressive disorder*. New York: Oxford University Press.

Hyman, P. (1977). I don't want to lose you [Recorded by Phyllis Hyman]. On *Phyllis Hyman* [CD]. New York: Buddah Records.

Hyman, P. (1979). Give a little more [Recorded by Phyllis Hyman]. On *You know how to love me* [CD]. New York: Arista.

Hyman, P. (1986a). Living all alone [Recorded by Phyllis Hyman]. On *Living all alone* [CD]. Philadelphia, PA: PIR.

Hyman, P. (1986b). Old friend [Recorded by Phyllis Hyman]. On *Living all alone* [CD]. Philadelphia, PA: PIR.

Hyman, P. (1991a). I found love [Recorded by Phyllis Hyman]. On *Prime of my life* [CD]. Philadelphia, PA: PIR.

Hyman, P. (1991b). Living in confusion [Recorded by Phyllis Hyman]. On *Prime of my life* [CD]. Philadelphia, PA: PIR.

Hyman, P. (1991c). Meet me on the moon [Recorded by Phyllis Hyman]. On *Prime of my life* [CD]. Philadelphia, PA: PIR.

Hyman, P. (1991d). Walk away [Recorded by Phyllis Hyman]. On *Prime of my life* [CD]. Philadelphia, PA: PIR.

Hyman, P. (1995a). Give me one good reason to stay [Recorded by Phyllis Hyman]. On *I refuse to be lonely* [CD]. Philadelphia, PA: PIR.

Hyman, P. (1995b). I refuse to be lonely [Recorded by Phyllis Hyman]. On *I refuse to be lonely* [CD]. Philadelphia, PA: PIR.

Hyman, P. (1995c). This too shall pass [Recorded by Phyllis Hyman]. On *I refuse to be lonely* [CD]. Philadelphia, PA: PIR.

Hyman, P. (1995d). Why not me [Recorded by Phyllis Hyman]. On *I refuse to be lonely* [CD]. Philadelphia, PA: PIR.

Isaacson, K. (2005). Divide and multiply: Comparative theory and methodology in multiple case psychobiography. In W. T. Schultz (ed.), *Handbook of psychobiography* (pp. 104–111). New York: Oxford University Press.

Jamison, K. (2000). *Night falls fast: Understanding suicide.* New York: Vintage.

Jamison, K. (2003). *Touched with fire: Manic-depressive illness and the artistic temperament.* New York: Free Press.

Jonze, T. (2014, June 12). Interview: Lana Del Ray: 'I wish I was dead already.' *The Guardian.* Retrieved from https://www.theguardian.com/music/2014/jun/12/lana-del-rey-ultraviolence-album.

Jung, C. G. (1968). *Man and his symbols.* New York: Dell Publishing.

Jung, C. G. (1973). *Mandala symbolism.* Trans. R. Hall. Princeton, NJ: Princeton University Press.

Kahlo, F. (1995). *The diary of Frida Kahlo: An intimate portrait.* New York: Harry N. Abrams.

Kamen, P. (2007). *Finding Iris Chang: Friendship, ambition, and the loss of an extraordinary mind.* Cambridge, MA: Da Capo.

Kantor, M. (2008). *Understanding paranoia: A guide for professionals, families, and sufferers.* Westport, CT: Praeger.

Kaplan, D. (2014, August 12). Laughter to tragedy: Suicide by asphyxiation likely. Stars in shock at loss of comedy great. *Daily News*, p. 4. Retrieved from www.lexisnexis.com.

Kaufman, J. C. (2001). The Sylvia Plath effect: Mental illness in eminent creative writers. *Journal of Creative Behavior, 35*, 37–50.

Kaysen, S. (1993). *Girl, interrupted.* New York: Turtle Bay.

Kennedy, K., Marshall, F., & Molen, G. R. (Producers), Spielberg, S. (Director). (1991). *Hook* [Motion picture]. United States: TriStar Pictures.

Kennedy, R. (2007, August 1). Jeremy Blake, 35, artist who used lush-toned video, dies. *The New York Times.* Retrieved from https://www.nytimes.com/2007/08/01/arts/design/01blake.html

Kirk, C. A. (2004). *Sylvia Plath: A biography.* Westport, CT: Greenwood Press.
Kohut, H. (1971). *The analysis of self.* New York: International Universities Press.
Kottler, J. (2006). *Divine madness: Ten stories of creative struggle.* San Francisco: Jossey-Bass.
Krauss, D. (Producer & Director). (2005). *The death of Kevin Carter: Casualty of the Bang Bang Club* [Motion picture]. United States: Kevin Carter Film.
Kroopf, S., & Teitler, W. (Producers), Johnston, J. (Director). (1995). *Jumanji* [Motion picture]. United States: TriStar Pictures.
Kvaale, E. P., Haslam, N., & Gottdiener, W. H. (2013). The 'side effects' of medicalization: a meta-analytic review of how biogenetic explanations affect stigma. *Clinical Psychology Review, 33*(6), 782–794.
Lacan, J. (1949/1982). The mirror stage as formative of the function of the I as revealed in psychoanalytic experience. In *Ecrits: A selection.* New York: W. W. Norton.
Laing, R. (1959). *The divided self: An existential study in sanity and madness.* New York: Penguin.
Leavitt, D. (2006). *The man who knew too much: Alan Turing and the invention of the computer.* New York, NY: Atlas.
Lee, C. (2007, August 3). In a cocoon of their making. *Los Angeles Times.* Retrieved from https://www.latimes.com/archives/la-xpm-2007-aug-03-et-doublesuicide3-story.html
Leffingwell, E. (2004). Jeremy Blake at Feigen Contemporary. *Art in America*, 119.
Lester, D. (1990). An analysis of poets and novelists who completed suicide. *Activitas Nervosa Superior, 32*(1), 6–11.
Lester, D. (1993). *Suicide in creative women.* Hauppauge, NY: Nova Science Publishers.
Lester, D. (1998a). Suicide in eminent persons. *Perceptual and Motor Skills, 87,* 90.
Lester, D. (1998b). Theories of suicidal behavior applied to Sylvia Plath. *Death Studies, 22,* 655–666.
Levine, P., & Kline, M. (2006). *Trauma through a child's eyes: Awakening the ordinary miracle of healing.* Berkeley, CA: North Atlantic.
Ludwig, A. M. (1995). *The price of greatness: Resolving the creativity and madness controversy.* New York: Guilford.
MacLeod, S. (2001, June 24). The life and death of Kevin Carter. *Time.* Retrieved from http://content.time.com/time/magazine/article/0,9171,165071,00.html
Maire, F. (1971). Van Gogh's suicide. *Journal of the American Medical Association, 217*(7), 938–939.
Malchiodi, C. (2007). *The art therapy sourcebook.* New York: McGraw Hill.
Marinovich, G., & Silva, J. (2000). *The Bang Bang Club: Snapshots from a hidden war.* New York: Basic.
Marr, J. (1991). The experience of living with Parkinson's Disease. *Journal of Neuroscience Nursing, 23*(5), 325–329.
Martin, S. C. (2016). The experience and communicative management of identity threats among people with Parkinson's disease: Implications for heath communication theory and practice. *Communication Monographs, 83*(3), 303–325.
Martindale, C. (1972). Father's absence, psychopathology, and poetic eminence. *Psychological Reports, 31*, 843–847.

Masaki, D., & Mishima, Y. (Director). (1966). *Yūkoku* [Motion picture]. Japan: Fuji Telecasting.

Masumura, Y. (Director). (1960). *Karakkaze yarō* [Motion picture]. Japan: Daiei Film Corp.

Max, D. T. (2009, March 1). The unfinished: David Foster Wallace's struggle to surpass "Infinite Jest." *The New Yorker.* Retrieved from https://www.newyorker.com/magazine/2009/03/09/the-unfinished

May, R. (1975). *The courage to create.* New York: Norton.

McAdams, D., & Bowman, P. (2001). Narrating life's turning points: Redemption and contamination. In D. McAdams, R. Josselson, & A. Lieblich (eds.), *Turns in the road: Narrative studies of lives in transition* (pp. 3–34). Washington, DC: APA.

McCann, I. L., & Pearlman, L. A. (1990). Vicarious traumatization: A framework for understanding the psychological effects of working with victims. *Journal of Traumatic Stress, 3,* 131–149.

McCarroll, J. E., et al. (1995). Working with traumatic material: Effects on Holocaust Memorial Museum staff. *American Journal of Orthopsychiatry, 65*(1), 66–75.

McClary, R. (2007). Healing the psyche through music, myth, and ritual. *Psychology of Aesthetics, Creativity, and the Arts, 1*(3), 155–159.

McLaughlin, K. (2004, November 20). Iris Chang's suicide stunned those she tried so hard to help -- the survivors of Japan's 'Rape of Nanking.' *San Francisco Chronicle.* Retrieved from https://www.sfgate.com/entertainment/article/Iris-Chang-s-suicide-stunned-those-she-tried-so-2634180.php

Menand, L. (2010, March 1). Head case: Can psychiatry be a science? *The New Yorker.* Retrieved from https://www.newyorker.com/magazine/2010/03/01/head-case-2

Mensa correspondence. (1983). Iris Chang Papers (Box 226, Folder 5). Stanford, CA: Herbert Hoover Archives.

Mestres, R., & Fuchs, F. (Producer), Coppola, F. F. (Producer/Director). (1996). *Jumanji* [Motion picture]. United States: Buena Vista Pictures.

Michael, J. A. (2017). *Strength of a woman: The Phyllis Hyman story.* Detroit, MI: JAM Books.

Miller, A. (1991). *The untouched key: Tracing childhood trauma in creativity and destructiveness.* New York: Anchor.

Miller, A. (1997). *The drama of the gifted child.* New York: Harper Perennial.

Miller, A. (2006). *The body never lies: The lingering effects of hurtful parenting.* New York: Norton.

Miller, A. (2008). *Breaking down the wall of silence: The liberating experience of facing painful truth.* New York: Basic.

Miller, H. (1972). *Reflections on the death of Mishima.* Santa Barbara, CA: Capra Press.

Mishima, Y. (1944). *A forest in full flower.* Tokyo, Japan: Shinchosha.

Mishima, Y. (1949). *Confessions of a mask.* New York: New Directions.

Mishima, Y. (1953). *Patriotism.* New York: New Directions.

Mishima, Y. (1954). *The sound of waves.* New York: Knopf.

Mishima, Y. (1956). *Five modern Noh plays.* New York: Knopf.

Mishima, Y. (1966). *Spring snow.* New York: Knopf.

Mishima, Y. (1968a). *Runaway horses*. New York: Knopf.
Mishima, Y. (1968b). *Sun and steel*. Paolo Alto, CA: Kodansha.
Mishima, Y. (1969). *The temple of dawn*. New York: Knopf.
Mishima, Y. (1970). *The decay of the angel*. New York: Knopf.
Moller, D. W. (2000). *Life's end: Technocratic dying in an age of spiritual yearning*. Amityville, NY: Baywood.
Monde, C., & Pesce, N. L. (2014, August 13). Depression: It can affect anybody – the rich, the famous and the rest of us. *Daily News*, p. 6. Retrieved from www.lexisnexis.com.
Monk, P. (2005). *Spirit hunter: The haunting of American culture by myths of violence*. Toronto, ON: Art Gallery of York University.
Mraz, W., & Runco, M. (1994). Suicide ideation and creative problem solving. *Suicide and Life-Threatening Behavior, 24*, 38–47.
Mueller, J. (2004, November 15). Letter of condolence to Brett Douglas and Chang family. Iris Chang Papers (Box 175, Folders 2-4). Stanford, CA: Herbert Hoover Archives.
Nagel, T. (1986). *The view from nowhere*. New York: Oxford University Press.
Nathan, D. (1999). *Soulful divas*. New York: Billboard Books.
Nathan, J. (1979). *Mishima: A biography*. New York: Da Capo.
Nettle, D. (2001). *Strong imagination: Madness, creativity and human nature*. New York: Oxford University Press.
Nijhof, G. (1995). Parkinson's Disease as a problem of shame in public appearance. *Sociology of Health and Illness, 17*(2), 193–205.
Nirvana. (2009, June 16). *Nirvana - Heart-shaped box* [Video file]. Retrieved from https://www.youtube.com/watch?v=n6P0SitRwy8
Norman, S., & Norman, M. (2009). *Tears in the darkness: The story of the Bataan Death March*. New York: Farrar, Strauss & Giroux.
Noyes, D. (2000). Authoring the social drama: Suicide, self, and narration in a French political scandal. *Narrative, 8*(2), 210–231.
O'Connor, A. (2009, March 24). Nicholas Hughes, 47, Sylvia Plath's son, dies. *The New York Times*. Retrived from https://www.nytimes.com/2009/03/24/books/24hughes.html
Orange, D., Atwood, G., & Stolorow, R. (2001). *Working intersubjectively: Contextualism in psychoanalytic practice*. Hillsdale, NJ: Analytic Press.
Orr, G. (2002a). *Poetry as survival*. Athens, GA: University of Georgia Press.
Orr, G. (2002b). *The blessing: A memoir*. San Francisco, CA: Council Oak.
Pennebaker, J., & Seagal, J. (1999). Forming a story: The health benefits of narrative. *Journal of Clinical Psychology, 55*, 1243–1254.
Phelan, J. C., Yang, L. H., & Cruz-Rojas, R. (2006). Effects of attributing serious mental illnesses to genetic causes on orientations to treatment. *Psychiatric Services, 57*(3), 382–387.
Phillips, T. (n.d.). In memoriam: Jeremy Blake and Theresa Duncan [Blog post]. *The Wit of the Staircase*. Retrieved from https://theresalduncan.typepad.com/witostaircase/terri-phillips.html
Plath, S. (1973). *The colossus and other poems*. New York: Alfred A. Knopf.

Plath, S. (1992). *Letters home: Correspondence 1950-1963*. A. S. Plath (ed.). New York: Harper Perennial.

Plath, S. (1996). *The bell jar*. New York: Harper & Row.

Plath, S. (1998). *The collected poems of Sylvia Plath*. T. Hughes (ed.). Cutchogue, NY: Buccaneer Books.

Plath, S. (2000). *The unabridged journals of Sylvia Plath, 1950-1962*. K. V. Kukil (ed.). New York: Anchor Books.

Plath, S. (2004). *Ariel: The restored edition*. New York: Harper Collins.

Preti, A., de Biasi, F., & Miotto, P. (2001). Musical creativity and suicide. *Psychological Reports, 89*, 719–727.

Ravin, J., Hartman, J., & Fried, R. (1978). Mark Rothko's paintings—suicide notes? *Ohio State Medical Journal, 74*, 78–79.

Reznek, L. (2016). *Peddling mental disorder: The crisis in modern psychiatry*. Jefferson, NC: McFarland.

Rogers, N. (1993). *The creative connection: Expressive arts as healing*. Palo Alto, CA: Science & Behavior Books.

Rogers, V. (1995). Elizabeth Layton: Maverick model of personality growth in later life. In B. Panter, M. Panter, E. Virshup, & B. Virshup (eds.), *Creativity and madness: Psychological studies of art and artists* (Vol. 1, pp. 249–261). Burbank, CA: AIMED Press.

Runyan, W. M. (2005). How to critically evaluate alternative explanations of life events: The case of Van Gogh's ear. In W. T. Schultz (ed.), *Handbook of psychobiography* (pp. 96–103). New York: Oxford University Press.

Runyon, B. (2005). *The burn journals*. New York: Knopf.

Sales, N. (2007, December 11). The golden suicides. *Vanity Fair*. Retrieved from https://www.vanityfair.com/news/2008/01/suicides200801

Salvo, V. (2013, March 29). Patrick Sammon on Codebreaker, his film about Alan Turing. *Windy City Times*. Retrieved from http://www.windycitymediagroup.com/lgbt/Patrick-Sammon-on-Codebreaker-his-film-about-Alan-Turing/42176.html

Sartre, J. (2001). *Being and nothingness: An essay on phenomenological ontology*. Camp Sherman, OR: Citadel.

Sartre, J. (2007). *Existentialism is a humanism*. New Haven, CT: Yale University Press.

Sass, L. (1994). *Madness and modernism: Insanity in the light of modern art, literature, and thought*. Cambridge, MA: Harvard University Press.

Sass, L. (2003). Lacan and 9/11. *Raritan, 23*(1), 162–166.

Sass, L. (2005). "Hyped on clarity": Diane Arbus and the postmodern condition. *Raritan, 25*(1), 1–37.

Schaffer, K., & Smith, S. (2004). *Human rights and narrated lives: The ethics of recognition*. New York: Palgrave Macmillan.

Schnabel, J. (Director). (2001). *Before night falls* [Motion picture]. USA: Fine Line Features.

Schnack, A. J. (Director). (2006). *Kurt Cobain: About a son* [Motion picture]. Los Angeles, CA: Sidetrack Films.

Schneider, S. (2016). The terrorist inside my husband's brain. *Neurology, 87*, 1308–1311.

Schultz, W. T. (2003). The prototypical scene: A method for generating psychobiographical hypotheses. In R. Josselson, A. Lieblich, & D. McAdams (eds.), *Up close and personal: The teaching and learning of narrative research* (pp. 151–175). Washington, DC: APA.

Schultz, W. T. (2005a). Introducing psychobiography. In W. T. Schultz (ed.), *Handbook of psychobiography* (pp. 3–18). New York: Oxford University Press.

Schultz, W. T. (2005b). Nothing alive can be calculated: The psychobiographical study of artists. In W. T. Schultz (ed.), *Handbook of psychobiography* (pp. 135–141). New York: Oxford University Press.

Scott-Stokes, H. (1974). *The life and death of Yukio Mishima.* Toronto: Doubleday.

Shlain, L. (2007). *Art & physics: Parallel visions in space, time, and light.* New York, NY: William Morrow.

Shneidman, E. (1971). Perturbation and lethality as precursors of suicide in a gifted group. *Life-Threatening Behavior, 1*(1), 23–45.

Shneidman, E. (2004). *Autopsy of a suicidal mind.* New York: Oxford University Press.

Shulman, E. (1992). Ibsen and the suicide enigma. *Omega, 25*(2), 109–126.

Siegel, R. (1996). *Whispers: The voices of paranoia.* New York: Touchstone.

Sobchack, V. (2004). *Carnal thoughts: Embodiment and moving image culture.* Oakland, CA: University of California Press.

Sorsoli, L. (2004). Echoes of silence: Remembering and repeating childhood trauma. In A. Lieblich, D. McAdams, & R. Josselson (eds.), *Healing plots: The narrative basis of psychotherapy.* Washington, DC: APA.

Soto, F. (1994). *Reinaldo Arenas: The Pentagonia.* Gainesville, FL: University Press of Florida.

Stack, S. (1996). Gender and suicide risk among artists: a multivariate analysis. *Suicide and Life-Threatening Behavior, 26,* 374–379.

Stack, S. (1997). Suicide among artists. *Journal of Social Psychology, 137,* 129–130.

Stewart, S. (2014, August 13). Blacklight: Shadows lurked behind the manic genius of Robin Williams – but he's far from the only comic to be plagued by demons. *The New York Post,* p. 38. Retrieved from www.lexisnexis.com.

Stolorow, R. (2007). *Trauma and human existence: Autobiographical, psychoanalytic, and philosophical reflections.* Hillsdale, NJ: Analytic Press.

Stolorow, R., & Atwood, G. E. (1994). Toward a science of human experience. In R. Stolorow, G. E. Atwood, & B. Brandchaft (eds.), *The intersubjective perspective* (pp. 15–30). Northvale, NJ: Jason Aronson.

Stolorow, R., & Atwood, G. E. (2018). *The power of phenomenology.* New York: Routledge.

Stolorow, R., Atwood, G. E., & Orange, D. (2002). *Worlds of experience: Interweaving philosophical and clinical dimensions in psychoanalysis.* Hillsdale, NJ: Analytic Press.

Styron, W. (1992). *Darkness visible: A memoir of madness.* New York: Vintage.

Szasz, T. (2002). *Liberation by oppression: A comparative study of psychiatry and slavery.* New Brunswick, NJ: Transaction.

Szasz, T. (2007). *The medicalization of everyday life.* Syracuse, NY: Syracuse University Press.

Tabachnick, N. (1973). Creative suicidal crises. *Archives of General Psychiatry, 29,* 258–263.

Tedeschi, R., & Calhoun, L. (1995). *Trauma and transformation: Growing in the aftermath of suffering.* London: Sage.

Terr, L. (1994). The Black Dahlia's son. In *Unchained memories: True stories of traumatic memories, lost and found* (pp. 183–219). New York: Basic.

Tillou Fine Art. (n.d.). Jeremy Blake. Retrieved from https://www.tilloufineart.com/artists/jeremy-blake

True, E. (2006). *Nirvana: The biography.* Cambridge, MA: Da Capo.

Ueland, B. (1987). *If you want to write: A book about art, independence and spirit.* Saint Paul, MN: Graywolf Press.

Vachon, C. (Producer) & Romanek, M. (Director). (2002). *One hour photo* [Motion picture]. United States: Fox Searchlight Pictures.

Valdez, S. (2002). Attack of the abstract. *Art in America,* 102–105.

Valenstein, E. (2000). *Blaming the brain: The truth about drugs and mental health.* New York: Free Press.

Vislocky, C. (2014, August 15). Death of a comedy icon: R.I.P., Robin Williams. *The New York Post,* p. 24. Retrieved from www.lexisnexis.com.

Watters, E. (2010, January 10). The Americanization of mental illness. *The New York Times.* Retrieved from https://www.nytimes.com/2010/01/10/magazine/10psyche-t.html

Weil, B., Schwarzer, M., & Blake, J. (2005). *Jeremy Blake: Winchester.* San Francisco, CA: San Francisco Museum of Modern Art.

Weintraub, K., & Kelly, D. (2014, August 12). All the on-screen laughs can't protect against depression. *USA Today,* p. 3D. Retrieved from www.lexisnexis.com.

Whitaker, R. (2003). *Mad in America: Bad science, bad medicine, and the enduring mistreatment of the mentally ill.* Cambridge, MA: Perseus.

Whitaker, R. (2010). *Anatomy of an epidemic: Magic bullets, psychiatric drugs, and the astonishing rise of mental illness in America.* New York: Broadway Books.

Whitehead, B. (2010). The psychosocial impact of communication changes in people with Parkinson's disease. *British Journal of Neuroscience Nursing, 6*(1), 30–36.

Whitemore, H. (1987). *Breaking the code.* Oxford, UK: Amber Lane Press.

Williams, M. G., Williams, R., & Radcliffe, M. (Producers), Columbus, C. (Director). (1993). *Mrs. Doubtfire* [Motion picture]. United States: 20th Century Fox.

Willings, D. (1984). Considerations in counseling the creatively gifted. *International Journal for the Advancement of Counseling, 7,* 3–13.

Willings, D., & Arseneault, M. (1986). Attempted suicide and creative promise. *Gifted Education International, 4,* 10–13.

Winnicott, D. W. (1955). The depressive position in normal emotional development. *British Journal of Medical Psychology, 28,* 89–100.

Winnicott, D. W. (1989). *Playing and reality.* New York: Routledge.

Wockner, R. (2009, September 23). British prime minister apologizes to Alan Turing. *Windy City Times.* Retrieved from http://www.windycitymediagroup.com/lgbt/WORLD-ROUNDUP/22976.html
Woolf, V. (1979). *The diary of Virginia Woolf, vol. 1: 1915-1919.* A. O. Bell (ed.). New York: Harvest/HBJ.
Woolf, V. (1981). *The diary of Virginia Woolf, vol. 3: 1925-1930.* A. O. Bell (ed.). New York: Harvest/HBJ.
Woolf, V. (1985). A sketch of the past. In *Moments of being: A collection of autobiographical writing* (pp. 61–159). New York: Harcourt.
Wurtzel, E. (1994). *Prozac nation: Young and depressed in America.* New York: Riverhead.
Yahr, E. (2014, August 13). Coroner releases details in death of Robin Williams. *The Washington Post*, p. C01. Retrieved from www.lexisnexis.com.
Yin, J., & Young, S. (1997). *The Rape of Nanking: An undeniable history in photographs.* Ed. R. Dorfman. Chicago, IL: Triumph Book.
Zilboorg, G. (1943). Fear of death. *Psychoanalytic Quarterly, 12,* 465–475.
Žižek, S. (1991). *Looking awry: An introduction to Jacques Lacan through 'popular' culture.* Cambridge, MA: MIT Press.

Index

About the Author

M. F. Alvarez is postdoctoral diversity and innovation scholar in the Department of Communication at the University of New Hampshire. He received his PhD from the University of Massachusetts Amherst, where he taught courses in film and media studies, television production, human communication and technology, and end of life communication. He is also a recipient of the Paul and Daisy Soros Fellowship. Visit him at mfalvarez.net or follow him on Twitter @mfalvarez121.

www.ingramcontent.com/pod-product-compliance
Ingram Content Group UK Ltd.
Pitfield, Milton Keynes, MK11 3LW, UK
UKHW041842031026
15587UKWH00002B/965

9 781498 523820